Donated
In Loving Memory Of

Marsha Auerbach

An avid reader and
Research Librarian

By
Her Children
Glenn Auerbach &
Karen Auerbach
Her Sister
Sandra Hammer

D1256759

THE HOUSE AT UJAZDOWSKIE 16

THE MODERN JEWISH EXPERIENCE

Deborah Dash Moore and Marsha L. Rozenblit, editors
Paula Hyman, founding coeditor

THE HOUSE AT UJAZDOWSKIE 16

JEWISH FAMILIES IN WARSAW AFTER THE HOLOCAUST

KAREN AUERBACH

INDIANA UNIVERSITY PRESS

Bloomington & Indianapolis

This book was made possible in part by support from the Schwartz Fund.

This book is a publication of

Indiana University Press
Office of Scholarly Publishing
Herman B Wells Library 350
1320 East 10th Street
Bloomington, Indiana 47405 USA

iupress.indiana.edu

Telephone orders	800-842-6796
Fax orders	812-855-7931

∞ The paper used in this publication meets the minimum requirements of the American National Standard for Information Sciences-Permanence of Paper for Printed Library Materials, ANSI Z39.48-1992.

Manufactured in the United States of America

Library of Congress Cataloging-in-Publication Data

Auerbach, Karen, author.
  The house at Ujazdowskie 16 : Jewish families in Warsaw after the Holocaust / Karen Auerbach.
    pages cm. — (The modern Jewish experience)
  Includes bibliographical references and index.
  ISBN 978-0-253-00907-4 (cl : alk. paper) — ISBN 978-0-253-00915-9 (eb) 1. Jews—Poland—Warsaw—Biography. 2. Jews—Poland—Warsaw—Social conditions—20th century. 3. Jews—Poland—Warsaw—Social conditions—21st century. 4. Jews—Poland—Warsaw—Social life and customs. 5. Jews—Homes and haunts—Poland—Warsaw—History. 6. Warsaw (Poland)—Buildings, structures, etc.—History. I. Title.
  DS134.7.A57 2013
  940.53′18140943841—dc23

                                                2013003910

1 2 2 3 4 5 18 17 16 15 14 13

FOR MY MOTHER,

Marsha Moses Auerbach,
In loving memory

Oh, gateways of Warsaw!

. . . Are there not apartment houses with gateways outside of Warsaw? There are. Perhaps they exist everywhere, yet only in Warsaw does the gateway of a home define somehow the life of several generations.

Oh, gateways of Warsaw! Whatever can I dedicate to you now, I, a chronicler searching for barely perceptible shadows? A handful of chaotic memories. . . . I know only that in your chilly semidarkness, among your strange and extravagant ornamental molding and pseudo-Renaissance cornices, we discovered our Dzikie Pola, we, boys from the floors, our first bruises and our first bloody noses. . . . And as with everything in this strange city, you, too, gateways of Warsaw, appeared in downright strangeness and misery in the noblest heroism without posing, pomposity or lofty words, rather with a lightly vulgar scream, just as it is done in Warsaw.

—LEOPOLD TYRMAND, ZŁY

Dzikie Pola: Wild fields, referring to the eastern steppes of the Polish-Lithuanian Commonwealth. The term here also refers to a children's role-playing game that is acted out in the term's historical context. Tyrmand, born in 1920, was from a prewar Polonized Jewish family in Warsaw. He was a journalist in postwar Poland before he emigrated in 1965 and settled in the United States.

CONTENTS

ACKNOWLEDGMENTS

This project has benefited from the assistance and generosity of many individuals. I would like first of all to express my gratitude to Antony Polonsky, whose guidance and wealth of knowledge as my doctoral advisor at Brandeis University influenced every aspect of this book. David Cesarani, ChaeRan Freeze, Seamus O'Hanlon, Jonathan Plaut, Jonathan Sarna, and Eugene Sheppard provided feedback on all or parts of the manuscript. The steadfast support of Marc Brettler and Ellie Kellman helped make it possible to see this project through to completion, and Michael Steinlauf's work on postwar Poland pointed me toward doctoral studies. Israel Bartal and Gabriella Safran commented on sections of the dissertation on which this book is based as part of the International Forum of Young Scholars on East European Jewry, as did David Biale, Laura Levitt, and other participants in the Posen Summer Seminar on Approaches to Jewish Secularism. Sylvia Fuks Fried was always willing to offer helpful advice. Deborah Dash Moore's comments significantly improved this book, and she facilitated its publication as coeditor of Indiana University Press's Modern Jewish Experience series. I am indebted as well to the late Paula Hyman, who was the series' coeditor, and to its current coeditor, Marsha Rozenblit, for their comments. This book would not have been possible without the support of Janet Rabinowitch at Indiana University Press, where Peter Froehlich and Nancy Lightfoot also shepherded me through the publishing process and freelancer Carol Kennedy copyedited the manuscript.

I pursued this project in several wonderfully supportive environments. I benefited from the insights of colleagues at the University of Southampton in England and the religious studies faculty at Virginia Tech, and I completed the final stages of writing at Monash University in Melbourne, Australia, where new colleagues in the European history research support group gave thoughtful feedback, and where the Australian Centre for Jewish Civilisation provided me with a home on the other side of the world. Conny Aust, Michael Cohen, Adam Mendelsohn, Simon Rabinovitch, Monika Rice, David Slucki, Melissa Weininger, and Kalman Weiser have helped to form a collegial circle in Jewish studies. I am especially grateful to the Frankel Institute for Advanced Judaic Studies at the University of Michigan, where a postdoctoral fellowship in 2010–2011 gave me the needed time to write this book, and to the American Council of Learned Societies, the American Society for Jewish Heritage in Poland, the Kościuszko Foundation, the YIVO Institute for Jewish Research, the Tauber Institute for the Study of European Jewry, and the Department of Near Eastern and Judaic Studies at Brandeis University for grants and fellowships that funded my research and training.

Previous versions of portions of chapter 4 of this book appeared in "'Nusekh Poyln'? Communism, Publishing, and Paths to Polishness among the Jewish Parents of 16 Ujazdowskie Avenue," *Polin: Studies in Polish Jewry* 24: 275–297, 2012. Previous versions of portions of chapter 6 and the epilogue appeared in "Elders Transmit Holocaust Memory in Vivid Detail to Younger Interviewers: In Warsaw, Ghetto Buildings Are a Palimpsest of the Past," *Forward* [New York, N.Y.], April 16, 1999, 15; "Youngsters Rebuild Life in Poland, Then Decamp for Israel, America: A Revival Turns Complicated in a Haunted Land," *Forward* [New York, N.Y.], December 18, 1998, 1; and "Natan Cywiak, 81, Was Stalwart of Warsaw Synagogue," *Forward* [New York, N.Y.], May 28, 1999, 6.

I am deeply indebted to my interviewees, who were generous with their time as they helped to reconstruct their family histories. This work would not have been possible without the assistance of the "children" of Ujazdowskie 16 and their relatives: Marian Adler, Halina Adler-Bramley, Lena Bergman, Feliks Falk, Krystyna Heldwein, Bernard Krutz, Jurek Neftalin, Włodek Paszyński, Szymon Rudnicki, Jan and Franek Sławny, Piotr Sztuczyński, Liliana Tyszelman, and the late Zofia Zarębska. I am particularly grateful to Marian Adler and Halina Adler-Bramley for allowing me access to their parents' personal papers.

At the Jewish Historical Institute, which provided me with an academic home in Warsaw, I was assisted by many individuals, especially Edyta Kurek, Monika Natkowska-Tarasowa, Yale Reisner, Agnieszka Reszka, and Feliks Tych. I am continuously inspired by their dedication. Monika Krawczyk has accompanied me through many years of friendship and conversations about postwar Polish Jewish life since my earliest research. I am grateful for the insights and camaraderie of Natalia Aleksiun, Robyn Berman, Michał Bilewicz, August Grabski, Joanna Nalewajko-Kulikov, Martyna Rusyniak, Piotr Rytka-Zandberg, Albert Stankowski, Karolina Szymaniak, Marcin Urynowicz, Wendy Widom, Zosia Wóycicka, and Kasia Żarnecka-Lasota during numerous extended stays in Warsaw. I also benefited from conversations with and assistance from Jerzy W. Borejsza, Helena Datner, Stanisław Krajewski, Adam Rok, Hanna Węgrzynek, and Andrzej Żbikowski. The late Joanna Wiszniewicz looked after me in Warsaw, and her research on the "1968" generation was a foundation for my own work. Archivists at numerous institutions facilitated my research, including the Polish Ministry of Education, the Institute for National Remembrance, and the Society for the Friends of Children, particularly Wojciech Stojanowski. At the U.S. Holocaust Memorial Museum, Teresa Pollin and Marcel and Ania Drimer shared their experiences in postwar Poland. Mentors and colleagues in journalism helped to shape my research in its earliest stages, especially David Lee Preston, who guided me at the very beginning of my journey, and Lisa Tracy, who encouraged me to embark upon this path. Andrzej Kołuszko and Gennady Kulikov provided help with photography.

My family and friends have sustained me through the many years it took to complete this project, especially Glenn Auerbach, Donna Davis, Sandra Hammer, the late Sheryl Lewart, Jeff and Joanna Bauman, Jeff Cioletti, Teri DelGiudice, Eric Fleisch, Tony Gallotto, Jennifer Golson, Rebecca Hartman, Randy Miller, Jenny Roth, and Emily Wax. Debra Margulies's support was a lifeline for many years. David B. saw me through every obstacle.

I am grateful above all to my parents. My father instilled in me a fascination with the past and shared my enthusiasm at every step. My mother taught me by her example what it means to persevere, and I could not have completed this project without her unwavering support. The joy of finishing this book was greatly diminished by the sadness of losing her before she could see the final result.

This project has its roots in a 1997 visit to Warsaw to see the childhood home of my grandmother, Hilda Yellin Auerbach, born Hinde Jelen. Her memory started me on this path and accompanied me along the way.

RESIDENTS OF 16 UJAZDOWSKIE AVENUE

ADLERS (APARTMENT 9)

Emil Adler, coeditor of Marxist-Leninist literature, with Stefan Bergman, for the Book and Knowledge publishing house until 1950 and professor of Marxist philosophy at Warsaw University. Born Mendel Adler in 1906 in Tarnów to Markus and Helena Adler and raised in Brody. Emil emigrated from Poland with his family to Göttingen, Germany, in 1968. Husband of Eugenia, father of Marian and Halina.

Eugenia (Genia) Adler, translator and editor at the Book and Knowledge publishing house. Born Eugenia (Gita) Sztarksztejn in Warsaw in 1922. Adler lived in the Warsaw ghetto and survived Majdanek, Auschwitz, and Gross-Rosen. After the war, before marrying Emil, she went by the name Eugenia Zagielska from the last name of her first husband, Jerzy Zagiel, who was killed during the war. Wife of Emil, mother of Marian and Halina.

Halina Adler-Bramley, daughter of Emil and Eugenia Adler. Born in Warsaw in 1948, Halina settled in the United States after her emigration from Poland in 1968.

Marian Adler, son of Emil and Eugenia. Born in 1947 in Łódź, he moved to Göttingen, Germany, with his family in 1968.

BERGMANS (APARTMENT 13)

Paulina Bergman, also known as Pesa, mother of Stefan Bergman and
Luba Rudnicka. Born in 1879. Paulina raised her children in Vilnius
and later cared for her grandchildren in the Soviet Union before
and during the Second World War while her children were in the
Gulag. Her married name was Epsztejn, but she went by Bergman
after the war.

Aleksandra Bergman, a prewar activist in the Communist Party of Western Belorussia and after the war a historian of the Belarusian minority in Poland. Aleksandra was born Chawa Kuczkowska in 1906 in
Hrodno; her party pseudonym was Aleksandra Malewska. She was
arrested in 1935 during the Stalinist purges and spent more than a
decade in the Gulag. Wife of Stefan, mother of Zofia and Lena.

Stefan Bergman, editor of Marxist-Leninist literature for the Book and
Knowledge publishing house in postwar Poland until 1963. Born
Beniamin Epsztejn in Vilnius in 1904 to Paulina and Szymon. Before
the war he was a typesetter and an activist in the Communist Party
of Western Belorussia. In 1935 he was arrested and sent to the Gulag.
Husband of Aleksandra, father of Zofia and Lena, son of Paulina,
brother of Luba Rudnicka.

Eleonora (Lena) Bergman, younger daughter of Stefan and Aleksandra
Bergman. Eleonora was born in Łódź in 1947. She is usually called
Lena, the diminutive of Eleonora.

Zofia (Zosia) Zarębska, elder daughter of Stefan and Aleksandra Bergman, born in Homel in 1934. She was cared for by her grandmother,
Paulina, while her parents were imprisoned in the Gulag. She was
originally named Zoria before her name was changed to Zofia following her family's arrival in Poland from the Soviet Union at the
end of the Second World War. She was usually called Zosia, the
diminutive of Zofia.

FALKS (APARTMENT 10)

Ernest Falk, board member and administrator of postwar Poland's publishing cooperative, RSW-Prasa, until his dismissal in 1964. Born

in Stanisławów in 1908, Ernest worked as a lawyer while serving as director of the propaganda section in Stanisławów of the Communist Party of Western Ukraine. Husband of Salomea, father of Feliks.

Salomea Falk, pediatrician from Stanisławów. Born as Salomea Zajfert in 1909, she studied medicine in Prague before marrying Ernest Falk. In the 1930s Salomea served as a doctor at a Jewish hospital in Warsaw called Czyste. She also worked as a doctor after the war. Wife of Ernest, mother of Feliks.

Feliks Falk, a film director in Poland, son of Ernest and Salomea Falk.

FEDECKA (APARTMENT 24)

Stefania Fedecka, born Stefania Kestenberg in Lublin in 1919. Stefania survived the Holocaust in Lublin and L'viv. After working in a publishing institution after the war, she held positions in the Ministry of Foreign Affairs and the Polish Institute for International Affairs. Married to Edward, a non-Jew whom she met after the war.

H. FAMILY (APARTMENT 16)

Barbara H., a pedagogue and editor, first editor-in-chief of Book and Knowledge. Barbara was born Bina in Końskie in 1907. After leaving Book and Knowledge in 1950, she was an editor at a literary monthly and at other publishing houses. Grandmother of Włodek Paszyński.

Włodzimierz (Włodek) Paszyński, born in 1951 in Warsaw. Grandson of Barbara H. He goes by the diminutive Włodek.

KACZYŃSKIS (APARTMENT 15)

Halina Kaczyńska, born in Warsaw in 1919. Halina gave birth to a son, Ryszard, in Warsaw during the Holocaust, and she and her husband, Zygmunt, lived on the "Aryan" side in Warsaw. She and Zygmunt had two daughters after the war as well.

Zygmunt Kaczyński, an administrator for the publishing cooperative RSW-Prasa immediately after the war and later a lawyer. Born in Baranowicze in 1914.

KRUCES (APARTMENT 20)

Ignacy Kruc, director of economic planning for Book and Knowledge. Born as Yitzhak Krancenblum in Warsaw in 1910. Before the war he helped his father run a grocery store and became an activist in the communist party youth movement, for which he distributed propaganda leaflets. Ignacy emigrated with his wife Stanisława to Sweden in 1971.

Stanisława Kruc, a nurse and pediatrician. Born Stanisława Szpigelman in Warsaw in 1915, she was a leader in the communist youth movement in Warsaw before the war. Married to Ignacy Kruc and mother of Bernard Krutz and Ela Kruc, she immigrated to Sweden with her husband Ignacy in 1971.

Bernard Krutz (Bolesław or Bolek Kruc), adopted son of Stanisława and Ignacy Kruc. Bernard lived in the L'viv ghetto as a young child and survived the Holocaust by hiding with a Catholic woman on the "Aryan" side. His birth date and his birth parents' names are unknown. He was known as Bernard Strzycki until his adoption in 1949 by Stanisława and Ignacy, who gave him the name Bolesław. Since immigrating to the United States in 1968, he has gone by the name Bernard Krutz. He lives with his family in New Jersey. Adoptive brother of Ela.

Ela Kruc, adopted daughter of Stanisława and Ignacy Kruc. Ela was born in 1942 or 1943 in the L'viv ghetto to Lili and Szymon Panach and survived as a hidden child on the "Aryan" side. The Kruces adopted her after the war from an orphanage near Łódź. Ela immigrated to Melbourne, Australia in 1970. Adoptive sister of Bernard.

RUDNICKAS (APARTMENT 13, THEN 6)

Luba Rudnicka, a prewar activist and youth leader in the Communist Party of Western Belorussia. Born Luba Bergman in Vilnius in 1909. Luba was arrested in 1935 during the Stalinist purges. She gave birth to her son, Szymon, while in the Gulag. Sister of Stefan Bergman, daughter of Paulina Bergman.

Szymon Rudnicki, historian of twentieth-century Poland. Born in 1938 in the Gulag to Luba Rudnicka. Grandson of Paulina, nephew of Stefan and Aleksandra Bergman.

SŁAWNYS (APARTMENT 17)

Antonina (Tosia) Sławny, born in Łódź in 1910 as Antonina Wajnberg, also called by the diminutive Tosia or by Tola. She immigrated to France in the 1930s and studied medicine at a university in Lyons. She survived the Holocaust in France before returning to Poland for six years with her family. Wife of Władysław, mother of Jan and Francis.

Władysław Sławny, photography editor for the weekly magazine *Świat* (World) from 1950 until he left Poland in 1957. Władysław was born as Wolf in 1907 in Nowy Korczyn and was raised in Łódź. He was active in the Communist youth movement in Łódź and emigrated to France before the war. Husband of Antonina, father of Jan and Francis.

Francis Sławny, elder son of Władysław and Antonina Sławny, brother of Jan.

Jan Sławny, younger son of Władysław and Antonina Sławny, brother of Francis.

SZTUCZYŃSKA/NEFTALIN (APARTMENT 18)

Nina Sztuczyńska, born in 1922 in Warsaw as Nina Kranc to a Jewish father and a Russian Orthodox mother. Nina was active in the communist underground in Warsaw during the Second World War. After the war she worked at *Gazeta Przyjaciółka* [Women's gazette] and in the research section for party history in the Central Committee of the Polish United Workers' Party. Mother of Piotr and Jurek.

Samuel Neftalin, engineer at an industrial architecture firm until his dismissal in 1968. Samuel was an administrator for the publishing cooperative RSW-Prasa in the early postwar years. Born in Łódź. Husband of Nina Sztuczyńska, father of Jurek, stepfather of Piotr Sztuczyński.

Jerzy (Jurek) Neftalin, born in 1947 in Warsaw, son of Nina Sztuczyńska and Samuel Neftalin. He emigrated from Poland to Göteberg, Sweden, in 1968. He goes by the diminutive Jurek.

Piotr Sztuczyński, born in 1944 in the Pruszków internment camp outside of Warsaw. His father, Kazimierz, died during the Warsaw Uprising before his birth. Son of Nina, stepson of Samuel Neftalin.

TYSZELMANS (APARTMENT 8)

Lea Herman, mother of Zina Tyszelman.

Józef Tyszelman, technical director for Book and Knowledge and vice president of its governing board until his dismissal in 1963. Józef was born in Warsaw in 1916. Husband of Zina, father of Liliana and Krystyna.

Zina Tyszelman, born Zina Herman in Warsaw in 1917. Zina worked at a chemical import-export firm after the war, among other positions. She was related to Judyta Herman, the wife of the historian and wartime ghetto archivist Emanuel Ringelblum. Zina's mother, Lea, lived with Zina's family at Ujazdowskie Avenue until her death in 1951. Wife of Józef, mother of Liliana and Krystyna.

Krystyna (Krysia) Minc, née *Tyszelman,* younger daughter of Józef and Zina. Krystyna was born in Warsaw in 1948. She left Poland in 1982 and works at the veterinary college of a university in Alabama. Sister of Liliana.

Liliana Kamionka, née *Tyszelman,* elder daughter of Józef and Zina. Liliana was born in 1942 in Tomsk in the Soviet Union, to which her parents fled during the war. Sister of Krystyna.

THE HOUSE AT UJAZDOWSKIE 16

Introduction

AT DAWN ONE MORNING in October 1945, eleven-year-old Zofia Bergman arrived with her mother, Aleksandra, by train into Warsaw, the
demolished capital of liberated Poland, after a long journey from the Soviet Union. The cold days of early winter had already set in. Mother and
daughter walked through rubble-lined streets, past skeletons of buildings in a barely living city that just six years earlier had been known as
the "Paris of the East."

Zofia did not want to make this journey. More than a decade earlier,
her parents, Polish Jews from Vilnius and Hrodno who were prewar
communists, had been arrested in the Soviet Union during the Stalinist
purges and sent to the Gulag. They were forced to leave Zofia in the care
of the infant's grandmother. Now, in 1945, the child had grown into a
serious young girl, strong-willed but good-natured, who wore her hair
in long braids and spoke only Russian. Zofia had only recently reunited
with a mother she did not know. The girl did not want to leave behind
her grandmother and cousins, who did not yet have permission to leave
the Soviet Union for Poland.

On Warsaw's right bank, called Praga, Zofia and her mother headed
to a crowded building where many Polish Jews returning from the Soviet
Union were finding temporary shelter. A few hours after their arrival,

mother and daughter walked across a makeshift bridge to the city center and toward the deserted streets of Muranów, the prewar Jewish neighborhood, where the Nazis had established the wartime ghetto. They walked in the area around Dzielna Street, where Aleksandra and her husband Stefan had lived briefly in the early 1930s. But it was difficult to make out the street grid in the rubble.

The Polish capital was a landscape of ruin, and the Nazi destruction of the wartime Jewish ghetto was only one element of the city's devastation. After the failed uprising led by the Polish underground in 1944, the Germans leveled the city center and sent remaining Warsaw residents to transit camps outside the city. Tens of thousands were deported to concentration and labor camps.

Among the few parts of the city center that escaped destruction was the area along Ujazdowskie Avenue, which extended south from the main thoroughfare of Jerusalem Avenue toward the picturesque Łazienki Park. German officials lived in Ujazdowskie Avenue's elegant buildings during the occupation. For this reason, the avenue and nearby streets suffered less devastation than the rest of the city center.

It was here that three generations of Zofia and Aleksandra Bergman's family would make their home in 1948, at 16 Ujazdowskie Avenue near the church of Saint Aleksander, in an area known before the war as Warsaw's "summer salon." Among their neighbors in the building were nine other families of Jewish background. Within the walls of their homes, they reconstructed their lives in a reconstructing city.

—⁓—

All along Ujazdowskie Avenue in the contemporary capital are architectural remnants of old Warsaw. At number 16, echoes of the past are displayed in the windows of the ground floor, where an antiquarian bookstore beckons passersby with maps from centuries past.

A visitor might pause in front of the bookstore's window before ringing an apartment upstairs, then passing through the wooden doors and arched entranceway before entering the building. The hallway is dim, but the stairway's expansive steps and open staircase are reminiscent of faded prewar elegance. On the second-floor landing, however, a window looking out onto the back of the building reveals dilapidated brick structures surrounding a courtyard on three sides, adjoined to the front but hidden from the street. Decades ago an empty stone fountain would have been visible below.

At apartment 13 on the second floor lives Aleksandra Bergman's younger daughter, Lena, who was born two years after her mother and sister Zofia first walked through the rubble of postwar Warsaw. Lena lives in the same apartment where her family had made its home for more than a half-century. A visitor might find her apartment door slightly ajar as she waits inside. In the foyer, where a framed nineteenth-century map of Warsaw hangs on the wall, glimpses of the high-ceilinged apartment come into view. The room to the right is spacious, dominated by a large wooden desk beside a window looking out onto the street. From the room just behind, the apartment's residents could lean over the iron railing of the balcony and take in the bustle of the city below. Long ago, Hitler oversaw a victory parade along the avenue.

Throughout the apartment, lining walls in every room but the small kitchen, are bookshelves that climb to the ceiling. Books were the "stage of their fate," as Walter Benjamin wrote, the re-creation of a lost past and the replacement of severed roots with new ones. The spines show titles in every language that Aleksandra and Stefan Bergman spoke during their lifetimes spanning the entire twentieth century: mainly Polish in the front rooms, and in the back room, shelves of books in Russian, Belorussian, and Yiddish.

In the hallway outside, on the opposite end of the corridor, lives Lena's older cousin, Szymon Rudnicki. Born in the Gulag in 1938, he was already a young boy when he came with his family to Poland from the Soviet Union at war's end. Today he is a historian of Poland and Polish Jewry. Like his cousin's apartment down the hall, his home is filled with books accumulated over a lifetime. On a side table in the small front room is a framed drawing of an unsmiling young woman. The picture depicts the two cousins' aunt in the 1930s, not long before she was shot in a Soviet prison.

—m—

More than six decades ago, when the cousins and their families moved into apartment 13 in early 1948, Lena Bergman was not yet one year old. Szymon Rudnicki was nearly ten. Accompanying them were Lena's sister Zofia and their parents, Szymon's mother, and the cousins' grandmother—an unusually large extended family in a Polish Jewish population decimated by the Holocaust. The Bergman/Rudnicka clan and nine other Jewish families that moved into the building in the following two years occupied nearly half of its twenty-three apartments at a time when surviving Jews made up a negligible percentage of Warsaw's population.

The families' common address resulted from social, political, and professional ties that connected one neighbor to another. Parents in all ten families worked for publishing institutions of the postwar Polish government, and in five of those families, they were founding editors and directors of the postwar Polish communist party's ideological publishing house, called Book and Knowledge, *Książka i Wiedza* in Polish.[1] The neighbors shared bonds of political passion and publishing work, friendship and casual acquaintance, and a common Jewish background that led to an understanding of where they had come from and what they had lost in wartime.

The postwar lives of the parents at 16 Ujazdowskie Avenue, the generation that survived the Second World War as adults, are replete with contradictions. More than half were internationalists in ideology, yet through their publishing work they immersed themselves in the Polish word. The families were distanced from their Jewish background, yet they lived in a building where nearly half of their neighbors were Jewish. Despite the integration of most of these parents into Polish culture to a greater or lesser degree both before and after the Second World War, their association with communism was an obstacle to their families' integration into surrounding society. One Jewish resident of 16 Ujazdowskie Avenue who moved there in the 1970s and whose father was a prewar communist described his parents' social circles as the "Jewish communist intellectual ghetto."[2]

The building's Jewish families were not typical of Poland's Jewish population before or after the Holocaust, since nearly half of the parents were communists, and the concentration at 16 Ujazdowskie Avenue is larger than the mostly smaller clusters of Jewish residents in other Warsaw buildings.[3] Nor were their networks exclusively Jewish; the connections that brought together the Jewish families at 16 Ujazdowskie Avenue included some of their non-Jewish neighbors, among them two who were involved in communist underground circles that provided help to Jews during the Holocaust. But their communist beliefs were an extreme form of the secularizing influences that shaped postwar Polish Jewry more broadly. The families' histories are an example of the paths by which Polonizing Jews sought entrance into nineteenth- and twentieth-century Polish society as well as the ambiguous fate of those aspirations. Their assimilation into Polish society over the course of the postwar generations in Poland coexisted in tension with antisemitism and emigration which underscored integration's limits.

The Jewish parents at 16 Ujazdowskie Avenue were entirely secular, nearly all of them radically so. Although they did not hide their Jewish roots from their children, the parents distanced themselves from that identity in postwar Poland. Yet the spaces they shared within the walls of their apartment building reflected the ties that continued to connect them with other Jewish families. The common setting of their homes, schools, social circles, and workplaces preserved the presence of the Jewish past in everyday life, and they understood how the Second World War and postwar political upheavals affected them differently than those events affected their non-Jewish neighbors. None of their children knew that so many of the other families had Jewish roots, but they were aware that some neighbors shared their own Jewish background. That identity was present in the spaces just outside their homes, if often only marginally. For one boy, the Yiddish sometimes spoken by the neighboring children's grandmother stood out in his memory; it was his own mother's native tongue but one that he almost never heard in his own home.

When the Polish government's antisemitic campaign in 1968 scapegoated Jews for student anticensorship protests, the Jewish identity that was present in the shadows of the children's everyday life rose to the surface as they were confronted with a Jewish past about which most of them knew little. About fifteen thousand Jews emigrated in the following two years.[4] Yet the departures did not put an end to Jewish integration in Poland. As the children who remained entered adulthood, they overcame the isolation from Polish society that had shaped their parents' lives.

Both the absence of Jewish identity on the surface of their childhoods and its presence beneath the surface led to their assimilation as adults. They grew up in homes where Polish culture filled the gaps resulting from their parents' suppression of the Jewish past. At the same time, the spaces that connected them to other Jews in childhood limited the impact of antisemitism, which often preserves Jewish identity in the absence of any other connection to that background. Some among them recalled encountering discrimination during the first postwar decades, but clusters of Jews among classmates, friends, and neighbors surrounded them in childhood with a concept of Polishness that did not exclude them. They identified mainly, sometimes entirely, with Poland and had little or no connection with their Jewish background.

Despite the antisemitic campaign of 1968, the spaces of everyday life that set them apart from other Poles at home, at school, and among friends in previous decades eventually helped those who remained in Poland after 1970 to fulfill their parents' hopes that their families would no longer experience life as the "other" in their native country. Of the nine children who grew up at 16 Ujazdowskie Avenue and remained in Poland after 1970, six who married had non-Jewish spouses, and those who had children raised them as Christians or with no religion at all. Of the two who married spouses of Jewish background, one left Poland in the 1980s.

Nonetheless, postwar Polish Jewish history is full of paradoxes. Even as Jewish families, not only at 16 Ujazdowskie Avenue, assimilated into surrounding society as children who grew up in Poland after the Second World War reached adulthood, some among them began to explore their Jewish background, however tentatively. Their interest stemmed not only from their individual family histories. They also were asserting a definition of Polishness with which they had grown up, one that could include Jews as equal members. Their explorations eventually strengthened the Jewish presence in Poland, creating identities that blurred boundaries between Christian and Jew, insider and outsider.

—⁂—

The youngest generation of Jews in contemporary Poland has emerged in part because shards of memory escaped attempts to forget the past: a grandmother's or a mother's unfamiliar way of washing her hands before meals, a few words remembered by a granddaughter who did not realize until much later that the words were in Yiddish. The windows of 16 Ujazdowskie Avenue offer a view onto the paths that led from suppression of the Jewish past among many surviving Jews who remained in Poland, particularly in Warsaw, to the reemergence of Jewish identity in the lives of their children and grandchildren.

As with many Jewish families, the rebuilt Polish capital also submerged the Jewish past beneath the traumas of the Holocaust, the politics of communist Poland, and reconstructed communities. Yet just as Jewish memory was still present on the margins of family life, so, too, did the city's postwar landscape preserve shadows of its once-thriving Jewish society, which made up about one-third of the capital's prewar population. That past remained beneath the surface of the rebuilt city and rebuilt families, fading into the background but never entirely erased.

Postwar Warsaw was a dynamic blend of continuity and change, both in the lives of its residents and in the spaces they inhabited. But its former Jewish quarters had been demolished. The rubble of the ghetto was quickly paved over to make way for new buildings; the neighborhoods' remnants were literally buried beneath the foundations of the new Warsaw. The absence of Jewish neighborhoods cast a particularly long shadow on the city's reconstruction. Not only people, but also the physical landscape of their lives had been erased when the Nazis quashed the final resistance of the Warsaw ghetto in 1943. "No more, the streets of mine are no more," a poet wrote in a Yiddish newspaper in Poland just after the war. "There are no Warsaw Jews left."[5]

And yet, in buildings throughout the city, surviving Jews continued to make the capital their home. Most transported the bonds of community from the street into the private spaces of their lives: homes, friendships, schools. Their histories are a missing thread of the narrative of Jewish history in Poland after the Holocaust.

Postwar Jewish life unfolded as part of the drama of Polish and Polish-Jewish history, reflecting the universal themes and complexities of human experience, evident in the most mundane histories but even more so in the tumultuous history of twentieth-century Poland and its Jewish population. There is the tension between memory and history, the desire to forget the past and the impossibility of doing so, the suppression of memory and the consequences of its absence. In this book we follow the narratives that individuals created to explain their present, built upon the past but always filtered through the lens of later experience, and the challenge of accessing the past beyond the narrative.

In this history we can trace the construction of identity and community: an individual's relationship to one's country, family, religion, surrounding society, political system, culture. From the vantage point of 16 Ujazdowskie Avenue we observe the interplay between private life and broader circumstances of time and place in shaping that identity and those communities. Emerging in the families' lives are commonalities in how individuals are shaped by the surroundings in which private life plays out, what Pierre Bourdieu termed the "habitus." We see the possibility for an individual to determine a life path and the limits to this ability when a history larger than an individual life intervenes. Rising to the surface is the accumulation of decisions by minor actors who determine the details of history—and perhaps the broader outlines as well—but also the influence of history writ large on what decisions an individual makes, often in a way that is invisible to those who are living this history.

The drama of private life itself unfolds: cycles of generational rebellion, the rootlessness that develops when history removes an individual from family and community, and the construction of new roots and new communities. Postwar Polish Jewish life underscores the role of family in preserving or rejecting Jewish identity, as decisions by one generation influence the identifications of the next, sometimes by continuing a previous generation's path and sometimes by rebelling against it. Shaping the lives of the residents at 16 Ujazdowskie Avenue are bonds that reach across borders, not only geographic, and at the same time the continued pull of the culture, language, and society in which they were raised. There is the tragedy of disillusionment with a chosen path, and the unquenchable longing and ruptured identity among those forced to leave their country. Above all we see the contradictions within an individual's identity and the continued influence of a previous identity despite its replacement with another.

Broader developments in modern Jewish history, too, thread through the families' lives despite the particular, perhaps exceptional, circumstances of Poland's Jewish population after the Second World War. In postwar Poland, the Holocaust and communist politics accelerated transformations of Jewish identity in modernity, bringing into sharp relief the processes of integration and its obstacles. These changes have unfolded not only in postwar Poland, but also in the United States, in Weimar Germany in an earlier period, and elsewhere. Their lives were marked by the vacuum of identity resulting from the absence of observance, when the texts and rituals that once united Jews across geographic borders no longer shaped everyday life. As in previous periods and other countries, Jews in Poland after the Holocaust often created informal communities in private spaces when Jewish institutions and public spaces no longer connected them.

In postwar Poland we witness the tensions in modern European Jewish history between the expectations of much of surrounding society that Jews would fully merge with it after emancipation, and the expectations of many Jews who believed they could be both Polish and Jewish, or French and Jewish, or German and Jewish at the same time. Cascading conflicts that developed since the second half of the nineteenth century saw surrounding society's redefinition of the relationship between nation and state in a way that could not include Jews, and many Jews' rejection of the desire for integration partly because of the antisemitism that accompanied these exclusionary ideas. We follow the decisions by some Jews to leave a hostile society behind for a country in which possibilities for acceptance seemed more promising, and the creation or re-creation of new Jewish group identifications, whether drawing on ancient ties or on the ideologies of surrounding European societies. In this history we confront in exaggerated form the very problem of defining Jewishness in modernity and the ever-present question of how to incorporate Jewish identity into a sense of belonging to the countries in which Jews live.

The search for an answer to that question shaped postwar paths of parents and children at 16 Ujazdowskie Avenue. Stripping away layers of history, we find the turning point of that search in 1968. As thousands of Jews left Poland during the government's antisemitic campaign, the Bergman-Rudnicki cousins who live today on opposite ends of the second floor at 16 Ujazdowskie Avenue cast their fate with the country in which they grew up. Every member of their family remained in Poland. They refused to accept the rejection of their identification as Poles.

Among the parents and children of Jewish background who lived at 16 Ujazdowskie Avenue for at least part of their lives in postwar Poland, members of more than half of the families followed a different path, boarding trains that led away from Poland. They learned new languages and struggled to incorporate not only their Jewish identity, but also their Polish identity into new roots in adopted countries. Their own children grew up in new cultures, even as some of the parents longed for a country and a language their children barely knew.

—⁕—

The families' twentieth-century histories began in cities and towns throughout prewar Poland, from the capital to the hometown *shtetlekh* of parents and grandparents. After the war their paths led not only to Warsaw, but also to Israel, France, Sweden, Germany, Australia, the United States, Canada, England, and in several cases back to Warsaw once more. Their lives were shaped by the Jewish past, the devastation of the Holocaust, and the evolution of Polish politics, culture, and society in the turbulent twentieth century.

A few preliminary comments about terms and methodology are in order. This book is a story of two generations: the parents who came of age in interwar Poland and were adults during the Second World War; and the generation of children who grew up and attended school in the decades between war's end and 1968. When relevant, however, the study examines differences between members of the children's generation who were born in the early postwar years and older children who were born just before or during the war, particularly those who survived the Holocaust as children. The term "assimilation," not only "acculturation," is appropriate for this history of Jewish life in postwar Poland. "Assimilation" in this study refers to a continuum of integration that can, but does not necessarily have to, continue through each stage of the process to full absorption into surrounding society.[6]

The framework of microhistory brings to light the influence of Jewish background and the evolution of identifications over the course of generations by creating a "thick description" of narrowly framed developments.[7] This approach allows a historian to analyze the relationship between "systems of belief, of values and representations on the one side, and social affiliations on the other."[8] I analyze the families' cultural backgrounds, upbringing, education, experiences of wartime survival, and other formative factors to understand how these influenced their social networks, their family life, their children's upbringing, and their reactions to variegations in postwar Polish politics.

Microhistory is a fruitful approach for researching postwar Polish Jewish history for two main reasons. First, most surviving Jews who remained in Poland into the 1950s were distanced from Jewish institutions. The researcher must therefore reach beyond institutional histories, whether political, religious, or cultural, to understand more completely the changed Jewish population of postwar Poland. Exploring Jewish life through the microhistorical framework of one building provides access to families who otherwise would not be included in postwar Polish Jewish history and whose experiences are not fully reflected in postwar demographic statistics and institutional records. Of Jewish residents at 16 Ujazdowskie Avenue, only four of ten families, and members of two other families, are listed in the registry of surviving Jews compiled by the Central Committee of Jews in Poland in the early postwar years.[9]

Microhistory also allows a historian to focus on individual lives to bring out both continuities and discontinuities before and after the Holocaust. This emphasis results in a different picture than that provided by a focus on postwar Poland's Jewish institutions, which, after the earliest postwar years, were largely uprooted from prewar Jewish life and therefore further the perception that the postwar period cannot be placed within the longer history of Polish Jewry.

The families I examine include nineteen members of the parents' generation and eighteen children. They comprise ten families, one of which, the Bergman-Rudnicka family, was made up of two branches that initially lived in the same apartment. The Adler, Kruc, and Fedecka families moved out of the building in the 1950s and early 1960s, and the Rudnicka family moved out of the Bergman home into one of their former apartments, occupying two residences in the building. Interviews indicated that another family from the building, the Kochanowskis, was Jewish and left Poland during an emigration wave, but they were not present on building lists and it was not possible to locate them. Another family, the Mieczkowskis, was close to the Bergmans and was present on one building list, but interviewees were not able to provide information with which to locate them, and there was no clear indication of their background from available documents or interviewees. I have therefore not included them when referring to the number of families of Jewish background from the building.

In one family, that of Włodek Paszyński, I have not included Włodek's mother when citing the number of parents and children in the building. She was thirteen years old at the outbreak of the Second World War and gave birth to Włodek in 1951, so she did not come of age between the world wars and was not an adult during the Second World War, as I have defined the parents' generation, nor was she raised or attended school after the war, as I have defined the generation of children. Because she declined to be interviewed, I do not use her name and refer to her mother as Barbara H., using the first initial of Barbara's prewar last name, since they shared a surname after the war. Barbara lived with her daughter and grandson at 16 Ujazdowskie Avenue. In the family of Stefania Fedecka, I have not used the name of her son, whom I interviewed but who asked that his name not appear. He and his mother do not share the same last name.

The sources for this book grew out of the study's focus on processes of integration and obstacles to this integration within individual families, as well as the ambiguous attitudes toward the Jewish past among the postwar residents of 16 Ujazdowskie Avenue. Limited transmission of knowledge from parents to children about the nature of the families' Jewish background challenged attempts to access information about this aspect of their past, making it difficult to place the postwar period within the context of the families' prewar and wartime lives. This, in turn, created an obstacle to tracing transformations in identifications.

These challenges determined the source base and the ways in which the study uses these sources to reconstruct the families' histories. Four groups of sources—oral histories, archival documents, personal papers and published writings—established a detailed understanding not only of the past as far as it was possible to reconstruct, but also of how the broader historical context compared both with the narratives transmitted from parents to children, and with the narratives presented in official postwar documents.

Thirty-nine oral histories, mainly from the generation of children and extended family,[10] in most cases provided a starting point to determine the specific areas of archival research. One extensive interview was possible with a member of the parents' generation from the building. Although other members of the parents' generation were no longer alive by the time I began research, this work also makes use of interviews with residents who were members of the parents' generation conducted by other individuals before the residents' deaths. Oral histories of extended social circles and members of the parents' generation who were not residents of the building, but whose postwar lives intersected with the families at 16 Ujazdowskie Avenue, supplemented interviews with the building's residents.

The study's focus on Warsaw is intentional. Distance from Jewish identity was more dominant in Warsaw than elsewhere in Poland, and communism played a greater role for its postwar Jewish population, since the capital attracted politically involved individuals more so than other parts of Poland. In Kraków, Łódź, and Poland's newly acquired western territories, the influence of politics was somewhat mitigated by distance from the central authorities. Thus, Warsaw is a more extreme case of the secularization and suppression of Jewish identity that threads through postwar Polish Jewish history more generally. Jewish communal life and populations outside of Warsaw are examined mainly as context.

Because the history of the families of Jewish background at 16 Ujazdowskie Avenue is also part of the history of Warsaw and its postwar transformations, the city is as much a character in this story as are the families and the building in which they lived.

—◊—

A final note: The address of 16 Ujazdowskie Avenue changed numerous times from its construction in the early twentieth century through 1956. Until just after the Second World War, the number was 28, and later its name changed to Stalin Avenue before reverting to Ujazdowskie Avenue. To avoid confusion, I have referred to the building throughout as 16 Ujazdowskie Avenue. The street name Ujazdowskie is pronounced u-yaz-DOVSK-ye. I have used the spellings of cities and towns according to their current usage, except in cases when a city had a different name entirely, such as Stanisławów, which is now in Ukraine and called Ivano-Frankivs'k.

CHAPTER ONE

History Brushed against Us

The Adlers and the Bergmans

FIVE MONTHS BEFORE Aleksandra Bergman and her daughter Zofia took a train from the Soviet Union across the rubble of the Polish landscape in October 1945, their future neighbor Eugenia Adler walked to freedom through the gates of the Nazi concentration camp Gross-Rosen in Germany. When the Red Army liberated the camp that May, she was a skeleton of her former self. But she had survived.

Eugenia, known as Genia, and five other Jewish women from the camp made their way by foot, wagon, and train back to their native country of Poland. As they traveled northward they carried with them few belongings, relying on their wits and the goodwill of strangers. In June the group finally reached Łódź, where Genia's friend Hela hoped to find relatives.[1]

Genia was her immediate family's only survivor, and her native city of Warsaw was destroyed. At twenty-three, she was alone and uncertain about the future. But a few weeks after arriving in Łódź, Genia found a job at the communist party's ideological publishing house, Book, which became known as Book and Knowledge in the fall of 1948 after absorbing the Polish Socialist Party's publishing house, Knowledge, upon the dissolution of the Polish Socialist Party. The Book and Knowledge publishing house became her anchor for the next two decades.

Just before beginning work that July, Genia boarded a train from
Łódź to Warsaw, the setting of her life until she was sent in a cattle car to
Majdanek in 1943. But there were few traces of the city she had known. A
half-century later, she recalled that first visit to postwar Warsaw:

> I ached to see my beloved city, to walk the streets, however damaged they might
> be by the war. I had already seen the destruction and burning of the ghetto. I
> knew that Warsaw was wounded and I was anxious not knowing how deep those
> wounds were.
>
> Seeing Warsaw was a crushing, devastating shock for me. Warsaw was a huge
> pile of ruins. That beautiful, elegant city was razed from the surface of the earth.
> . . . Rubble and ruins. Nothing else.
>
> I walked along Jerusalem Avenue, the beautiful thoroughfare was no more.
> . . . I walked to the Praga section, where the Jewish Center was located. I hoped
> against reason that maybe I would come across someone I knew, or maybe
> someone from my family had left a message for me and is looking for me. I don't
> know what I hoped for. A miracle.
>
> I walked across a floating bridge on the Vistula River. My Vistula. My beloved
> Warsaw, where I was born and raised, where my mother and her parents were
> born and raised. I found nothing and nobody at the Jewish Center.[2]

So Genia boarded a train once more and returned to Łódź. Thus she
began her postwar life.

—⚏—

Jews who remained in Poland after the early postwar years were a
remnant of remnants. But the drastic rupture of the Holocaust did not
severe their roots entirely, and postwar Jewish life was not only one of
discontinuity. At war's end they were freed from Nazi camps, emerged
from forests, came out of hiding places on the "Aryan" side, and returned
from the depths of the Soviet Union. Then they rebuilt on the very landscape of their losses.

After early postwar emigration, the remaining Jewish population was
increasingly made up of those for whom secular life had already overtaken
religious observance even before the Second World War. Many struggled
before the war with tensions between their Jewish background and increasing attachment to the country in which they lived, while others grew
up in families that were distanced from their Jewish background even
in previous generations. Some had left behind Jewish traditions before
the war for communist politics, whose internationalist ideology rejected
religion and, often, the relevance of Jewish identity to their worldviews.

Beneath the surface of the postwar lives of Genia Adler and her Jewish neighbors at 16 Ujazdowskie Avenue is the prewar history of a transitional generation on the borders of identities. They came of age between the world wars at a time when Polish Jewry and the newly independent Polish state struggled to define themselves and their relationship to one another. The Holocaust and its aftermath, together with the postwar communist government's secularizing policies, accelerated transformations in how Jews defined the boundaries of community. Only by understanding their lives before the Holocaust can postwar paths come into full view.

Polish Jewish life before the Second World War was shaped by contradictions. An increasing number of young people lived in multiple worlds: Polish and Jewish cultures, religious tradition and secular life, Jewish and non-Jewish languages, the shtetl and the big city. Their world was often a cacophony of languages. Most young Jews between the wars were educated in Polish at public elementary schools established specifically for Jews, called the *szabasówki,* with a day off on Saturday, and they sometimes spoke Yiddish with their parents while conversing with friends in Polish. Even those who joined Zionist youth groups but whose parents could not afford to send them to private schools grew up learning in Polish at the szabasówki.

Yet identification with Polish culture and with their native country before the Second World War found an increasingly uneasy place in Jewish life as antisemitism challenged the possibility for Jews to be equal citizens of the independent Polish state. Antisemites insisted that Jews could never be truly Polish, no matter how perfectly they spoke the language and how well they knew the classics of Polish literature. Young Jews searched for new solutions and new identities. They imagined what the future should hold, debating every possibility, from communism to Zionism in all hues.

Isaac Deutscher would have referred to the parents' generation at 16 Ujazdowskie Avenue as "non-Jewish Jews." Yet while they were distanced from Jewish observance, culture, and identity after the war, they were only one or at most two generations removed from the religious traditions of traditional Jewish society, and most of them grew up in that world. Despite their identification with Poland, despite their severance from Jewish culture and religion, their history is part of the fate of Jews who survived the Holocaust as well as the larger history of how Jews became part of European societies in modernity. Their histories are, in Yuri Slezkine's words, the story of "what happened to Tevye's children, no matter what they thought of Tevye and his faith. The central subjects of the story are those of Tevye's children who abandoned him and his faith and were, for a time and for that reason, forgotten by the rest of the family."[3]

THE ADLER FAMILY

Genia

By the time Genia Adler was born in Warsaw in 1922, her family, the Sztarksztejns, had already begun to drift away from a strictly observant Jewish life. Her parents worked on Saturdays, but they attended synagogue on Jewish holidays, fasted during Yom Kippur, and built a *sukkah* in their backyard during Sukkot. In Genia's early years the family lived on Krochmalna, the bustling street romanticized in the stories of the Yiddish writer Isaac Bashevis Singer. It was crowded with peddlers and fiddlers, Genia later reminisced, "an unforgettable, colorful world, my world."[4] Her parents made a living selling imported food and spices, and the family later moved to a more middle-class Jewish neighborhood nearby.

Genia was a pretty but plump girl who excelled in school and dreamed of becoming a doctor. Her parents usually spoke Polish and sometimes Yiddish at home, and at her Jewish girls' high school she learned in Polish while studying Latin, French, and Hebrew. Genia never focused on politics, but the Jewish political youth groups of interwar Poland were as much about community as they were about ideology, and in the late 1930s she joined the Socialist-Zionist youth movement Hashomer Hatzair.

During the summers Genia attended a Jewish camp that melded the Polish and Jewish cultures in which she was growing up. The summer before the Second World War, she recounted in an interview late in life, the campers staged a production of the drama *Dziady* (Forefathers' eve) by Adam Mickiewicz, the most beloved Polish poet of the nineteenth century. Three decades later, in 1968, the play was at the center of student anticensorship protests that sparked the political turmoil and antisemitic campaign leading to Genia's emigration that year with her husband and children. Perhaps her memories of the months before her leave-taking from Poland in 1968 became blurred in her own mind with that summer three decades earlier, in those last days before the outbreak of a war that forced her to leave behind an earlier home. Or perhaps, as often occurred in the lives of the families at 16 Ujazdowskie Avenue, history really did create its own ironies.

By the late 1930s Genia had high hopes for the future, but at home she and her father began to argue over her plans to become a doctor. She eventually prevailed, yet quotas on Jewish students in some university departments in Poland, particularly in medicine, stymied her plans.[5] So Genia set her sights on studying abroad and began tutoring to save money in Depression-era Poland. For months Poles had feared that war was imminent. The Second World War broke out before she could realize her ambitions.

During more than five years of war, it seemed as though decades passed. The Holocaust erased Genia's roots in Warsaw almost entirely. When she sat down with an interviewer in 1996, Genia recalled the smallest details of her childhood and wartime survival: the names of friends, addresses, important dates. Sometimes the chronology of her narrative was muddled. But as she recounted her life, she sought to reconstruct in her mind's eye a lost world.[6]

Genia's younger sister, Cesia, was the first in her family to die. On October 31, 1939, less than two months after the war began and before Warsaw Jews were imprisoned in a ghetto, Genia held her sister as she succumbed to typhus. Cesia was the only member of her immediate family who had a funeral and a proper burial.[7] Years later, when Genia returned to Warsaw after the war and visited the city's Jewish cemetery, her sister's grave had been badly damaged.

Genia's younger brother Natek was just ten years old when he was caught in the mass deportations in the Warsaw ghetto between July and September 1942, when at least 300,000 Jews were herded onto trains and sent to Treblinka. Older youth and young adults such as Genia, who was twenty by then, had a better chance of surviving than young children such as Natek. The Holocaust destroyed a generation of Jewish youth who were too young for the Nazis to consider them "useful" enough to remain living.

Jews of Genia's generation in the Warsaw ghetto often lived for the present at a time when their futures were so uncertain. Even in the dire conditions of the ghetto, where corpses lay on the streets and several families resided together in desperately overcrowded rooms, young people found love and infants were born. Genia, too, began her own family in those desperate times. In the ghetto she married an upstairs neighbor, Jerzy Zagiel, in a ceremony performed by Majer Bałaban, a rabbi and leading historian of Polish Jewry.

The young couple and their parents struggled together to survive. They found hiding places in the ghetto during the deportations to Treblinka, and they crowded into a cellar bunker when the ghetto resistance staged a desperate uprising the following April. After the Nazis bombed the building above the hiding place and they were forced to emerge onto the street, the family was herded to the *Umschlagplatz,* the train platform from which Warsaw Jews were deported to camps. Jerzy, Genia, and their parents were forced together into cattle cars and sent to Majdanek. Her mother never made it past the selection. Genia last saw her father and husband when she was sent without them from Majdanek to Auschwitz.

Soon after the Holocaust, Genia returned to the Umschlagplatz and took a train to the forest clearing that was once the death camp of Treblinka, where her brother had been killed. But if she ever visited the Nożyk synagogue, where she married her first husband in wartime, her children did not know it. Even when her son Marian was approaching sixty, he was not aware that the prayerhouse where his mother had married her first husband continued to exist in the postwar city, on the "Jewish street"—a few blocks surrounding the synagogue—where the small postwar religious community was based.[8]

Genia Adler, a Warsaw native like five other adults among her postwar Jewish neighbors at 16 Ujazdowskie Avenue, sought to rebuild her life from entirely new roots, even while living in the city where she witnessed the beginning of her family's wartime destruction. "I buried my childhood, my family, the camps," she later recounted. "It all got buried deep inside while I attempted to start a new life."[9]

Emil

After the Holocaust, as Genia recovered from wartime deprivations, she met an editor and philosopher named Emil Adler in the crowded offices of the Book publishing house. Emil was sixteen years older, but his short stature and boyish face gave him the look of a much younger man. He, too, was widowed during the Holocaust and was his immediate family's only survivor. Emil and Genia soon became a couple, helping one another through those first postwar years.

Genia was never passionate about politics, and she worked at the publishing house out of need for a job, not because of political faith. But Emil had been a communist since young adulthood, and after the war he became an editor at the party's publishing house with the hope of seeing its ideology prevail in his native country.

Emil's path to communism was a gradual one. It began with a childhood in a traditional but modernizing Jewish home, where his mother wore European clothes and his father's beard was closely cropped. Born in 1906, Emil grew up in the Galician city of Brody in the area of Poland that Austria annexed in the late eighteenth century. The city was a trade crossroads, located just across the border from the area of Poland annexed by Russia, and Emil's parents owned a small inn catering to merchants and other travelers.[10] In the century before Emil's birth Brody had been an important center of the East European *haskalah,* the Jewish Enlightenment, whose promoters saw themselves as bringing modernity to an insular Jewish world: secular schools, European dress, the languages of their non-Jewish neighbors. Emil's adult life and those of other communists of Jewish background, who radicalized and transformed aspirations for integration, can be seen as one of the roads that led from that path.

At nineteen Emil left his childhood home to study at a university in Vienna, which was still a magnet for young Galician Jews even after Poland regained its independence. In Vienna Emil immersed himself in books and European intellectual life, not politics, but he had not yet left behind his connection to Jewish culture: in addition to German, he also studied Hebrew, though no longer in the religious context of his childhood. After the war he obscured this reference to his Jewish background in the records that documented his life. Whenever he filled out a form in postwar Poland asking what he studied in Vienna, he gave different answers: philosophy and psychology, or German linguistics, or "Oriental subjects." Only in prewar files and in records he filled out after he emigrated from Poland in 1968 did he include Hebrew among his university interests.[11] That was not the kind of past a Marxist philosopher and loyal communist was expected to have; perhaps he listed "Oriental subjects" on documents in postwar Poland as a kind of coded reference to a Jewish language that the communist government associated with Zionism.

In 1927 Emil moved to the Polish capital. He was twenty-one, full of intellectual passion and plans for the future as he pursued a doctorate at Warsaw University. Throughout Emil's later wartime wanderings in the Soviet Union he held on to his diploma, one of few original documents that survived from his prewar life. The degree was awarded not to Emil Adler, but to Mendel, the Jewish first name with which he was born.

Warsaw between the world wars was a cauldron of political turmoil, and even before Emil finished his doctorate, the intensity of that world drew him in. As with his future neighbors at 16 Ujazdowskie Avenue who were communists, publishing was his entrance into politics. He helped to lead an underground cell of the illegal Communist Party of Poland while working as a clerk in a publishing house, called Rój, which was founded just a few years earlier but was already an important publisher of Polish literature.

Emil began his family in the uncertain years of the late 1930s, when the rise of Nazi Germany posed a danger to all of Europe and the prospect of war loomed. Just over a year before the Second World War, a snapshot was taken of Emil with his new wife, Helena, both of them dressed in stylish clothes and fashionable hats. Accompanying them was Emil's mother, who was stout and serious. They walked along the streets of a city whose residents could not have predicted the devastation soon to come.

―⁂―

Nazi Germany began bombing Poland on September 1, 1939, putting an abrupt end to the more peaceful years of Emil and Helena's young marriage. In Warsaw, as Emil's future wife Genia hid in cellars with her family, he joined the men who mobilized to defend the capital. On September 27, Warsaw fell to the Germans. Years later Emil remembered only the quiet that prevailed on the streets that day.

The country fell victim not just to the Nazis, but also to the Soviets, who had secretly agreed with the Germans to carve up Poland. As Poles were desperately defending the capital against the Germans, the Red Army invaded from the east, and Emil and Helena fled from Warsaw to eastern Poland, which the Soviets occupied. Many other Poles saw little difference between the Germans and the Soviets; for them, both countries were occupiers and enemies. Many Polish Jews, however, had been reading for years about increasingly violent antisemitism in Germany and were convinced they would be safer under Soviet rule. And for the minority of Jews who were communists, the Soviet Union represented an ideology that drove their political passion. The Soviets would defeat Nazism, communists believed. For Jews among them, that hope was all the more significant.

Emil and Helena found refuge in the eastern Polish city of L'viv, where they settled into the routine of family life as best they could and brought into the world a baby girl, Józefina. Emil worked for the Soviet censorship office before finding a job at a Polish bookstore. War was not far behind, however. Nearly two years after the Nazi invasion of Poland, Germany attacked the Soviet Union, and among the first areas to face the German army were the Soviet-occupied areas of eastern Poland and Lithuania. Mobilized into the Red Army during the chaos of retreat, Emil had to leave behind his wife and newborn daughter. Neither one survived the Holocaust. In Emil's native city of Brody, his parents, siblings, and nieces were killed.

In the Soviet interior, working as a woodcutter far from the war front, Emil tried to establish contacts with his prewar friends and political comrades. Letters were sometimes delivered from hand to hand in the Soviet Union during wartime, and through this patchy mail system Emil kept in touch with the leader of his prewar communist cell in Warsaw, Jakub Prawin. Emil Adler was a minor actor in communist politics, but Jakub was a prominent figure, leading troops at Stalingrad as a major in the Red Army. He maintained contact during the war with Polish communists at high levels and became a prominent army general in Poland after the war.

Jakub and Emil were close friends in prewar Warsaw. Although Jakub was five years older, the two men followed similar life paths from Jewish families in eastern Galicia, to university studies in Vienna, to the illegal communist cells of the Polish capital and survival in the Soviet

Union. Jakub grew up in Tarnów, where Emil was born before his family moved to Brody, and Jakub also fled Warsaw for L'viv at the outbreak of the Second World War. Like Emil, Jakub left behind his wife in L'viv when he joined the Red Army after the German invasion.[12]

Jakub's wartime letters to Emil were filled with political hope and personal anguish. Communication was especially difficult across the war front, and Jakub wrote to Emil that his main political task was maintaining contact with other party members in Nazi-occupied Poland. Jakub sent cryptic messages. Moscow had dissolved the Communist Party of Poland in 1938, accusing it of harboring spies, and most of its leaders and many rank-and-file members were shot or died in Soviet labor camps. In letters to Emil in 1942 Jakub hinted at the reestablishment of a Polish communist party. Aside from politics, Jakub also wrote to Emil as a Jew who had left behind close relatives and friends in L'viv. "I am very worried about [illegible], ach, how much I regret about Ariela!" Jakub wrote. "Why did I not advise them to leave on Saturday? They should not have been left, I have great pangs of conscience as a result of this, although I received the order to leave L'viv in such circumstances that I absolutely could not have rushed to them!"[13]

Emil and Jakub remained close friends long after war's end, until Jakub's death in 1957, and Jakub visited Emil some evenings at his apartment at Ujazdowskie Avenue and later at the Adlers' home elsewhere in the city. In a commemorative book for Jakub after his death, Emil mused about their shared wartime experiences, when they were filled with hope even as their families and communities were destroyed. "History brushed against us—Kuba [Jakub] constantly saw our individual fates connected with the development of events," Emil wrote. He quoted a wartime letter he had received from Jakub: "I know only this much, that in the country [Poland], important events are taking place," Emil's old friend wrote. "The main thing now is to halt Hitler and defeat him. And so it will be!"[14]

THE BERGMAN AND RUDNICKA FAMILIES

Three years later, after the chasm of the Holocaust and the murder of his wife and child, Emil Adler married Genia. They became fast friends with another couple, Stefan and Aleksandra Bergman, who were survivors of the Soviet Gulag. The Adlers and Bergmans would follow similar paths for the next twenty-three years.

Stefan Bergman arrived in Łódź that May of 1945, just weeks before Genia reached the city. Genia's journey was an arduous one, but Stefan traveled by military transport from the Soviet Union, where he and most of his family lived during wartime. He had been a committed communist since his youth, but during the Stalinist purges the Soviets had deemed him and other communists in Poland a traitor and sent him to the Gulag, where he, his wife Aleksandra, and his sister Luba suffered in terrible conditions for years. But that very fate saved them from the Holocaust. Now, at war's end, Stefan was needed as the communists prepared to take power in Poland.

Through the window of the train heading west to Poland, Stefan would have seen the detritus of wartime and a country coming back to life: small towns dotted with bombed-out buildings and the shells of factories on the outskirts of cities. His train finally arrived in Łódź, where his political comrades were expecting him.

It would be years before Stefan walked the streets of his native city of Vilnius again. Vilnius was known before the war as the "Jerusalem of Lithuania," a center of religious life and Jewish culture, and both old traditions and new currents shaped Stefan's childhood. Born in 1904, he grew up in a crowded, working-class Jewish neighborhood in a one-room apartment with his parents, brother, and three sisters. His pious father sent him to *cheder,* the traditional Jewish elementary school, but his mother, Paulina, born Pesa, was drawn to Russian culture before the First World War, when Vilnius was still under tsarist rule. Paulina read Russian newspapers, and the works of Russian writers lined the small bookshelf of their cramped apartment.[15] Far from being an anomaly in East European Jewish life, Paulina's affinity for the Russian word reflected the role of Jewish women in exposing their sons and daughter to the languages and cultures of non-Jewish societies, at times paving the way for the children's rejection of the traditional Jewish world.[16]

Stefan's father died when the son was only twelve or thirteen, and religion faded into the background. The boy spent only one year in a Russian secondary school before going to work, helping to support his large family. He took many jobs: as a shoeshine boy, a courier, and other menial work. But even then Stefan began to learn the tools of the publishing trade. He delivered newspapers and became a typesetter for the Yiddish press, as his father had been.

Despite his family's drift away from Jewish observance, Stefan, known then as Beniamin Epsztejn, lived in the orbit of Vilnius's Jewish world. Although he spoke Russian and Polish, at work he was immersed in the Yiddish word, and most of his neighbors were Jewish. Only later, in prison for his communist politics in the 1920s and 1930s, did he become friends with non-Jews.

In an interview he gave late in life, Stefan emphasized that his Jewish background did not push him toward communist politics. "I never felt that we [Jews and non-Jews] were made from different cloth, foreign to one another," he later recalled to an interviewer. "But one of the deepest and most painful memories of my youth was the pogrom against Jews just after the Polish military entered Vilnius in April 1919."[17] At that time, both Poland and Lithuania claimed Vilnius, and when Polish troops took control of the city in the border dispute between the two countries, violence broke out against the Jews. Pogromists broke the windows of Jewish shops, ransacked Jewish homes, and beat up the residents. As many as eighty-one Jews were killed.

Stefan was still working as a typesetter for a Yiddish newspaper at the time, and he set in type the words that reported those events. A year later, Vilnius's daily Yiddish newspapers published on their front pages the names of those killed. Recollections of those commemorative publications and of the pogrom itself never left Stefan. Six decades later, he recalled: "I still have these pages before my eyes."[18]

Stefan joined the youth group of the communist party the same year as the pogrom. It was the start of decades of Stefan's faith in communism, outlasting his and his wife's imprisonment in the Stalinist Gulag and waves of antisemitism in postwar Poland. Only in December 1981, when Stefan gave back his party card in anger over the government's declaration of martial law, did his dedication to the party officially end.

As a leader in the Communist Party of Western Belorussia, formally part of the illegal Communist Party of Poland, Stefan lived a dangerous but exciting life as he traveled around the country to help set up party presses. In 1924 he took the train to Białystok in northern Poland and toiled in secret in the home of another conspirator to teach the masses what he viewed as the truths of communism. He had been working in printing since youth, but this was a risky operation. He was establishing the party's first press in the city, and the authorities might raid the home at any moment. So with the few tools at hand, he set up a crude contraption hidden inside a tabletop, covered it with a tablecloth, and went about the task of printing flyers with party propaganda.[19]

Stefan was an industrious man, and the Communist Party considered him promising enough to study Marxist-Leninist ideology at the International Lenin School in Moscow, a prestigious assignment for a young communist. In old age, after the fall of the communist government, he found in a Warsaw archive a portrait of himself that had been taken during those Moscow studies. He was a handsome, dignified-looking man, and he was looking away from the camera. Stefan insisted to his younger daughter that the photograph had been taken without his knowledge.

—⁓—

In his political circles before the Second World War, Stefan met an equally passionate young communist activist, Aleksandra Kuczkowska, born Chawa. Youthful pictures of her before the Second World War belie the dangers of her work. Her family left their small town in an earlier generation, and she was born in the northeastern Polish city of Hrodno, just ninety miles from Stefan's hometown. Aleksandra was the baby in a family of four siblings, and life was not easy for their large family. Her father worked in a warehouse, struggling to provide for his children.[20]

Aleksandra's father was strict about Jewish observance. In the narrative she threaded from her past and recounted to one of her daughters, her father's search for crumbs of bread in every corner of their small apartment just before Passover, after Aleksandra had cleaned the apartment thoroughly, helped to prompt her rebellion against Jewish tradition and her path to radicalism.

Aleksandra, like Stefan, was drawn early on to the idealism of communist politics, joining the party's youth group while still in her teens. By her early twenties she was a leader in the Communist Party of Western Belorussia, which was part of the Communist Party of Poland and was focused on the areas of eastern Poland that were predominantly Belorussian. Poland's communist party wanted to unite the region with Belorussia's eastern part, which was already part of the Soviet Union. That goal was anathema to most Poles.

Politics consumed Aleksandra's and Stefan's days. Their work for an illegal party put them in constant jeopardy, and they risked prison as they traveled across regions and borders. During numerous imprisonments Stefan passed the endless tide of hours by reading books he had not had the opportunity to study in school. He learned German, immersed himself in the works of Marx and Lenin, and began to develop the skills of the meticulous editor and translator he would become after the Second World War.

By the mid-1930s, Stefan and Aleksandra Bergman were already a couple and had begun a family, living for a time in the Jewish neighborhood of Muranów in Warsaw and then in the Soviet city of Homel, where their elder daughter, Zofia, was born. In the terror and chaos of their arrests in 1935, just six months apart, the Bergmans left the baby in the hands of Stefan's mother, Paulina.

From that one-bedroom apartment in Vilnius where Paulina Bergman raised her family, all five siblings turned to communism. There was almost always at least one member of the Epsztejn family in prison, Stefan's younger sister, Luba, later recalled. Paulina was a stern woman, but she regularly visited her children in prison.

Luba's communist activism interrupted her budding career as a teacher. Despite her family's poverty, Luba had been able to study at both Belorussian and Jewish secondary schools before attending the Jewish teacher's seminary in Vilnius, and at twenty-one she began working in a Jewish elementary school. But she made her radical politics known when she helped to organize a strike over teachers' salaries, and afterward she could not find work in the classroom.[21]

Luba began her own family during the terror of the Stalinist purges. Imprisoned in a Siberian labor camp, Luba became pregnant and gave birth in 1938 to her son, Szymon, who was named after his long-deceased grandfather. Prisoners often had little to eat and suffered through hard labor, and the conditions of Szymon's birth must have been difficult. Luba gave him the last name Rudnicki.

Stefan, Aleksandra, and Luba avoided the fate of many prewar comrades who were arrested and killed, but among those who were murdered
during the purges was a sister of Stefan and Luba. Three of Paulina Bergman's five children survived both the Stalinist purges and the Second
World War, all of them in the Soviet Union after imprisonment in labor
camps: Stefan, Luba, and their brother, the latter of whom stayed in the
Soviet Union after the war. Another sister was killed by the Nazis after
trying to escape from the Otwock ghetto just outside Warsaw. Only
when Stefan died more than five decades later were his murdered sisters'
names placed on a grave, listed symbolically on his tombstone in the
Warsaw Jewish cemetery.

Although Paulina Epsztejn, three of her children, and her grandchildren survived in the Soviet Union, even this small nucleus of their
family was scattered by imprisonments and the chaos of wartime. Stefan
was released from a Soviet labor camp after the beginning of the Ger-
man-Soviet war in late June 1941 and reunited with his daughter Zofia
(born Zoria), his mother Paulina, sister Luba, Luba's three-year-old son
Szymon, and another of Paulina's grandsons, Oleś.

The Bergmans' daughter Zofia later recalled the hurried evacua-
tion from Minsk to Troitsk, a city in the Urals in the far eastern regions
of the Soviet Union, as the Germans invaded. A train was prepared to
carry workers of the factory where Stefan's sister Luba was working from
Minsk to the Soviet interior, away from the war front. One car was reserved for other family members wanting to flee. Stefan was mobilized
into the Red Army but had not yet left, and he, along with Luba, Paulina,
Zofia, Oleś, and the baby Szymon, crowded into the basement. Aleksandra was still in a Siberian labor camp, her future still uncertain. She
would not be allowed to rejoin her family for another four years.

As the Bergman family prepared to depart, in a pit in the middle
of the basement was a decorated wooden box containing the family's
photographs, and the adults selected a few to take with them. Only those
pictures, along with the most basic necessities and a collection of books
that included the writings of Marx and Engels, were among the family's
possessions that they brought with them upon their return to Poland
after war's end.[22]

RETURN

If the Adlers or Bergmans debated in the early postwar years whether to remain in Poland or rebuild elsewhere, neither couple left a trace of such discussions. Returning to Poland from the Soviet Union after the deluge of war, Emil Adler and Stefan Bergman hoped to help create a new society, and they took up with fervor the publishing work they had begun in their youth, although Aleksandra Bergman, who spent a decade in the Gulag, seemed to have already lost her political passion. Communists no longer risked imprisonment after the war; their political involvement bestowed privileges under the new communist authorities, whose party, initially called the Polish Workers' Party, gradually consolidated its power over the following three years. The ideological works of Marx and Lenin whose translations Stefan and Emil oversaw were the foundation of the communist government's official ideology.

For Genia Adler, remaining in Poland in those early postwar months after the traumas of her survival seems to have been rooted not in any clear-cut decision but in the tide of mundane matters as life began anew: finding a place to sleep, looking for a job, meeting new friends. An orphan and a widow with no surviving family in Poland, Genia found a community at the Book publishing house. So she rebuilt in the country of her birth.

In 1947 the extended Bergman family reunited in Łódź when Stefan's mother Paulina, sister Luba, and nephews Szymon and Oleś were finally allowed to return from the Soviet Union. While three generations and three branches of Stefan Bergman's family lived to see war's end, no one from Aleksandra's immediate family survived the Holocaust. Nearly six decades later, when Aleksandra was buried in the Warsaw Jewish cemetery next to her husband's grave, there were too many names of murdered relatives to list each one separately on her tombstone.

CHAPTER TWO

The Families of 16 Ujazdowskie Avenue, 1900–1948

IN 1930, BARBARA H. arrived in Warsaw at twenty-three years old, yearning for knowledge and access to the wider world. The Polish capital was still an impressive European city then, its avenues lined with ornate buildings and the pastels of its medieval old town lending it a quaint atmosphere. The trip from Barbara's hometown of Końskie to Warsaw was just eighty miles, but the capital was a world away.[1]

Nearly all of Barbara H.'s postwar neighbors of Jewish background at 16 Ujazdowskie Avenue were raised in the large cities of prewar Poland, but she was already a young adult when she left behind the provincial town of her youth. After the Second World War Barbara's grandson Włodek and her neighbors' children knew her as a Polonized intellectual who had never known Yiddish or Jewish traditions. It was an identity she adopted even before the Second World War. In postwar Poland, that identity became further cut off from her Jewish background, scarcely evident to her grandson or to outsiders in the postwar papers that documented her life.

For Barbara H. and neighboring families of Jewish background after the war, reconstruction masked diverse backgrounds of prewar lives and obscured porous boundaries of identities among Jews before the Holocaust. When they remade themselves and their families after wartime survival, the connections to Jewish life that they had maintained before the Holocaust were barely visible to their children.

The mundane facts of prewar lives bring to the surface evolving prewar identities: the languages they spoke in childhood, given names, the neighborhoods they lived in, where they attended school, nascent political involvement. Individual histories build a collective portrait by reconstructing what bonds connected the families and what differences separated them.

ON THE BORDERS OF IDENTITIES: BEFORE THE DELUGE

To the Big City: Barbara H.

Like Genia Adler, Barbara H., born Bina, never immersed herself in politics. Growing up in Końskie, where about 6,500 Jews made up nearly half of the town's residents, Barbara hoped to study Polish culture and ancient history, and she impressed her teachers at a Polish-language secondary school with her aptitude. She arrived in Warsaw aspiring to an intellectual life.

Barbara's early years were a time of turmoil in Poland. She was born toward the end of the failed revolution in the Russian empire between 1905 and 1907, and by the time she entered young adulthood, her country had been transformed dramatically. With the end of the First World War, Poland was no longer governed by foreign powers for the first time in more than one hundred and forty years. Barbara's family life was also in transition. Her father died when she was young, leaving her dependent on two older brothers, including one, Mojżesz, who taught Judaism at a school in Końskie, she wrote in prewar documents.[2]

When Barbara's train pulled into Warsaw, she might have walked along the bustling main avenues of the capital to the predominantly Jewish neighborhoods, where she lived for most of the following years before the outbreak of war. Many of her future postwar neighbors of Jewish background at 16 Ujazdowskie Avenue lived nearby. Stanisława Kruc, known then as Stanisława Szpigelman and just eleven years old, joined a Zionist youth group that year, having her first taste of the political world. Józef Tyszelman worked at a printing house while helping to publish illegal communist propaganda. Genia Adler was just four years old and lived with her family on Krochmalna Street.

Jewish life in all its diversity thrived on the streets of Warsaw then. On Friday evenings and Saturdays the synagogues were full and the streets were quieter—a public marker of difference in the passing of time in contrast with most of the rest of Warsaw. Stores advertised their wares in Yiddish and often in Polish as well, and newspapers and books in both languages were sold from stores and along the streets. Clean-shaven young men and women in European dress were as visible on the streets of Jewish Warsaw as were long-bearded men in capotes and skullcaps and women in covered hair.

At Warsaw University Barbara H. began listening to lectures about philosophy, the ancient world, and Polish culture. Perhaps she crossed paths there with her future postwar neighbor Emil Adler, who was studying in the same department where Barbara was also a student. A university education was often reserved for the privileged then, and those years could not have been easy for a young woman with limited means from a provincial town. But Barbara excelled at her studies.

Life for a young person in Poland, especially for Jewish youth, was becoming considerably more complicated as Barbara pursued her goals. The Great Depression made economic prospects dim for everyone in the 1930s, but for Jews, fewer jobs and more desperate times also meant greater hostility from surrounding society. Economic competition bred resentment from non-Jews, and boycotts of Jewish stores left many even more impoverished than the Depression had done on its own. As Barbara H. pursued her studies, universities moved to the forefront of antisemitic agitation. Decades later, Barbara told her grandson Włodek about university admissions quotas on Jews between the wars, referred to as the *numerus clausus,* and the "ghetto benches" at the back of the classroom, where students intimidated their Jewish peers into sitting. It was one of the few conversations she had with her grandson about her life as a Jew in prewar Poland.

Studying abroad was a way to evade the quotas, and those whose parents had enough money to support them left for Vienna, Prague, Paris, and other European cities. If Barbara had the means, she might have left Poland to study as well, as three of her future postwar neighbors did before the war. Barbara had little choice but to remain in Poland, and she appealed repeatedly to Warsaw University for financial help.

The effects of antisemitism on Barbara's life in Warsaw left few traces in the surviving paper trail of her prewar history. From nearly the beginning of her Warsaw years, she earned money by teaching at a Jewish girls' secondary school, a choice that might have been the result of limited options for employment at a non-Jewish school at the time rather than an indication of a desire to remain connected with a Jewish community. Only in one of her earliest university records did she list Yiddish as her native tongue, perhaps a hint of ambivalence, even before the Holocaust, about her identity as a Jew from a traditional background.

Despite her struggles, Barbara enjoyed the social life of the big city. At Warsaw University she met a medical student named Leopold, who probably was also from a traditional Jewish home if his parents' names— Hersz and Fajga—are any indication. Like Barbara, Leopold felt the pull of Polish culture while attending a Polish secondary school, but those earlier years of his education also brought challenges. He quickly withdrew from one school, he later wrote in a university document, because he was "soon convinced about the absolute impossibility of work in this educational establishment and I withdrew from it."[3] This was a time when restrictions limited the admission of Jews to Polish secondary schools as well; perhaps his vague statement refers to discrimination, though this, too, is unclear.

Leopold was already studying medicine at Warsaw University when Barbara H. began her studies. He, too, worked in a Jewish institution, as a doctor in the Berson and Bauman Jewish Children's Hospital, where one of Barbara's future neighbors, Stanisława Kruc, later worked as a nurse. The hospital was founded in the late nineteenth century and held on even in Warsaw Jewry's worst years, closing only when most of its staff and patients were killed during the Holocaust.

Leopold and Barbara married in 1929 and gave birth to a daughter, Barbara recorded in postwar documents. After war broke out a decade later, Leopold was killed as a medic in the Polish officers' corps, whose members were shot en masse by the Soviets in the Katyń forest in 1940. Leopold died not because he was Jewish, but because he was Polish.

To the Broader World and Back: Salomea Falk and the Sławny Family

As Barbara H. began her university studies, further east her post-war neighbor Salomea Falk was preparing to leave her hometown of Stanisławów for medical school in Prague.[4] Salomea's father, Herman, also known in documents as Hersz-Lejb, and her mother, Helena, grew up in nearby small towns before they moved to the large Galician city, where nearly a third of its 75,000 residents were Jewish. Herman and Helena owned a candy and chocolate store and must have struggled to scrape together enough money to send their daughter abroad.[5]

Salomea was never particularly political, and in Prague she focused on becoming a doctor. But in Stanisławów she met a law student named Ernest Falk, who was deeply involved in communist politics. Soon after completing her studies abroad she returned to her hometown, where she married Ernest while beginning work as a pediatrician. Even after the Second World War, when Salomea and Ernest lived at 16 Ujazdowskie Avenue, the lawyers and doctors of Salomea's hometown of Stanisławów who survived the Holocaust remained her closest friends, sharing memories, perhaps unspoken, of their native city.[6]

—⁂—

If Salomea Falk ever considered building her life permanently outside of Poland between the world wars, she soon decided to return to their native country. But two other postwar residents of 16 Ujazdowskie Avenue, Władysław and Antonina Sławny, were more ambivalent.

The Sławnys grew up not far from one another in Poland, Antonina in Łódź, and Władysław in a small town nearby. Both immigrated to France between the world wars when they were still young adults. By the time they began their romance in Lyons, Władysław, who was born Wolf, had already begun a career as a photographer, while Antonina, known also as Tola or Tosia, was a university student studying medicine and science.[7]

Only a generation earlier, their families lived in the insular but rapidly changing world of shtetl life. The Sławnys' parents were raised in religious homes in small towns whose mills wove fabric for Łódź's garment factories, yet the families were also shaped by secular Jewish cultures. Tola's uncle Jakub-Ber Gips became a Yiddish poet after moving from

his small town of Brzeziny to Łódź, and her sister Judyta began performing as a dancer there in the troupes led by Moyshe Broderzon, a Yiddish newspaper editor and playwright whose cabaret theater performed
throughout Poland and Western Europe.[8] Tola and her two sisters all
attended a Polish-language high school.

In France, Tola and Władysław moved back and forth across borders
of languages and cultures. Even as they began making the language of
their adopted country their own, Władysław worked for a Polish-language newspaper in France, while Tola still spoke Yiddish and Polish
with one of her sisters, Fajga, who had also moved to France. The third
sister, the dancer Judyta, also straddled identities as she absorbed the
new currents of European dance to help innovate Jewish culture. While
Tola and Fajga established themselves in France, Judyta went instead
to Dresden to study the latest dance techniques, returning to Poland
only in 1933 when the Nazis rose to power. In Warsaw Judyta became
well-known in Yiddish theater and film, and she choreographed the 1938
filmed version of S. An-ski's classic play, *The Dybbuk,* drawing on the
folk traditions that her grandmother had described to Judyta from the
Chasidic environment in which she grew up.[9]

Władysław and Tola Sławny survived the Holocaust in France, and
they were not in a rush to return to Poland. Władysław's brother Roman had been killed while fighting with partisans in Białystok, and Tola
Sławny's brother Eliezar died there as well. A letter from her parents in
the Warsaw ghetto made its way to France in 1941, but it was the last Tola
heard from them.

The new communist authorities in Poland were not a particular
attraction for the Sławnys. Although Władysław had been arrested in
his youth in prewar Łódź after joining a communist youth organization and he worked for a leftist Polish newspaper in France, he never
was a party member. Even in postwar Poland, where party membership brought privileges rather than danger, neither Władysław nor Tola
joined the party. The Sławnys returned to Poland in 1950, however, because Władysław was invited to be photography editor of an illustrated
journal, called *Świat* (World). He was eager for the chance to hold a
prestigious position and bring the newest trends in photography to his
native country.

The Sławnys did not stay long in Poland. During the emigration wave of Jews in the second half of the 1950s, they returned with their young sons to France, and the Sławny boys, who had arrived in Poland in 1950 speaking only French, now had to relearn the language of their native country.

Two Paths to Communism: Ernest Falk and the Kruc Family

The political cauldron of Poland between the world wars was the stage on which the parents of Jewish background who lived after the war at 16 Ujazdowskie Avenue began their young adulthoods. For eight of the nineteen parents, illegal communist politics consumed their lives before the deluge of the Second World War. But they followed varied paths to radicalism. Six of the communist parents came from working-class families, while the two others who joined the party before the war grew up in middle-class, Polonized families, and they embraced an ideology that rebelled against their parents' bourgeois world.

The parents were among only a small fraction of Jews who turned to communism in the fraught political climate of interwar Poland, and the antisemitic stereotype of *Żydokomuna*, or "Judeo-communism," which blamed Jews for communism before, during and after the Second World War, has greatly exaggerated Jewish involvement in communist parties. Yet the concentration of employees of Jewish background at the post-war Polish party's ideological publishing house Book and Knowledge is rooted in the fact that most prewar communists in charge of publishing and distributing propaganda were Jewish.[10] When the printed word became a tool of government control after the war, the communist authorities initially viewed communist intellectuals in publishing and press institutions, among them a disproportionate number of individuals of Jewish background, as playing an important role in the party's consolidation of power over the country.

Communists among the Jewish parents of 16 Ujazdowskie Avenue shared with other young Polish Jews the experiences that helped to define their generation: the political turmoil of interwar Poland, increasing secularization that left many Jews searching for new communities, and coming of age at a time when antisemitism was an increasing presence. Why a disproportionate number of Jews turned to communism in this atmosphere has been much debated by historians. Communism's promise to uproot identity from national background would likely have been an attractive idea for Jews who struggled with the label of "other" in a country to which they felt they belonged, and class ideology must have been an important element for those who came from poor families that struggled to get by. Some historians have posited that the Chasidic world imbued in Jews a messianic worldview that drew a minority to the utopian ethos of communism.

Jews were not the only marginal group attracted disproportionately to communism in interwar Poland, however, and at least some residents of 16 Ujazdowskie Avenue after the war who were prewar communists from Jewish families were unlikely to have attributed their political radicalization to antisemitism.[11] According to their ideology, national and religious background was supposed to lose importance as the utopian vision of socialism became a reality. Stefania Fedecka, on the other hand, a native of Lublin who lived at 16 Ujazdowskie Avenue in the first postwar decade, did not hesitate after the war to explain how her experiences as a Jew drew her toward leftist politics in her youth. Stefania grew up in what she later described as a "half-assimilated," well-to-do family, and although she never joined the communist party before the war, she had a glimpse of political intrigue while still in secondary school. The experience that stood out in her memory was sneaking into the coatroom at school to stuff propaganda leaflets into the pockets of her classmates' coats.

Stefania's friends from leftist circles were almost entirely Jewish, she remembered in an interview she gave in 1996, when she was seventy-seven. "Which is entirely understandable," she commented. When she was a student at a journalism school in Warsaw in the 1930s, Stefania recalled, only one professor signaled his dissent with a brief silence when some students intimidated their Jewish peers into standing in the back of his class. "I was forced to stand during lectures," Stefania remembered. "I did not find any non-Jews who . . . came to us during breaks, no one showed sympathy to those who were suffering. Suffering for what, exactly? For the fact that we were born Jews."[12]

—⁓—

Another postwar neighbor, Ignacy Kruc, took a different path to communism. The son of a grocer in Warsaw's right-bank neighborhood, known as Praga and generally poorer than the city center, Ignacy watched his siblings emigrate one by one as they escaped from limited economic prospects to Western Europe in the 1920s and 1930s. Ignacy stayed behind, cutting short his education to work in his father's small store.

Like other postwar residents of 16 Ujazdowskie Avenue, Ignacy, whose name was Yitzhak Krancenblum until just after the war, was drawn to conspiratorial communist circles early on. By fifteen he was already a foot soldier in the party as he and his peers took charge of distributing political leaflets that older comrades printed on party presses. Propaganda was central to spreading communist ideology, and all of the communist parents among the Jewish families at 16 Ujazdowskie Avenue played a role in printing and publishing in the party's illegal, prewar days.

Ignacy and his friends risked prison as they handed out fliers to workers at factories, the unemployed on Praga streets, and young people in front of libraries. They hid piles of leaflets in Ignacy's neighborhood with a janitor, near a theater, or in other secret locations. In conspiratorial meetings in the apartments of one or another of Ignacy's comrades, the young communists of right-bank Warsaw, many of them from poor and working-class families and stymied in their hopes for education, sought to satiate their "hunger for knowledge," Ignacy later recalled. They read literature, economic news, and political journals in a "kind of ideological school of the youth, who were fervently drawn at that time to knowledge." Ignacy was still fifteen when he served his first prison sentence.[13]

The dangers that communists faced as members of an illegal party drew them into close circles, and romance flourished together with political passion. Like Stefan and Aleksandra Bergman, Ignacy Kruc began his family in this intimate atmosphere, meeting his wife, Stanisława Szpigelman, in the capital's communist underground.

Five years younger than her husband, Stanisława also became involved in politics as an adolescent, but she turned only gradually to communism. As with many young Jews in interwar Poland, where youth organizations of secular political parties created new communities as the bonds of religious observance weakened, Stanisława drifted from one political ideology to the next. At eleven she joined a left-wing Zionist youth movement before switching to the Polish Socialist Party, and in her late teens she took up the more radical politics of communism. Her life played out on the opposite side of the Vistula River from her future husband Ignacy's childhood home. In the predominantly Jewish neighborhood of Muranów, not far from where her future postwar neighbor Genia Adler lived, Stanisława studied nursing at the Berson and Bauman Jewish Children's Hospital. She made trouble for the hospital administration as she earned her party stripes by organizing strikes among the nurses. Like Ignacy, she traveled to factories around Warsaw distributing communist propaganda leaflets.[14]

Among Stanisława's and Ignacy's prewar comrades was Józef Tyszelman, who secretly printed many of those illegal pamphlets at the printing house where he worked. The son of a printer, Józef studied at a secondary school in Warsaw before himself becoming a typesetter. Not long before the Second World War he met Zina Herman, who was from a middle-class family and never took great interest in politics. One of her mother's relatives was Judyta Ringelblum, whose husband, Emanuel, was a well-known historian of Polish Jewry. After the outbreak of war less than a decade later, as Józef, Zina, and Zina's mother, Lea, found refuge in eastern Poland under Soviet control, Emanuel Ringelblum led the underground archive of the Warsaw ghetto, documenting the suffering of Warsaw Jewry and the genocide that led to the death of Józef's parents, brother, and many of the Tyszelmans' other relatives.[15]

—◌◌◌—

If communism's class ideology attracted working-class and poorer youth, then the communism of assimilating young Jews from wealthier families was rooted in different soil. Long before the Ujazdowskie Avenue parents were old enough to read political literature, and before nearly all of them were born, Maks Horwitz, one of the founders of the Communist Party of Poland and the descendent of a well-off, assimilated Jewish family in Warsaw, made clear that his ideology was rooted in his experiences as a Jew who had sought to leave behind his Jewish identity, only to have his identity as a Pole rejected. Assimilation, he wrote in 1905 in a pamphlet titled "The Jewish Question," was "the bankrupt ideology of the Jewish bourgeoisie and intelligentsia. A Jew, in order to become a person, had to stop being a Jew . . . to become entirely a Pole, to the point of illusion." Maks sought to escape from his Jewish background not by continuing to immerse himself in the Polish culture in which he was raised, but by creating a new society that sought to break the bonds of nation and state that excluded him.[16]

Ernest Falk, who lived at 16 Ujazdowskie Avenue for more than a half century after the Second World War, might not have explained his politics through his Jewish background, as Maks Horwitz did, but Ernest's path to communism rebelled against a privileged background as well. He was the son of a lawyer in Stanisławów and spent his earliest years in Vienna, to which his family had fled during the First World War, and he took up radical politics while studying law at Jagiellonian University in Kraków. In addition to working in his father's law office in Stanisławów, he also organized the illegal press and propaganda of the Communist Party of Western Ukraine, which, like its Western Belorussian counterpart, was formally part of the Communist Party of Poland. His conspiratorial work as director of the party's propaganda section in the city might have brought him into contact with one of his postwar neighbors on Ujazdowskie Avenue, Emil Adler, who traveled to Stanisławów to establish connections with political comrades there. One can imagine the disappointment of Ernest's father when his son was arrested in 1935 and sentenced to seven years in prison with other party members in connection with the printing of illegal political leaflets.[17]

After Ernest's arrest, his new wife, Salomea, the pediatrician who had returned from Prague just two years earlier, was held in a solitary cell for weeks because of her husband's politics. Salomea moved to Warsaw after she was released, away from the tenuous situation in her hometown, and found work in a Jewish hospital while her husband remained in prison. Four years later, she took the train in the opposite direction, returning to Stanisławów as the Second World War began.

UNDER NAZIS AND SOVIETS

When German bombs began falling on Poland on September 1, 1939, and Soviet troops invaded Poland from the other direction seventeen days later, thirteen future residents of 16 Ujazdowskie Avenue who were of Jewish background were in Warsaw struggling to keep themselves and their families safe.

The men of Warsaw mobilized to defend a besieged city. Barbara H.'s husband, Leopold, was a reserve officer and was hurriedly mobilized into the Polish army as a medic, while Leopold's brother Aleksander, an avant-garde artist, fled east to Soviet-occupied Poland, fearing immediate persecution by the Nazis because of anti-Hitler caricatures he had published. Aleksander later recalled that his family gathered in their Warsaw home in those chaotic first days of war to bid farewell. "We sat around the table," Aleksander wrote in his memoirs. "Only our eyes spoke.... We said goodbye. I do not remember whether the words 'goodbye,' or even 'see you later' were spoken."[18]

Aleksander prepared for the long journey eastward while his brother Leopold and the rest of the Polish officers' corps retreated eastward with the Polish army into Soviet-occupied territory. The officers disappeared; the Soviets shot them in the spring of 1940 in the Katyń forest near Smolensk. The Soviet Union, which later became a wartime refuge for Leopold's wife, Barbara H., was the same country responsible for the murder of her husband. But for decades the Soviets blamed the massacre on the Nazis, and for decades Barbara and her daughter refused to accept, at least openly, that the Soviets, not the Germans, had killed Leopold.

Tens of thousands of Jews fled to Soviet-occupied eastern Poland in those early weeks after the Nazi invasion, often leaving behind parents, children, and spouses. Refugees reached the border by foot, train, cart, and any other means they could find. As Stefan and Aleksandra Bergman and Stefan's sister Luba Rudnicka struggled to survive in the Gulag in the depths of the Soviet Union, all of their postwar neighbors at 16 Ujazdowskie Avenue who had been communist party members before the Second World War found temporary refuge in eastern Poland with their spouses. Emil Adler and his wife, Helena, left for L'viv, which Ignacy and Stanisława Kruc also reached after parting with their parents in Warsaw. Zina and Józef Tyszelman, together with Zina's mother, Lea, settled further north in Białystok. Barbara H. found herself in Białystok as well, fleeing not because of her politics—like most Jewish refugees, she was not a communist—but because Soviet-controlled eastern Poland seemed safer than Nazi-occupied territory. Tola Sławny's sister Judyta Berg also escaped from Warsaw to Białystok, while Samuel Neftalin, a

Jewish man from Łódź who married Nina Sztuczyńska after the war, found refuge in the town of Łomża.[19]

Back in Warsaw, four future residents of 16 Ujazdowskie Avenue faced the early tribulations of Nazi rule. Genia Adler remained in the Polish capital with her family, as did her postwar neighbor Nina Sztuczyńska, the daughter of a marriage between a Jewish father and a Russian Orthodox mother. Zygmunt and Halina Kaczyński, who lived with their three young children on the fourth floor of the Ujazdowskie Avenue building after the war, stayed in the besieged city as well. The decision to stay behind was a fateful one, but at the time, no one knew just how extreme Nazi persecution of European Jewry would become.

On the "Aryan" Side: Stefania Fedecka

Stefania Fedecka, who did not lose her poise even in old age, must have been a savvy woman in her youth and young adulthood. On the "Aryan" side of L'viv during the Holocaust, she evaded informants, blackmailers, Nazi interrogators, and every other danger. Living "on the surface" with false papers, as Stefania did, was often even riskier than hiding in a secret space behind a wall or in a primitive dugout underground. Surviving meant masking her fear and paying attention to the smallest detail that might give away her identity as a Jew.[20]

Before the war Stefania's family was well known in Lublin to Jews and non-Jews alike. Her father, Salomon, and an uncle owned a large stationery and bookstore prominently located on the city's main boulevard, and they had many non-Jewish customers. Stefania, born in 1919 with the last name Kestenberg, spoke only Polish, and her family was "assimilating," as she later described them. They maintained Jewish traditions and a kosher home, however, and her father was a leader in Lublin's Jewish community.

Stefania had her heart set on becoming a journalist, and in her young adulthood she went to Warsaw to study. She took in the city's cultural life, visiting coffeehouses and seeing the latest films. Only when marriage drew her back did she return to Lublin. Just two weeks before the outbreak of war, she and her new husband, Mieczysław, vacationed in the quaint town of Kazimierz Dolny near Lublin; preserved photographs show her carefree in a bathing suit and smiling for the camera.[21]

Stefania was guided by stubborn determination from the very beginning of the war. As bombs fell on Lublin that September of 1939 and her family and neighbors hid in a cellar, Stefania went outside to a nearby park and took cover in the city gardens. Her husband rushed to his parents in L'viv, which soon fell under Soviet rule, and Stefania left Lublin with a friend to join her husband. She packed a few belongings and wrote a letter to her parents, apologizing for leaving. It was the first of many agonizing leave-takings from her family.

Although Stefania dabbled in leftist politics before the war, her experiences in Soviet-occupied L'viv cast doubt on her nascent political beliefs. In their apartment she and her husband lived in cramped quarters with several other families, among them an employee for the Soviet security police, who left a distinctly negative impression. "I did not have a good feeling toward Russians," she later recalled. She remained prepared to flee at any time, keeping a stash of food and other necessities. "Uncertainty," she recalled many years later. "We did not know what would happen tomorrow."[22]

The prominence of Stefania's family in Lublin, her father's position as vice president of the Judenrat, and connections with non-Jewish customers of the stationery store failed to save Stefania's family during the Holocaust. Not her pious grandparents, nor her parents, nor her younger brother lived to see war's end. Her husband was also killed. Only her older brother, who had emigrated from Poland before the war, survived from her immediate family. But her dual identity as both a Pole and a Jew shaped Stefania's wartime survival. In the Lublin ghetto, to which she returned for a time when the Nazis invaded L'viv, Jewish leaders who knew her family as well as non-Jewish customers from their store helped her escape from danger at critical moments. She spoke Polish with no trace of an accent that could betray her Jewish identity to the Nazis or to blackmailers, since she never knew Yiddish. For much of her postwar life Stefania struggled to reconcile those identities.

Between the Ghetto and the "Aryan" Side: Nina Sztuczyńska,
the Kruc Children, and the Kaczyński Family

In the same city where Stefania braved life on the "Aryan" side, two young children who grew up at 16 Ujazdowskie Avenue after the war were struggling to survive in the care of strangers. Ela Kruc, as she was known after the war, was born in the dire conditions of the L'viv ghetto before being secreted out to a Polish woman on the "Aryan" side. Another young child in the city's ghetto, Bernard, known as Bolek in postwar Poland, also parted with his mother, who, desperate to save her son, found a Catholic woman to hide him. Neither child saw their families again.[23]

In the Polish capital, meanwhile, Zygmunt and Halina Kaczyński moved back and forth across the boundaries of the ghetto. After the Great Deportation in the summer of 1942, when at least 300,000 Jews were sent from the city to Treblinka, the Kaczyńskis escaped from the ghetto. On the "Aryan" side, Halina gave birth to their son Ryszard in the dangerous conditions of their wartime existence. Yet they continued to visit the ghetto secretly, maintaining contact with resistance circles.[24]

A fourth-floor neighbor on Ujazdowskie Avenue after the war, Nina Sztuczyńska, also straddled the borders of Jewish and "Aryan" Warsaw. Nina had a Jewish father but had been baptized in her mother's Russian Orthodox faith, so she had identification papers to survive on the capital's "Aryan" side without adopting a new identity. Members of her extended family suffered a different fate, succumbing to the dire conditions of the Warsaw ghetto, while her father, Dawid Kranc, died of cancer. Connections beyond the Jewish world did not ensure their survival.[25]

Even in previous generations, Dawid's family had shed the trappings of Jewish piety, with pictures showing family members wearing European dress and trimmed beards. The family's construction company made them relatively well-to-do. Dawid worked for a family member's company manufacturing bronze and iron casts for monuments, bringing them into contact with the Polish artistic circles of the sculptors who worked for them. Before the war Dawid and his Russian wife took Nina and her two siblings to live in France, but when the marriage fell apart, Dawid returned to Poland before the outbreak of war.

The Nazi occupation separated the extended Kranc family between the divided worlds of wartime Warsaw. Dawid's daughter Nina as well as her brother and sister found apartments on the "Aryan" side, ignoring the Nazi racial laws that considered them Jewish. One of Dawid's cousins, Gustawa Maślankiewicz, had also married a non-Jew before the war, and she took refuge with her husband and their two young daughters on the "Aryan" side as well.

Nina and her siblings traveled back and forth between "Jewish" and "Aryan" Warsaw. They crossed illegally into the Warsaw ghetto to visit their sick father and then to smuggle him out to Nina's apartment, where he died of cancer. The elderly mother of Dawid's cousin became ill, too, and was taken from the Warsaw ghetto's old-age home to Treblinka on one of the earliest transports. On the other side of the ghetto walls, meanwhile, Nina became active in the communist underground and traveled around city districts to conspiratorial meetings in private apartments, where young people read illegal newspapers and planned sabotage activities. Nina's small home on Krakowskie Przedmieście Street in the city center was a distribution point for the movement's underground press, and she was involved in the communist underground's assistance to Jews in Warsaw.[26]

The last months of war were just as trying for Nina as the earlier years had been. Her sister was killed during the Polish underground's Warsaw Uprising in 1944, and her brother died as a partisan in the communist underground. Nina, meanwhile, met and married a sculptor, Kazimierz Sztuczyński, a non-Jewish Pole of aristocratic heritage. She was nearly nine months pregnant when her new husband was killed in the Warsaw Uprising. Their infant son became a link between Nina's wartime losses and her postwar reconstruction.[27]

Soviet Exile and Soviet Refuge

For the vast majority of Polish Jews who survived the Holocaust, the Soviet Union loomed large in their memories of wartime survival. Nine of the Jewish residents of 16 Ujazdowskie Avenue who survived the Second World War as adults fled east after the German invasion of Poland in September 1939, living in Soviet-occupied eastern Poland for nearly two years before escaping eastward again when the Germans attacked the Soviet Union.

Soviet control of eastern Poland was a relative respite before the Nazi invasion, but nearly all of the region's population, Jews and non-Jews alike, suffered under the Soviets. The new authorities closed churches and synagogues and disbanded private organizations as well as noncommunist political parties, while a change from Polish to Soviet currency impoverished the population, wiping out their savings. Politicians and other leaders were imprisoned in harsh conditions, many were killed, and hundreds of thousands of people were forcibly sent to the Gulag or elsewhere in the eastern reaches of the Soviet Union during periodic deportations. But even in those times of uncertainty, future neighbors of 16 Ujazdowskie Avenue began their families in eastern Poland. Salomea Falk and Emil Adler's wife, Helena, gave birth—Salomea to a son, Feliks, and Helena to a daughter, Józefina. Barbara H. began her career as a pedagogue and editor, translating Russian textbooks into Polish.

Life under the Soviets ended on June 22, 1941, when the German army invaded and advanced rapidly as the Red Army retreated in haste. In thirty-one towns in eastern Poland and a dozen places in the countryside, Jews fell victim to pogroms even before Nazi authorities arrived, as their non-Jewish neighbors scapegoated them for the terror of the Soviet occupation.[28] Nine future neighbors at 16 Ujazdowskie Avenue sought refuge from the Nazis further east. Salomea and Ernest Falk escaped with their newborn son, Feliks, from Stanisławów, which initially fell under Hungarian control with the German invasion of the Soviet Union, while further north Barbara H. made her way east with her daughter. The Soviets moved entire factories into the Soviet interior, and Józef and Zina Tyszelman were evacuated from Białystok with other employees of the printing press where Józef worked. Tola Sławny's sister Judyta fled from Białystok as well, seeing her brother Eliezar for the last name. Stanisława and Ignacy Kruc fled from L'viv, while Emil Adler and Samuel Neftalin headed east as they were mobilized into the Red Army.

Jews who fled from eastern Poland and Lithuania escaped the mass shootings that destroyed entire communities in the early stages of the Nazi genocide, but conditions in the Soviet interior were difficult. Food was short, and work was often back-breaking. But here, too, as in the much more dire circumstances of the Nazi ghettos, children attended school and young people began their families. Zina and Józef's elder daughter, Liliana, was born in the city of Tomsk deep in the Soviet interior, and the Falks began raising their son Feliks. Barbara H. found herself in the far reaches of the Soviet Union on a collective farm, but she escaped from the difficult labor when her brother-in-law, who had political connections, found her work as an editor at *Wolna Polska* (Free Poland), the Polish organ of the Soviet-backed Union of Polish Patriots. Although Barbara had been involved with leftist teachers' circles in Warsaw, only in the Soviet Union toward the end of the war did she join the reconstructed Polish communist party.[29]

—∿∿—

For the families of Jewish background at 16 Ujazdowskie Avenue, the markers of their experiences during the Second World War are not only the Warsaw ghetto uprising of 1943, the Umschlagplatz, and the Nazi death camps, but also the murder of Polish officers at Katyń, the Warsaw uprising of 1944, and internment at the Pruszków camp near Warsaw as the Nazis destroyed the capital. For others, wartime survival was connected with their prewar communist involvement: the Stalinist purges, the Gulag, the arrests and murder of Communist Party of Poland members and its leadership. Most of the families marked their wartime survival through a combination of these symbols of memory.

But nearly every Polish Jew who lived to see war's end, whether in the Nazi death camps or in the depths of the Soviet Union, in the forests and dugouts of Nazi-occupied Poland or on streets of the "Aryan" side, had to rebuild from the wartime destruction of families and communities. Although most surviving Polish Jews had not themselves experienced the desperate years of ghettoization and death camps, the generation that came of age in Poland before the Holocaust was shaped after the war by the loss of families and communities and of a way of life that had surrounded most of them as they grew up, even among those who had fallen away from religious observance long before. They were survivors of the cataclysm that engulfed Polish Jewry.

In Końskie, Barbara H.'s brother Mojżesz was killed in 1941, even before the Germans sent the Jews of the ghetto to Treblinka. The Jews of Nowy Korczyn, where Władysław Sławny was born, were deported to the death camp a month earlier, leaving empty streets and homes in a town where 2,500 Jews made up 80 percent of the population before the war. Stefania Fedecka's native city of Lublin lost nearly a third of its population when most of the 38,000 Jews who had lived there were killed. Brody's 10,000 Jews, more than half of the city's population, were wiped out, including nearly all of Emil Adler's family. In the Falks' city of Stanisławów, Stefan Bergman and Luba Rudnicka's home of Vilnius, Aleksandra Bergman's Hrodno, Zygmunt Kaczyński's Baranowicze, the narratives were variations of the same story.

REBUILDING

At war's end the future neighbors of 16 Ujazdowskie Avenue began to emerge from wartime devastation. Genia Adler made her way back to Poland from Gross-Rosen, and Bernard and Ela, the two children who were hidden by Catholic families in L'viv and later adopted by the Kruc family, were taken to an orphanage near Łódź. Stefania Fedecka returned home to Lublin, where she went back to her family's prewar apartment and their stationery store, inquired at the makeshift Jewish community office, and asked old acquaintances if they had any information about her family. "I walked on the streets with eyes wide open so that people would see that I exist, that I had survived, so that perhaps someone would come up to me," she later recalled. She found no trace of her family, but for the first time in years, she ventured outside without having to mask fear that her Jewish identity would be discovered.[30]

Lublin was the first major Polish city to be liberated from Nazi control, and Stefania found a job in a publishing office of Poland's temporary government, which was based there as Warsaw still struggled to free itself of German rule. Many institutions moved to Łódź after its liberation, and when Stefania began working in the office of a printing press there, she met a non-Jewish man named Edward from a Polish village who was twenty-three years her senior. A few months later they married and settled in Warsaw. Of all the families at 16 Ujazdowskie Avenue aside from the Bergmans and Stefan Bergman's sister Luba Rudnicka, Edward, a non-Jew, was the only one who referred to Jewish background in the communist party's personnel files. During the Second World War, Edward wrote in one document, he was part of underground circles in Warsaw that provided help to Jews, including false passports, money, and food packages. He noted, in parentheses, that his wife was of Jewish background.[31] Stefania never changed her name from Fedecka, the Slavic name she assumed using the false documents that allowed her to survive the Holocaust.

While Stefania was searching for family in Lublin, her future fourth-floor neighbor at 16 Ujazdowskie Avenue, Nina Sztuczyńska, was struggling through the final months of war in Warsaw, which was still under Nazi control. After the failed uprising Nina was sent with the rest of the remaining population in Warsaw's city center to an internment camp in Pruszków, just outside the capital, as the Nazis bombed building after building. Nina was still mourning her husband Kazimierz's death when their baby was born in Pruszków in October 1944. She named him Piotr.

As a young war widow with an infant son, Nina returned with other Varsovians to the ruins of their city. Soon afterward she met an engineer, Samuel Neftalin, a Jewish man from Łódź who was the grandson of pious Jews. Although Samuel's family had begun to drift away from strict religious observance in his parents' generation, he knew Yiddish and Hebrew, and Jewish traditions were part of his childhood home. After the war he raised Nina's son Piotr as his own.[32]

Nina, the daughter of a Russian mother and Jewish father, did not consider herself Jewish before the Second World War, and she did not adopt that identity afterward. But her marriage to Samuel and her experiences of wartime survival transformed her family's assimilation, bringing shadows of Jewish background—a few melodies of Yiddish songs, a Hebrew book—into their home. And like many of her postwar neighbors at 16 Ujazdowskie Avenue, Nina was the only member of her immediate family in Poland who survived. Among her few remaining relatives was Gustawa Maślankiewicz, her father's cousin, who survived on the "Aryan" side of Warsaw with Gustawa's non-Jewish husband and daughter. Gustawa's daughter Krystyna was only five years old at the outbreak of war, and the girl learned of the dangers of her wartime existence only in 1946. Only after forty Jews were killed in the Kielce pogrom that July did Gustawa tell her daughter about her Jewish background.

―⁂―

The remnants of Polish Jewry numbered about 300,000 to 350,000, but only about 50,000 survived in Nazi-occupied territory.[33] Most had lived to see war's end in the Soviet Union, and they began their postwar lives on trains heading west back to Poland. For Jews, as for all of Europe, those early postwar years were a period of frequent migration and emigration. Trains carried Jews back to Poland from the Soviet Union even as other Jews were leaving their native country by train or by foot, legally or illegally, making their way to Palestine or to displaced persons camps in Germany. Often they waited years for visas to countries where they could rebuild.[34]

When Genia Adler arrived in Łódź in June 1945, fewer than 43,000 surviving Polish Jews had registered with the Central Committee of Jews in Poland, most of them former prisoners of German camps. Genia later recalled the feeling of loneliness that accompanied her arrival: "We used to fantasize in the camp that one day when we became free, we would be greeted like heroes. People would carry us on their hands. In Łódź, we stood for hours just taking in the bustling city, and not one person looked at us."[35]

As more and more Jews arrived from the Soviet Union, Łódź became a center of the nascent Jewish leadership and institutions. The newly established Yiddish newspaper *Dos Naye Lebn* (The new life) enthusiastically tracked the arrivals. "Polish Jews in Magnitogorsk—the beginning of the repatriation from the Urals," heralded one banner headline in the newspaper on March 23, 1946.[36] By the time the transports ended, an estimated 230,000 Jews had returned to Poland from the Soviet Union. Others remained in the Soviet Union, from which they would be allowed to return only a decade later.

The new Jewish institutions provided a foundation of support, connections, and financial help, and postwar Jewish life was initially characterized by a similar ideological diversity as it had been between the wars, though on a vastly diminished scale. Bundists, communists, and Zionists of all stripes established schools, youth groups, and newspapers in Yiddish, Polish, and Hebrew. Stefan Bergman's sister Luba Rudnicka began working as a writer and editor for *Dos Naye Lebn,* but most future residents of 16 Ujazdowskie Avenue who lived in Łódź at the time had little contact with Jewish communal life. They created new circles outside of Jewish institutions, even as their common Jewish background helped to bring them together.

Decisions about where to settle were based as much on happenstance and individual choices as on efforts by government authorities and Jewish communal leaders to take control of mass migrations. Trains arriving from the Soviet Union often directed Jews to Poland's new western territories acquired from Germany, as German residents were expelled westward across the border, leaving behind empty homes. The cities of Szczecin, Wrocław, and nearby Wałbrzych as well as a small town, Dzierżoniów, became new centers of Jewish culture. Tola Sławny's sister Judyta Berg, the dancer who choreographed *The Dybbuk* on the eve of war, opened a dance school for Jewish youth in Wrocław. Their sister Fajga joined Judyta in Wrocław for just a month in 1947 before returning home to France. Fajga's eight-year-old daughter Yvette, who was born in France just weeks before the Second World War began, remained behind in Wrocław for a year, staying with her aunt Judyta and attending a Jewish summer camp.[37]

Salomea and Ernest Falk's postwar lives began in western Poland as well. When a train brought the Falks from the Soviet Union to the coal-mining city of Wałbrzych in March 1946, the family was assigned a spacious apartment with furniture and other belongings left over from German residents. Their son Feliks had still been an infant when his parents fled from eastern Poland as the Nazis invaded in 1941, and he had only ever known the harsh conditions of wartime. Now, in Wałbrzych, the family's large new apartment and the German servant woman who had stayed behind made an impression on the five-year-old. More than a half-century later, as a prominent film director in Poland, Feliks set one of his best-known works in the city.

The Falks did not immediately distance themselves from their Jewish past, and in Wałbrzych they sent their young son to a Jewish preschool. Only with the family's move two years later to Warsaw, where Ernest was assigned an important position in the government's publishing administration, did they begin raising their son in a world almost entirely devoid of Jewish identity.[38]

Józef and Zina Tyszelman began their postwar lives in Łódź with Józef's colleagues at the Book publishing house, where he was in charge of its technical department, but their stay there was brief. Just months after arriving in Poland from the Soviet Union in 1946, the Tyszelmans moved with their four-year-old daughter Liliana and Zina's mother, Lea, to an apartment in Warsaw's right-bank Praga neighborhood when the printing department moved to the still-devastated capital ahead of its editorial operations. Their second daughter, Joanna Krystyna, known as Krysia, was born in 1948. Like the Bergmans, the Tyszelmans were a family of three generations in early postwar Poland, unusual among Jewish survivors.

Ignacy and Stanisława Kruc returned to Poland with other repatriates from the Soviet Union a year after the Tyszelmans did. The parents of both had been killed, but Stanisława's two brothers had survived, one in a German camp, the other on the "Aryan" side of Warsaw. Her brother Henryk left Poland before he and Stanisława were able to locate one another, and he made his way to Palestine, where he settled in Jaffa. The second brother was killed just after the war by bandits in western Poland, in an unknown city where, according to family lore, he was involved in the illegal black market of goods taken from the homes of expelled German residents.[39]

Ignacy and Stanisława, meanwhile, settled into their postwar lives in Łódź, where they changed their last name to Kruc from Krancenblum, Ignacy's given last name. Ignacy was assigned to the Book publishing house as director of economic planning, while Stanisława began working as a doctor in a Łódź hospital. There she began treating a little girl, just about five years old, who was severely malnourished and clinging to life. Despite her grave condition, the girl had been left alone in the hospital and did not have any visitors. When Stanisława inquired, she learned that her young patient, named Elżbieta, or Ela, was Jewish and was born in the L'viv ghetto. Stanisława and Ignacy, who were childless, adopted the girl along with a second child from an orphanage, an older boy named Bernard Strzycki. Neither the orphanage officials nor Bernard himself knew his age. The boy appeared to be about eight or nine. The Kruces gave him a Polish name, Bolesław, or Bolek, and a birth date: December 26, 1939. In postwar documents, the Kruces avoided mentioning either their own Jewish background or their children's adoptions.

Bolek joined the family only in 1949, after the orphanage and Jewish communal institutions exhausted their search for his identity and any surviving family members. By that time, the Kruces were already living in Warsaw, having moved from Łódź early that year into an apartment on the second floor of 16 Ujazdowskie Avenue. Their son Bolek grew up playing with a neighboring boy, Szymon Rudnicki, who lived down the hall. Bolek's younger sister, Ela, sent paper messages out the window to her neighbor just above, Liliana Tyszelman, whose father had known Ela's mother, Stanisława, when they were young radicals in the communist circles of prewar Warsaw.

AT 16 UJAZDOWSKIE AVENUE

In early 1948, with rubble still scarring the Polish landscape, residents of the newly renovated building at 16 Ujazdowskie Avenue began moving into their apartments, which were allocated to the Book publishing house for its workers. The Jewish employees among them had lost their families and communities during the Holocaust. Yet they had already begun the process of reconstruction.

Among the families were eight children born before or during the Second World War and five other children who were born by the time the last Jewish family, the Sławnys, arrived from France in 1950. The new residents had traveled from Łódź, western Poland, and the right bank of Warsaw before arriving at their new homes. For most, their belongings were few, lost during their wartime survival, and the generous spaces of the building's prewar homes had been carved up.

One family, the Kaczyńskis, moved into an empty apartment they could not furnish. They had obtained the home through the father Zygmunt's administrative position at the government's umbrella publishing institution, but his political leanings are unclear from documents; when he wrote to the Jewish Colonization Association in Paris asking for help furnishing the family's apartment, the agency's representative appealed to the Hebrew Immigrant Aid Society on his behalf, calling him an "old colleague of our office in Warsaw."[40] Decades later, Zygmunt's son Ryszard still remembered the bicycle of two neighboring brothers from a Jewish family, Jan and Francis Sławny (known then as Janek and Franek), who had survived in less desperate conditions in France. The Bergmans were somewhat better situated by then, having acquired a heavy wooden credenza and large desk from the apartment they had just left behind in Łódź.

As the reconstituted communist party in Poland consolidated its rule and Warsaw gradually returned to life, the new leaders signaled their authority over the very streets of the Polish capital. Perhaps nowhere else was that message clearer in those first postwar years than along Ujazdowskie Avenue. Nine years earlier, in 1939, the Nazis renamed the thoroughfare Avenue of Victory. After war's end the avenue reverted to Ujazdowskie. But on January 1, 1948, the government authorities renamed it Stalin Avenue, inscribing the new politics on the streets of a reconstructing city.[41]

CHAPTER THREE

The Entire Nation Builds Its Capital

Ujazdowskie Avenue and Reconstructed Warsaw

The Jewish quarter in Warsaw occupied one-fifth of the city, two-hundred fifty thousand people were concentrated there, so one-third of the city's residents. . . . This little world seemed very big to me. I admired the passageway of Friedman on Świętojerska [Street] with an exit onto Wałowa [Street]. It was possible to live there without going out onto the street at all. There were two prayerhouses, a shtibl for Ger Hasidim, two chederim, a bakery, grocery stories, several eateries and cafes, one hotel and two institutions with the strange name "furnished rooms." . . .

Lace, haberdashery and stockings were sold on Nalewki [Street]. Gęsia [Street] traded in goods made in Moscow and Łódź. . . . Merchants lived most often close to their stores. They prayed not far from their apartments.

—*Bernard Singer (Regnis), Moje Nalewki*

Warsaw dust . . .

Warsaw dust and the dust of the years of reconstruction . . .

One of the philosophers calculated that Varsovians inhaled four bricks each year at that time. Varsovians breathe construction—this was not a metaphor, but a heavy, brick and dusty truth. One must love one's city in order to rebuild it at the cost of one's own breathing. And it is perhaps for this reason that from the battlefield of rubble and ruins Warsaw became once more the old Warsaw, eternal Warsaw, the same Warsaw—despite the new shapes of the streets and the new contours of the homes—that Varsovians brought it to life, filling its brick body with their own, hot breath.

—*Leopold Tyrmand, Zły*

As the families of 16 Ujazdowskie Avenue rebuilt from the ashes of wartime, so, too, was Warsaw being reconstructed and transformed.

Few cities in Nazi-occupied Europe were destroyed on the same scale as Warsaw was, and nowhere else was the size of a city's murdered Jewish population so large. Wartime destruction dispersed prewar communities. Neighbors were scattered, many prewar political leaders fled, and throughout Poland thousands of priests were killed in wartime.

The rupture in Jewish life was deeper. Approximately ninety percent of Warsaw Jewry had been killed, and rubble lined the streets of former Jewish neighborhoods. The Yiddish signs, the men in the long black coats called capotes worn by Chasidic Jews, and the women with covered hair were gone. Gray apartment blocs that were built on the remains of the ghetto had few storefronts on the ground level, depriving the neighborhoods of the shops, busy streets, and courtyards that once characterized this part of the city. After the war Jewish life on Warsaw's landscape was reduced to a square around the only operating synagogue, a nearby community building, a Yiddish theater in the city center, and a handful of other locations.

Jewish absence resulted not only from the murder of Warsaw Jewry, however. Even in 1955, after early postwar emigration, nearly 70,000 Jews still lived in Poland, and a more visible Jewish neighborhood might have been resurrected in the capital, even if a mere shadow of the past.[1] But just after the war Warsaw's devastated infrastructure made it difficult to settle there, and later on, the stronger presence of central political authorities discouraged religious observance while drawing individuals whose association with the government often made involvement in Jewish institutions untenable. The absence of more than a shadow of a Jewish presence on the streets of postwar Warsaw was rooted not in the complete absence of Jews, but in the distance from Jewish tradition, culture, and often from Jewish identity itself.

In 1960, when the Jewish communal leadership took stock of the population that remained in Poland after the emigration wave of the late 1950s, its report seemed to recognize the distance of many Warsaw Jews from Jewish institutions: while the leadership provided detailed demographic estimates of Jewish populations elsewhere in Poland, it gave only a rough number of 10,000 for the capital. It was perhaps an acknowledgment of the hesitancy of many Warsaw Jews to declare affiliation with Jewish institutions and of the difficulty of defining who could be considered Jewish in assimilating circles.[2]

As in the postwar capital more broadly, however, surviving Jews sought refuge in old bonds, even if those bonds were with new acquaintances after the wartime murder of friends and family. Often traces of shared Jewish background remained confined to their home and friendships with others of Jewish background. The boundaries of community turned inward, while Jewish absence prevailed on the streetscape outside.

—m—

Reconstructed Warsaw was a new city superimposed on the ruins of the old. The rebuilt capital magnified the intermingling of permanence and change that characterizes life in big cities, where streetscapes are in constant flux even as mainstays of a city's geography become symbols of continuity. Urban dwellers are surrounded by new architecture side by side with buildings in old styles; restaurants and stores with the latest trends open next to romanticized gathering places of writers and artists that recall old traditions; historic churches stand near the financial institutions of changing economies. Newcomers to big-city life often form enclaves that preserve bonds from previous homes and identities, even as the move from the village and small town to the big city eventually alters worldviews, ways of life, and the boundaries of community. "In the city remote forces and influences intermingle: their conflicts are no less significant than their harmonies," the urban historian Lewis Mumford wrote. "And here, through the concentration of the means of intercourse, in the market and the meeting place, alternative modes of living present themselves: the deeply rutted ways of the village cease to be coercive and the ancestral goals cease to be all-sufficient: strange men and women, strange interests, and stranger gods loosen the traditional ties of blood and neighborhood."[3]

In postwar Warsaw, change prevailed over continuity. Wartime destruction and postwar reconstruction accelerated the remaking of the streetscape and communal ties even as shadows of the past remained. For the capital's postwar Jewish population, that transformation was even more acute.

PAST AND PRESENT IN RECONSTRUCTED WARSAW

The center of Warsaw was a barren landscape at war's end. When the Polish underground's two-month uprising collapsed in October 1944, the Nazi authorities sent most of the surviving residents—about 550,000 people—to transit and internment camps just outside the capital, and tens of thousands were sent on to concentration camps. Then the Nazis bombed building after building, destroying the already devastated city. The rebels had planned the uprising with the hope of retaking Warsaw as the Nazis retreated but before the Red Army arrived, and its failure, followed by the city's destruction, demoralized the Polish population even further.[4]

Social ties born of prewar communities throughout Poland were partially broken by wartime displacement and postwar resettlement. Ethnic Poles from the former eastern territories, which were annexed to the Soviet Union in the fall of 1939, were transported westward to the territories that Poland acquired from Germany after war's end, while more than three million German residents in the western regions fled or were forced across Poland's new border with Germany. Wrocław, which the Germans called Breslau but which was now in Poland, became a blend of the city's existing streetscape and the society of L'viv, now in Ukraine but part of Poland before the Second World War; many of L'viv's ethnic Polish residents were settled in Wrocław after the war. Surviving Jews formed new communities in the western territories as well. Ethnic Ukrainians within Poland's new eastern borders, meanwhile, resettled or fled eastward to Soviet Ukraine, while in the space of three months in 1947, nearly 150,000 mountain people in southeastern Poland known as Lemkos, whom the Soviet-Polish accord on resettlement did not recognize as a distinct national group, were forcibly relocated to the country's new western lands. Polish authorities dispersed the Lemkos in small numbers, uprooting their communities and separating them from the mountains that were central to their identities. With the Nazi genocide of Jews, the forced postwar resettlements, and the redrawing of borders, Poland came much closer to being the ethnically homogenous state that prewar nationalists had sought.

In Warsaw, residents began trickling back into the capital from camps just outside the city and from all corners of Poland soon after the Red Army entered Warsaw in January 1945, and the spontaneous influx in the chaos of war's end left the city unprepared. Transportation, sewage systems, bridges, and other infrastructure were destroyed, and people lived among the ruins, even as corpses were being exhumed from under the wreckage. Rubble marred the landscape into the 1950s, a constant reminder of wartime destruction and demoralization. The physical devastation of the capital, wrote the historian Krystyna Kersten, led to a "defeat of hope, of a certain order, of a system of values."[5]

Moving into hastily built apartment houses were not only prewar residents but also tens of thousands of peasants from the Polish countryside who arrived to work in newly built factories, enticed by the government's economic incentives as they repopulated the capital. Migration and rapid industrialization facilitated social mobility.

The temporary government's new leaders initially were ambivalent about the monumental task of rebuilding Warsaw almost from scratch, a project that would strain the resources of an economy that was already crippled by war. Politicians agonized and quarreled over Warsaw's future. Soon after the Red Army arrived in the capital in January 1945, the fate of the city was the focus of a dramatic, all-night meeting of Polish politicians in Lublin. Many leaders felt that running a country from Warsaw, with its destroyed infrastructure, was unrealistic. They supported the temporary relocation of the government to Łódź or Kraków, both of which had survived mostly intact, while recognizing Warsaw as the symbolic capital.[6]

But it was Stalin who seemed to have decided the city's fate. With the capital's future still uncertain at the end of January in 1945, Bolesław Bierut, the Stalinist head of the provisional Polish government, traveled to Moscow to discuss the problem with Stalin. The Soviet leader promised funds to reconstruct the capital, and when Bierut returned to Poland, he and other Polish leaders did an about-face: they decided to move the government seat to Warsaw immediately.[7] Many cultural institutions relocated to Łódź, but the temporary Parliament, ministries, and other symbols of power began establishing themselves in Warsaw.

The symbolism was ambiguous and ironic: the Soviet Union, which was taking steps to dominate Poland's new government, helped the Poles to undertake the seemingly impossible task of rebuilding their capital, an assertion of Polish resilience and national pride.

Warsaw was gradually remade on the skeletons of the ruined city, retaining echoes of the prewar capital. In the medieval Old Town, architects and artists helped to recreate the facades of buildings that existed now only in old drawings and photographs, and some monuments to heroes of Poland's past—the bard Adam Mickiewicz and King Zygmunt III, who moved Poland's capital to Warsaw in the sixteenth century— were rebuilt. The Blikle café, the haunt of high society since the nineteenth century, continued operating through most of the communist years, even as workers' cafeterias called "milk bars," with their stark interiors and rudimentary meals, became a staple of city streets. The grid of postwar Warsaw resembled the map of the prewar city.

"The entire nation builds its capital" was inscribed into the façade of a building not far from the northern end of Ujazdowskie Avenue and became the motto of the government's early reconstruction plan for Warsaw, but it was a new society and a new city that the communist government wanted to create. The authorities overseeing reconstruction sought to remake the capital not in the image of the old, but as a mirror of the new ruling ideology. Buildings were intended to make a political statement and shape new identities. Images of strong, working men and women were carved into the exteriors of buildings that rose on Constitution Square just south of the city center, and further north, remnants of an entire neighborhood were razed and rubble was cleared to make way for the imposing Palace of Culture and Science, a "gift" from Stalin, with its drab brown façade and tall spire. It was an enduring and much-resented symbol of a Soviet presence in Poland. From everywhere in the city center, it seemed, Varsovians could see its spire and keep time by its clock. Symbols of the new politics, from street names to architecture, became the settings of everyday life. In most of the rebuilt capital, the streetscape was no longer the familiar space of the past.

Monuments of a shared history, the bonds of a national community, were often present only in absence as empty spaces reminded passersby of what existed in those locations just a few years earlier. The land where the King's Castle once stood on the edge of the Old Town and where the Saski Palace once rose in the heart of the city might have reminded older Varsovians of the country's aristocratic past, but that emptiness also evoked memories of defeat and destruction. The communist authorities never allowed Poles to memorialize the Warsaw Uprising of 1944 as a reminder of wartime suffering.

Absence preserved memory of the Jewish past even more so than in the city as a whole. In the prewar Jewish neighborhood of Muranów, where the Nazis established the largest section of the wartime ghetto, a memorial to the 1943 ghetto uprising was built in an empty space where rubble was removed but no new buildings were constructed. The monument became a place of shared memory, where the remnants of Polish Jewry, including some who were otherwise distanced from Jewish communal life, gathered each year to remember those absent, even though the commemorations created a skewed political narrative that placed communists at the center of resistance. Further south, the plot of land where the monumental Great Synagogue had stood before the war remained empty for decades.

Some Warsaw Jews could not escape reminders of absence and wartime losses. Among the first new buildings constructed in the capital after the war were those that rose on the ruins of the ghetto, and most Varsovians had little choice but to accept whatever home they could find. Survivors from Jewish families who found apartments there spent their postwar lives surrounded by physical reminders of loss. "As soon as we walked down Zamenhof Street, she immediately cried!" recalled a daughter about her mother, who grew up in Muranów before the Holocaust and continued to live in her old-new neighborhood after the war. "And at the ghetto monument she said: 'This is not the Warsaw that I remember from childhood. My school stood over there, I played with my friends over there—it does not exist! All of this is so foreign now!' And it was an ironic fate that we would live after the war on the terrain of the former ghetto, in the same area where mother lived before the war."[8]

—⁂—

Nostalgia and loss were not the sole sentiments of Poles toward the capital. Before the war, it was a city not only of palaces and ostentatious homes of aristocrats, but also of poverty: crowded tenement houses, apartments without indoor plumbing, and long hours of factory work. In letters to political leaders, some Poles expressed support for the prospect of equality and the privileging of ordinary workers. They viewed Warsaw as a tabula rasa that could become a city where everyday comforts were not dependent on wealth and aristocratic background. The new capital could be the symbol of a new society. "From the Warsaw of yesterday, only its general character and the traditional names of the streets must remain," an engineer from Lublin wrote in 1945 to a top party official Władysław Gomułka. "Warsaw must be a modern city, as the society of Poland must be modern. Let us leave behind the past, or rather let us not use it as a model, it was not that beautiful or cheerful. . . . Let us break with the past, at least in building our capital. New Warsaw must not be a copy of the old."[9]

Control over housing assignments was part of communism's attempt to reshape society, identity, and the bonds of community by restructuring social relations, helping to sever society's ties with past traditions. But a state's attempts to infringe on the private settings of everyday life inevitably prompt individuals to seek autonomy in personal space, the sociologist and philosopher Henri Lefebvre has argued.[10] In the postwar Polish capital, Varsovians sought to create places beyond the reach of government within the walls of their homes and among friends, challenging the intrusion of politics into private life and the alienation of an unfamiliar landscape outside: prewar furniture and art that evoked old cultures, long strolls where conversations were less likely to be subject to surveillance.

Among strangers, meanwhile, the city outside their homes sometimes became a place of estrangement between individuals and from one's inner self. In the eyes of one bard of postwar Warsaw, public spaces often did not foster ties of community. "The Warsaw tram is a perpetual symbol and existential retort," commented the writer Leopold Tyrmand in his diary from 1954. "It is dirty and squalid by nature. Its purpose is to liberate the instinct of mutual hatred in people. The most compassionate Christian transforms into his base nature and evil on a Warsaw tram."[11]

The intimacy of friends and family was sometimes a refuge even in public spaces of the city. On the tram, a symbol for Leopold Tyrmand of the atomization of society, Barbara H.'s grandson Włodek, still a child who was not fully aware of the ideology that surrounded him, took comfort in rides throughout the city with his older cousin Piotr with no particular destination in mind, while his great-uncle Stanisław used to take the boy for walks around Warsaw. But the capital developed a different atmosphere from its prewar existence as the new architecture of socialist realism, which viewed art as a tool of political ideology, transformed the streetscape. Warsaw developed a gruff exterior, permanently altered.

UJAZDOWSKIE AVENUE AND THE POLITICS OF HOUSING

The presence of old Warsaw in the landscape of the new city was most apparent in the neighborhood around Ujazdowskie Avenue. Since the nineteenth century the thoroughfare had been a microcosm of changes in Poland's national life, and in communist Poland it once again reflected transformations in Polish society. Where Warsaw's "summer salon" once stood for wealth, after the war it was the neighborhood of political privilege.

Before the Second World War, Ujazdowskie Avenue and nearby streets were home to aristocrats, bankers, and industrialists, who hired architects from Western Europe to build their villas and apartment houses in Renaissance and secessionist styles. It was the "center of . . . big-city Warsaw," a pianist who grew up there, Roman Jasiński, recalled after the war. "Ujazdowskie Avenue was to a certain degree a snobbish address, similar to the avenue du Bois de Boulogne . . . and the neighborhood of Grosvenor or Berkeley Square in London."[12] In the late nineteenth century, horse-drawn carriages carried residents down the avenue until electric trams brought modernity to the capital's streets. New financial elites and industrialists of Poland's modernizing economy built their own homes alongside the Polish aristocracy.

With the end of the First World War, Ujazdowskie Avenue heralded Poland's regained independence from the surrounding empires, which had divided up the country at the end of the eighteenth century. The embassies and consulates that were built along the avenue reflected Warsaw's old-new political role as the capital of independent Poland between the world wars, and the city's main Russian Orthodox church, a symbol of Russian rule, was taken down in 1923. By then, a handful of Warsaw Jews, mainly assimilating financiers who were prominent in Poland's modernizing economy, had built apartment houses on Ujazdowskie Avenue. Their presence in this neighborhood of the Polish aristocracy underscored their distance from the Jewish traditions that governed life in predominantly Jewish neighborhoods further north.[13]

The building at 16 Ujazdowskie Avenue had its roots in this history. Before the war it was owned by Jakub Lindenfeld, an administrator in the Polish Bank, who built an apartment house there in the first years of the twentieth century. Its street number was 28 at that time, becoming 16 Ujazdowskie Avenue (and, for a time, 16 Stalin Avenue) only after the Second World War.[14] Jakub was a dour man, not particularly prominent in business or cultural life, but a position in the Polish Bank gave him the means to build on the capital's most prestigious avenue. His tenants were a mix of Polish society, from minor aristocrats, to clerks and tailors in the less desirable apartments behind the main building. Among the residents of the front section overlooking the street was a financier from a prominent Jewish family, Kazimierz Natanson, who was a "representative of assimilation," an interwar Polish Jewish politician later recalled, and "the last member of the Natanson family who remained in the Mosaic faith."[15]

Like many Jews who were part of assimilating circles, Jakub Lindenfeld's son Henryk was attracted to Polish culture and intellectual life. Just after his father had the apartment house built on Ujazdowskie Avenue, Henryk purchased a well-known Polish bookstore from another Jewish family, the Centnerszwers. Henryk's business partner, Jakub Mortkowicz, the son of a Yiddish-speaking Jew from Łódź, soon rose to prominence as one of the most important publishers of Polish literature.[16] It was a road to integration through the Polish book, one that the families who lived at 16 Ujazdowskie Avenue after the war transformed into their own path to integration—often in tension with an internationalist ideology that sought to alter the very definition of Polish identity.

The aristocrats and financiers who lived on Ujazdowskie Avenue before the Second World War were not spared when the Germans attacked Warsaw in September 1939. Buildings were damaged during the early bombardment, and when the Germans commandeered the neighborhood for their own residences the following year, all of its residents, both Polish and Jewish, had to find homes elsewhere in the city. In the Warsaw ghetto, assimilating Jews as well as converts to Christianity lived side by side with traditional Jews from whose way of life they had long been distanced.

A search for the wartime fate of the Lindenfeld family, the prewar owners of the building at 16 Ujazdowskie Avenue, turned up few traces. Perhaps a Władysław Lindenfeld who found an infant in the front stairway of a ghetto building in March 1941 and turned the baby over to an orphanage was the same Władysław who was an heir to Jakub Lindenfeld's building, and a Berta Lindenfeld whose Swiss bank account went unclaimed after the war is possibly the same woman who was listed in building records as another inheritor of the apartment house. None of the five heirs were included in the postwar registry of Polish Jewish survivors. They might have been killed with the masses of Warsaw Jewry, or perhaps they survived in hiding. Whether privilege and connections with Polish cultural and economic circles helped the family to survive is unclear.[17]

The Lindenfelds' building stood empty at war's end. Although the neighborhood escaped the worst of Warsaw's destruction, rubble dotted the thoroughfare, and the tops of some buildings had jagged edges. At the north end of the avenue, on Three Crosses Square (Plac Trzech Krzyży), bombs had badly damaged the monumental Church of Saint Aleksander. On a corner further south, an empty lot where a building had been destroyed was a kind of playground for the neighborhood's children into the 1950s.

But destruction in this most elegant of Warsaw neighborhoods was less severe than in the rest of the city, the result of its wartime role as part of the German quarter, and homes on the avenue and some nearby streets were among the most desirable in the postwar city. As reconstruction began, the authorities allocated apartments in the area to government offices, communist elites, and others who were helping to build the new political system. Their importance in rebuilding Warsaw, the city's mayor explained in January 1947, gave them priority.[18] The party seat was located at the corner of Chopin Street and Ujazdowskie Avenue, while the prewar General Inspectorate of the Armed Forces, which was established on the thoroughfare in 1928, now housed the communist government's Council of State and Council of Ministers.

Yet Warsaw society before the Second World War left its mark on the very structure of apartment houses on Ujazdowskie Avenue. From the street passersby could view the elaborate prewar architecture, but hidden behind the buildings overlooking the avenue, called the "front," were the back sections of the *oficyna,* or annex, which was built around one or more courtyards and was usually home to families of lesser means. It was the style of the late nineteenth century until the Second World War, as the contemporary Polish Jewish writer Henryk Grynberg wrote through the eyes of a narrator whose father owned a similar building in Lublin: "in the front wealth, in the back poverty, and at the bottom destitution."[19] The continued division between "front" and "back" in a neighborhood of new political elites represented a way of life that communism was supposed to erase.

"BACK AND FRONT" AT 16 UJAZDOWSKIE AVENUE

In the early months of 1945, a war widow and her young son, Wojciech Chodorowski, stood in the courtyard of 16 Ujazdowskie Avenue and looked around at the scarred facade of the annex, where they had lived until the occupying German authorities took over the neighborhood in 1940. Months before mother and son returned to their prewar home at war's end, Wojciech's father, who had been a guard for an aristocratic family before the war, was killed in the Warsaw Uprising.

The housing shortage was at its most dire then, and having a roof over one's head was a feat in those chaotic first postwar months. So Wojciech and his mother began their postwar lives in the place they had been forced to leave behind more than four years earlier. Wojciech grew old in the same apartment, where he and his wife raised their children. The couple still lived there in the early twenty-first century. Few, if any, other prewar residents remained.[20]

In the summer of 1947 construction began at 16 Ujazdowskie Avenue on the damaged front section, which the communist authorities set aside for employees of the Book publishing house. Its founding editors and directors began moving into apartments in the front building beginning in early 1948, and top employees of other government publishing institutions soon joined them. Initially the ground level was used as the publishing house's warehouse, protected by a guard, but later the publishing house turned it into a store selling its books.[21]

The apartments of the annex, meanwhile, fell under the jurisdiction of the municipal housing authorities, and the façade remained in a state of disrepair for years after the front was renovated. One resident of the annex recalled that relations between front and back were not strained, but that money for building renovations went first to the front and only later to the annex, causing some resentment.[22]

None of the front's residents was among the most privileged intellectuals associated with the new authorities, nor were they visible in public life, and most of the prewar apartments were divided up, so the homes were far from luxurious. Some were not much larger than those in the annex, while on the bottom floor of the front building lived the publishing house's driver, a position with little prestige. But the communist party's ideological publishing house played an important role in those early years, when the government sought to win over a wary society through propaganda. That role gave its employees political status despite their increasing marginalization in the party in the coming years.

At 16 Ujazdowskie Avenue one of the few spaces of contact between the front and the annex was the courtyard, where young boys from Jewish families in the front sometimes played with Wojciech Chodorowski and other non-Jewish children from the annex around an empty stone fountain. The older children and adults from the front rarely ventured into the courtyard, and by the time Włodek Paszyński, the youngest of the children's generation among the Jewish families, was old enough to play, he had little contact with the annex's children. Books occupied his spare time.[23]

A Polish writer in the 1960s reflected on the atmosphere of surviving prewar buildings with a "front" and "back":

> In the Home [the front] lived polite children who did not dirty their clothes in
> the sandbox, did not carry matches or stones in their pockets, studied English,
> painting, music and piano, and not dirty words. . . . On the other hand the chil-
> dren from the old home, arranged on three sides around the courtyard—that
> is from the Tenement [the back section]—are their opposite in every way. No
> wonder, then, that when children from the Tenement go out in the area of the
> Home's property: to the sandbox and the swings . . . suddenly the clatter of the
> typewriter stops coming from many windows of the Home and screams cry
> out: "Magda!" "Ola!" "Jacek!"[24]

The allocation of apartments in prestigious prewar buildings to individuals connected with the communist government meant that the
"front" residents of 16 Ujazdowskie Avenue, not only the families of
Jewish background, were intricately connected with sudden shifts in
privilege. The divide at 16 Ujazdowskie Avenue between the politically
privileged and the "ordinary" Varsovian was not a clear boundary, however, particularly in the first postwar years. That difference was blurred
even before the war, when laborers and tailors who lived in the annex
were neighbors of clerks and nurses, while the wife of an industrialist
and an engineer who was director of a factory lived in other apartments
in the back. Just after the war, when housing was scarce, the economic
and social status of the annex's residents was also mixed. A shoemaker
and laborers lived down the hall from a medical doctor, a dentist, and
a bookkeeper. Among the postwar residents of other apartments in the
annex were soldiers in the Polish military that had been formed in the
Soviet Union during the war and others with political connections.[25]

Postwar divisions between front and back overlapped with distance
between Jews and non-Jews. In the early postwar years, when building
registration lists still included a column for "religious confession," the
vast majority of the residents of the back were Catholic, and at least one
resident of the annex was under the incorrect impression that all of the
front building's residents, whom he associated with the communist government, were Jewish or families of mixed marriages.[26] But postwar distance between Jews and non-Jews was far from being a clear boundary.
Just over half of the front building's residents did not have Jewish roots,
a percentage that increased with the emigration waves of the late 1950s
and 1960s.[27] In the back, meanwhile, the neighbors included a handful
of Jewish families in the early postwar years. As in the front, the Jewish

families of the annex just after the war were clustered together, partly though not entirely isolated from their non-Jewish neighbors. Apartments in the back were cramped, as housing generally was in Warsaw in the first postwar decade, with nearly 350 people living in the annex's thirty-seven apartments—an average of ten individuals in each one. Among its postwar residents were as many as six Jewish families. In one apartment, three Jewish families lived among fourteen people who crowded together in what could not have been more than a few rooms. Sharing the kitchen and bathrooms with them, and perhaps the same rooms, were a Catholic family with two children and four other Catholic women.[28]

In 1950, however, as the Sławny family arrived from France and moved into the front section at 16 Ujazdowskie Avenue, one of the annex's Jewish families, the Gelbfiszes, boarded a train in the other direction. They planned to travel with their teenage son to Paris before boarding a ship to Tel Aviv. Traces of the annex's other Jewish families disappeared by then in the building's records and documents of Jewish institutions.[29]

—⁓—

Communist rule might have turned society upside down, taking privilege away from the wealthy and the aristocracy, but the comforts of everyday life in postwar Warsaw were rooted in status just as before the war, even though the factors that determined status were transformed. The result was a lasting irony of the city during the communist years: political leaders and intellectuals connected with the government often lived in buildings whose architecture and prestige represented a way of life officially opposed by the new politics. The neighborhood around Ujazdowskie Avenue, which was once the home of old elites, was now a symbol of their replacement by a politically privileged class.

The new regime promised that the city center would be the domain of workers, and disparities in housing were the most concrete evidence of the gap between communism's egalitarian ideology and the realities of everyday life. Housing was a constant preoccupation for the residents of postwar Warsaw. Typical conditions in the first postwar decade recalled the communal apartments of the Soviet Union, even if the arrangement in Poland resulted from pragmatic needs rather than government planning. The confinement of individual family space to "a room or a nook behind a partition" within an apartment and the sharing of common kitchens and bathrooms eroded the boundaries of private and public space. Only with the Five-Year Plan for Housing, announced in 1960, did the state's construction of new housing projects on the city's outskirts began accommodating large numbers of residents, soon bringing the number of residents per room back to prewar levels.[30]

Newcomers to Warsaw and others who did not have influential connections often lived for years, sometimes longer, in shared apartments while waiting for their own home. Political ideology alone did not mean that individuals had acquaintances who might help them obtain proper housing. One woman, Waleria M., whose school friend Zofia Zarębska grew up at 16 Ujazdowskie Avenue, recalled that her father, a prewar communist from a Jewish family, was not skilled at handling matters of everyday life, and he found only a small room when he arrived in Warsaw in 1945. Only when Waleria and her mother joined him in the city did they succeed in finding proper living quarters. Gustawa Maślankiewicz, whose cousin Nina Sztuczyńska lived at 16 Ujazdowskie Avenue after the war, had an even more difficult time, perhaps the result of her husband's involvement with the wartime Polish underground. While Nina and her husband, Samuel Neftalin, moved into a fourth-floor apartment on Ujazdowskie Avenue, benefiting from Samuel's position as a publishing-house administrator, Gustawa and her husband, with their young daughter, rented a small room in another family's apartment elsewhere in the city for more than a decade after the war.[31]

Individuals who obtained their apartments through association with the new government found themselves in a compromising situation, dependent on the regime for privileges in everyday life, from drivers to news from abroad and in some cases permission to travel to other countries. Intellectuals were particularly vulnerable, the poet Czesław Milosz wrote. A writer who cooperates with the new regime in his work, Milosz wrote,

> changes completely within the four walls of his home. There one finds (if he is a well situated intellectual) reproductions of works of art officially condemned as bourgeois, records of modern music, and a rich collection of ancient authors

in various languages. This luxury of splendid isolation is pardoned him so long as his creative work is effectively propaganda. To protect his position and his apartment (which he has by the grace of the State), the intellectual is prepared to make any sacrifice or compromise; for the value of privacy in a society that affords little if any isolation is greater than the saying "my home is my castle" can lead one to surmise.[32]

Bernard Kruc remembered that in 1968, his parents' apartment, which by then was just down the street from 16 Ujazdowskie Avenue, contributed to a feeling of security that initially made them wary of emigrating even after Bernard and his sister Ela left Poland. Only after Bernard's parents began to receive harassing phone calls did they decide to leave.[33] But a comfortable apartment was not enough to discourage the departure of disillusioned communists of Jewish background at times when the government itself was espousing antisemitism. One émigré who settled in France after the "anti-Zionist" campaign of the late 1960s wrote to a correspondent in Poland in 1972 that friends found it difficult to understand why he left behind the privileges of his life in Warsaw, including his apartment, which the letter's recipient had helped him to obtain: "Poland will be with me everywhere I go and this is without any pathos or patriotic frenzy, but simply because of nationality understood as culture, language, tradition," the émigré wrote. But, he continued,

> We are happy with the decision that we made two years ago, although it is not understood either there or here. We were not persecuted personally by anyone, the March-Zionist turmoil did not affect anyone in my family, and it is because of this that the question is constantly asked in disbelief, that after all we decided to leave a beautiful (thanks to you) apartment, "social position" and other such nonsense.[34]

—⁂—

Jews were never more than a minority of communists after the Second World War, just as they had not been beforehand, nor were most Jews communists. Yet the presence of a minority of individuals of Jewish background in postwar positions of political privilege reinforced the stereotype that blamed Jews for communism. Everyday comforts obtained through connections with the government made them part of the government's attempt to uproot old social structures and, as a result, of the replacement of old elites with new ones.

Isolated from much of Polish society and, for the communists among them, increasingly marginalized within the party itself, families of Jewish background were often drawn together despite their desire to keep that identity below the surface of their lives. Their circles were informal, no longer rooted in shared religious traditions, Jewish languages, and culture, and the identity that connected them was often fragmented. The boundaries of community were unclear, and networks that brought together families of Jewish background also included non-Jews.[35] Yet if communism can be viewed as a radical attempt at integration, the cluster of Jewish residents at 16 Ujazdowskie Avenue represented the limitations of that path. Just as shadows of old Warsaw remained in the reconstructed streets and society of the new city, so, too, did prewar ties of identity persist.

The continuity of old identities in new forms in postwar Warsaw was not an anomaly, however, and the history of Polish Jewry after the Holocaust is not entirely one of rupture. The genocide and the communist government's secularizing policies accelerated the breakdown of traditional Jewish communities that took place in Central and Western Europe in the previous century and that began tentatively in Poland even before the Second World War. In earlier centuries, Jewish neighborhoods reinforced the cohesiveness of communities, yet even after integration began to erode the religious foundations of communal life, Jews who were distanced from observance and Jewish culture often continued to share living spaces that shaped and reflected common identities.[36] In Vienna and Berlin, Paris and London, when the synagogue and its courtyard no longer were centers of everyday life for many Jews and restrictions on where they could live were lifted, Jews often continued to cluster together in neighborhoods and buildings, and they became friends with other Jews while immersing themselves in German or French or British culture.[37]

In postwar Warsaw the rupture with the past was more abrupt and far-reaching than during the more gradual changes over the course of European Jewish history, bringing into sharp relief the ambiguities of identity and the bonds of community in modernity. If postwar Warsaw Jewry was not entirely cut off from its history before the Holocaust

despite its vastly reduced size, but rather was a population that under-
went vastly accelerated transformations in identity and the ties of community, then the lives of Jewish families in the postwar Polish capital
become part of the history of Jewish populations in modern Poland
and beyond.

Emil Adler's parents, Markus and Helena, *née* Citterspieler.
Brody, 1911. *Courtesy of Marian Adler.*

Józef Tyszelman's family in Warsaw before the Second World War:
Józef (*bottom right*); sister Ewa; father, Cal, and mother, Łucja,
née Halperin. *Courtesy of Liliana Kamionka.*

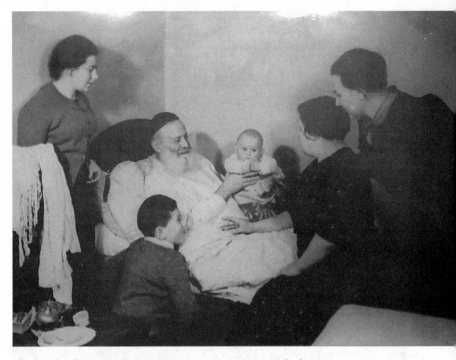

The family of Zina Tyszelman, *née* Herman, in Warsaw before
the Second World War. *Courtesy of Liliana Kamionka.*

Stefan Bergman, Moscow,
1931. Stefan sent the picture
in a letter to Genia and
Emil Adler in Germany.
Courtesy of Marian Adler.

Emil Adler with his first wife, Helena (*left*), and his mother, also named Helena, in Warsaw, June 1938. *Courtesy of Marian Adler.*

Paulina Bergman with her granddaughter Zofia, 1935, Homel. *Courtesy of Zofia Zarębska. All photos of the Bergman family that are courtesy of Zofia Zarębska were archived and researched by her.*

Zofia Zarębska (*née* Bergman) (*left*) and Aleksandra Bergman,
Troitsk, September 1945. *Courtesy of Zofia Zarębska.*

Employees in the offices of the Book and Knowledge publishing house
in Łódź, 1947. Emil and Eugenia Adler are on the far right.
Courtesy of Marian Adler.

Emil Adler, 1949. *Courtesy of Marian Adler.*

First of May parade, Warsaw, 1949. Eugenia Adler is on the right, and Stefan Bergman is behind her. *Courtesy of Marian Adler.*

First of May parade, Warsaw, 1958. Eugenia Adler is on the far left looking
at the camera, Stefan Bergman is behind the pole, and Aleksandra Bergman
is to his right. Halina Adler is in the front with glasses. Her brother Marian
is to her left, and Lena Bergman is behind them, holding the pole.
Courtesy of Marian Adler.

Left to right: Lena
Bergman, Marian Adler,
and Halina Adler in the
Park of Culture in Warsaw.
According to Zofia
Zarębska (*née* Bergman),
the photograph was taken
after the First of May
parade in 1959. *Courtesy
of Zofia Zarębska and
Eleonora Bergman.*

Józef Tyszelman (*left*) in his office at the Book and Knowledge publishing house in Warsaw. The photograph was taken in the 1950s or 1960s. *Courtesy of Liliana Kamionka.*

Ujazdowskie Avenue during the visit of Pope John Paul II in 1983, taken from the balcony of 16 Ujazdowskie Avenue. Among those standing on the balcony are members of the Tyszelman family. *Courtesy of Liliana Kamionka.*

CHAPTER FOUR

Stamp of a Generation

Parents and Children

"There exists in humanity a desire, inherited from generations long dead, to display heroism. Those who have no opportunity to do that elsewhere come to us. It is the 'professional' revolutionary type that does that mostly, a type very common among us Jews. With us this desire is a desire for martyrdom inherited from our forefathers, a natural need, nurtured through generations, to sacrifice oneself for the faith; one might also put it down to romanticism. Those of us who have lost the old faith fashion a new god to whom we can sacrifice ourselves. . . ."

But presently Anatol seemed to become ashamed of his sentimentality and to regret his lapse into idealism; with a contemptuous smile he went on: "Nevertheless, young man, you must resign yourself to the fact that our role—I mean us intellectuals—the role of all those who join battle merely out of idealism, as you call it, is a wretched one. We are fated to destruction. When the great moment comes the revolution will crush us, for with our useless baggage, our idealism and romanticism, we should only be in the way. We must be prepared to play the role of . . . slaves, whose labor is welcomed as long as it is of use, and cast off when it is not. Among us Jews there are saints, Zaddikim, who renounce all reward. That must be our role."

—*Sholem Asch, Three Cities*

Is it possible that that reality has transformed itself over the years into a nightmare? How did that happen? Instead of blood pulsing in its veins, instead of animal warmth, instead of love—a nightmare. The faces have changed into wolf snouts, the faces of my generation have changed into my own face, into wolf hair growing on the palms of these people. This is unjust. The wolf smell on my hands. It is unfair to forget about all the distinctions, about the fact that many people then were guided by noble intentions.

And you dare say that I was a Stalinist! How can one demand that a defenseless boy oppose the entire epoch? Do you think, perhaps, that I did not have an immortal soul? That I was an idiot who did not know Leśmian? Who had not read and had not thought about Rilke? My dear sir, people who were much older than I, men whom I considered experienced intellectuals, who were authorities for me, accepted the new faith. They did not share their doubts with me. If they shared anything at all, it was enthusiasm.

—Adam Zagajewski, Two Cities

IN JULY 1959 EMIL ADLER sat down at his desk in Warsaw and addressed a handwritten letter to his only son, Marian, who was celebrating his twelfth birthday. As Emil remembered Marian's birth in the aftermath of the Holocaust, the father's thoughts turned to the vanished Jewish world of Emil's childhood home. Despite the handful of Hebrew grammar books interspersed with Polish literature and political tracts on the bookshelves of Emil and Genia's home, their postwar distance from the Jewish past created a blank spot that separated their son Marian and their daughter Halina from the way of life that had defined their own youth. On Emil's twelfth birthday nearly a half-century earlier, his father had begun to prepare him for his bar mitzvah. Now the traditional Jewish marker of adulthood for Emil's son loomed just a year away.[1]

Three years before Emil wrote to Marian, political turmoil in Poland had challenged his political faith as the end of Stalinism exposed the bankruptcy of the communist government. He began to rethink the absence of Jewishness in his postwar home, which was shaping the identities of his children. They had no understanding of the Jewish rituals that linked Emil and his wife Genia to their own parents and grandparents.

The words that came to Emil on Marian's birthday in 1959 maintained an atheist's rejection of the father's childhood faith but sought nevertheless to fill in those blank spots. Underlying the letter's sentiments is the ambivalence of a Jewish communist in post-Holocaust Poland, whose longing for his murdered family was intertwined with recollections of the Jewish traditions he had long since left behind.

From the first sentences Emil sought to connect his son to memory of his prewar family, though he initially hesitated to emphasize the Jewish past that eventually emerges as his reason for writing. Ruminating on his first glimpse of Marian as a newborn just two years after war's end, Emil recalled that in the sea of babies at the maternity ward he had immediately picked out his son, who looked exactly like Emil's memory of his own father. "On that day, July 29, you were a few hours, perhaps a dozen hours, into the first year of your life. Today, July 29, 1959, you have already begun your thirteenth year. Today you are a few hours, a dozen hours into your thirteenth year."[2]

Then Emil Adler broached his main reason for writing. In a four-page letter, he tried to make up for the previous twelve years in which Jewishness had meant for his son only a sign of difference, a vague understanding of where his parents came from and why they had lost so much in wartime. Emil wrote:

> 13—this number is treated differently by various nations. Some consider it to be an unfortunate rite of passage, some—otherwise, in any case it is not possible to experience the 13th year with indifference. An interesting date, for example, is the 13th year of life for Jewish children. For them, a new period of life begins in the thirteenth year. By new I mean here mature, more serious.
>
> I will describe to you how this [his thirteenth year] was with me. My parents were believing people, believing Jews, and they raised me in the Jewish tradition. According to this tradition, the age of childhood ends with the twelfth year.
>
> For twelve years the father takes upon himself all the sins arising from the behavior of the child (a son! A girl, this is another matter) and when the boy reaches the thirteenth year, the father brings a prayer to god and says "*baruch shepatrani*," which means "blessed are you who liberated me," and so he withdraws from responsibility for his son. The boy receives the liturgical vestments, the so-called "*tefillin*" (boxes made of leather, containing the basic prayer written on parchment), which he puts on daily from now until the end of life for the morning prayer, takes part in fasts (very difficult and rigorous among Jews) and in other rituals. The rituals are like rituals always are, every religion has its own and for as long as they are believed in, they exert influence.[3]

Emil then hinted at his own struggle to make his Jewish past relevant to his secular world view despite his childhood loss of faith. He emphasized a humanistic interpretation of Judaism that transformed religious belief into universal values, which he judged to be compatible not only with his own atheism and political ideology, but also with his son's secular upbringing:

> This is how it was with me. Then came education, knowledge and all of these fairy-tales and myths were cast off into a corner. But one thing in all of this is worthy of attention, and this is why I have described these things to you. Remember that I experienced my thirteenth birthday very deeply!
>
> I think to myself, dear little son, that you are raised in a secular spirit, with-out any superstitious rites. But I also think that from the various traditions, we should keep from the discarded myths that which is true and sensible in them. In this case, I believe that this sensible thing is the <u>feeling of responsibility</u> that should accompany a thirteen-year-old. When I went through those days, when the thirteenth year of life began it was the feeling that a new period was begin-ning in my life, when <u>I will be responsible for myself</u>. At that time I saw this responsibility through the eyes of a stupefied boy first of all as responsibility to God. But on a daily basis this meant responsibility for actions concerning people and in reality, when I was 13 years old, I already felt serious, adult, in short <u>responsible</u>. You should think about this, reflect on how your greater maturity and responsibility will manifest itself from this moment on. This will be responsibility not to God, but significantly more difficult—to people. . . . It is not God [in Polish Pan Bóg, the Lord God] who will judge your results but people.[4]

Forty-seven years later, living in Göttingen, Germany, with his Ger-man wife but still longing for Poland, Marian Adler did not recall receiv-ing the letter that his father wrote on his twelfth birthday. In 2006, a decade after Emil's death, Marian still had not looked through the piles of letters and papers that his parents had left behind, a hesitancy that was not uncommon among the generation that grew up at 16 Ujazdowskie Avenue. Even after rereading the letter as an adult, Marian did not real-ize that his father was trying to explain the preparations for a ceremony that would not take place.

At age twelve and at age fifty-nine, Marian could not have under-stood his father's sentiments. Although Marian was aware from early childhood that his parents were Jewish, neither the thoroughly secular home in which he and his sister were raised nor their education in Pol-ish schools could have helped them comprehend the substance of that identity or the traditions of their parents' prewar homes. In place of Jew-ishness, there was mainly absence. It was a barrier to understanding not only their parents' world view, but also their own identities.

ON THE BORDERS OF POSTWAR IDENTITIES

From the earliest years after the Holocaust, Emil Adler and other Jewish communists at 16 Ujazdowskie Avenue rebuilt their families around their political ideals. They were internationalists who believed that community transcended religion and nation, and they embraced the government's secular ideology. For those of Jewish background, political faith often left no room for Jewishness on the surface of their lives.

Yet every individual lives with contradictions in their outlook on the world, and identity is never seamless. The parents at 16 Ujazdowskie Avenue lived on the borders of identities, often never fully reconciling their politics with their desire for acceptance as Poles or with the ambiguous role of Jewishness in their postwar homes. Even as political ideology suppressed their Jewish background, Jewishness continued to shape their private lives and bonds of community. The parents shared with their neighbors common memories of the Jewish past and the loneliness of wartime survival, and they understood how political upheavals affected the other parents not only as Poles, but also as individuals of Jewish background.

Polish culture was deeply ingrained in them just as memories of the Jewish past were. Symbols of Polishness defined their everyday lives, from the classics of Polish literature that lined their apartments to the melody of the Polish language. Their desire for acceptance as Poles only deepened the suppression of Jewishness that their internationalism entailed. For those who were communists, remaining in Poland after the Holocaust meant not only casting their fate with the new political system, but also maintaining the hope that in People's Poland they could resolve the contradictions in their identities.

—⚊—

In war's early aftermath, when Emil Adler saw his newborn son for the first time, he was still flush with political passion. As a top editor at the Polish communist party's ideological publishing house, Emil was helping to establish a government representing the political ideology for which his comrades had been imprisoned in prewar Poland. The Holocaust cemented his political faith. He expected communism to create a just society after the genocide and a war that had devastated Europe and its Jewish populations.

Prewar memories and wartime losses were still fresh then, and Emil and his new wife, Genia, sought solace in one another. Emil's travels for the Book publishing house and Genia's recovery from tuberculosis in a sanatorium separated them for long periods, so they wrote to each other often.

In those early postwar years, emptiness began to give way to new friends and new families. The Adlers shared an apartment for a short time with Aleksandra and Stefan Bergman, and in Genia's letters to Emil she sometimes enclosed a note for them.[5] Soon after Marian Adler was born, Aleksandra Bergman also gave birth. She and Stefan named their daughter Eleonora, known as Lena. She was the first member of her immediate family whose first language was Polish.

In the Adlers' frequent letters to one another they occasionally wrote about their wartime losses. They never mentioned the Jewish past directly, but recollections of their prewar families were intertwined with the Jewish world of their youth. Nearly all traces of their childhood lives were gone. Even as Genia and Emil began building a new family together, they were still mourning their relatives.

"Everything else is already passing," Emil wrote to Genia on July 24, 1946, "but loneliness leads me to dwell on various things: thoughts come back about my brothers, my parents—categorically, dear baby, we should not allow a separation from such experiences. But it will not be long before we are together." Listening to a concert in a park that day, Emil wrote, he remembered a vacation with his mother in the Bohemian spa town of Carlsbad (Karlovy Vary, Czech Republic) when he was four years old. The young Emil, known then as Mendel, wandered away and became captivated by an orchestra. The musicians took him into the orchestra pit while his mother searched for him frantically in a nearby park.[6]

Shortly after she located Emil, a photograph was taken of mother and son. "Always when we looked at this picture, we remembered the events [of the trip], which remain in my memory in all of their detail," he wrote to Genia. "Not even one photograph! I am certain that if I go to Brody I will find a few pictures there. I am thinking seriously about a trip there—even more so because it is necessary to sell my home."[7]

Nostalgia and mourning soon disappeared from their letters. Memories of wartime losses were painful as they sought to rebuild, and under the very political system they were helping to establish, the strict censorship and repressions of the Stalinist years forced their memories beneath the surface. And while surviving Jews who rebuilt in other countries physically separated themselves from places of trauma, those who remained in Poland lived in their shadow.

By 1947 the Adlers stopped writing about the past, neither their lost families nor their wartime survival. Their letters were now filled with news about Emil's political work, Genia's updates on her health, and mundane matters of everyday life. As they raised their children, Marian and Halina, the parents created the very barrier against the past that Emil cautioned Genia in his letter not to erect.

—␣—

Looking back in 1962 at his early postwar years in Łódź, Emil remembered not the pain of building life anew, but the hope and idealism of his publishing-house colleagues. Political faith was nearly all that remained of his prewar life.

Emil arrived in Łódź in May 1945 on one of the trains carrying Polish citizens back to Poland from their wartime exile in the Soviet Union, and most of his future publishing-house colleagues had not yet returned. Those who had already arrived in Poland, including Stefan Bergman, were awaiting orders from party leaders. But they quickly set up offices in a few rooms in an apartment, eager to begin work.

Soon the makeshift office was crowded with editors and translators. Colleagues often met for the first time after the war, but they quickly became a close-knit group who worked and socialized together as the devastation of wartime gave way to the routines of daily life. Emil later remembered "more than one shared moment at work and leisure, especially during our small celebrations, [which] are documented to this day in photographs of the group gathered at tables set with food and drink."[8] The black-and-white pictures preserved scenes of men in suits and women in plain dresses crowded around a simple wooden table. The Adlers sat together at the edge of the group, looking directly into the camera. Genia had begun to recover from the extreme depravations of Auschwitz, and her round face and soft features were relaxed into a smile.

As the Adlers and other Jewish families were rebuilding, so, too, was Poland beginning to emerge from wartime devastation. Political chaos engulfed the country as the resurrected, Soviet-backed Polish communist party consolidated control. Leaders of the wartime Polish underground, the Home Army, were arrested, and within a few years the communists had forced their political opponents to flee the country. The Polish masses often blamed the Jews, whom they viewed as outsiders helping to impose communism on an unwilling population—a continuation of the decades-old stereotype of Żydokomuna, roughly translated as "Judeo-communism." For the minority of Jews who were in fact communists, the hostility meant that they experienced postwar political turmoil differently from their non-Jewish comrades. They became isolated not only from Polish society, but also within the communist party itself.

Antisemitism sometimes turned violent in those first postwar years. In 1945 and 1946 surviving Jews were attacked in a series of pogroms, the most devastating of which occurred in July 1946 in the city of Kielce, where more than forty Jews were killed. Smaller pogroms in previous months elsewhere in Poland did not create the same panic as the Kielce attacks did. One year earlier, several Jews were killed and injured in a pogrom in Kraków, but thousands of Jews continued to resettle there, with more than four thousand moving to Kraków in the first half of 1946 alone despite simultaneous emigration from the city. But the Kielce pogrom alarmed Jews throughout Poland, and mass emigration picked up its pace. In the following six months more than ninety thousand Jews left Poland.[9]

The Kielce pogrom awakened old memories for the Adlers. Just three weeks afterward, Emil wrote to Genia about the childhood vacation with his mother to the Bohemia spa town, though the letter never mentioned the pogrom. Genia later recalled that the murders in Kielce convinced her to change her parents' first and last names to less "Jewish-sounding" ones on government documents. The Adlers eventually decided to keep their own, non-Slavic last name. But wartime fear never left Genia.[10]

The editors at the Book publishing house clung to their political faith. Old bonds of community—religion and nation—were part of the world that had given birth to the Holocaust, and now communism would reshape what connected individuals to one another and to their country, they believed. In the utopia they envisioned, Jewish background would no longer mark them as the "other" in their native country, even if they did not emphasize that view as central to their political beliefs.

In those early Łódź years the publishing-house editors spoke late into the night about politics, Poland's past and its future, and the world events they learned about on the radio. They had orders from the party to print propaganda and ideological works, but the editors had other tasks, too. Libraries and personal collections had been decimated throughout Poland during the war, and the editors satiated the public's hunger for books with reissued Polish novels and translations of literature from English, French, and other European languages.

As they debated about what to publish, the editors seemed at times to reach out to readers about the "Jewish issue" through words written in the previous century. The literature they published included nineteenth-century books written by novelists known as Polish positivists, who discussed similar preoccupations as the ones facing Polish and Jewish society after the war: what it meant to be Polish, and how—whether—Jews could be included in that identity.

These nineteenth-century novelists were not Jewish, and their books were above all about Poland at a time when the country was divided up among the surrounding powers. After Poles revolted unsuccessfully against Russian rule in 1863–1864, the Polish positivists had called for the abandonment of quixotic notions of rebellion. They believed that aristocrats and peasants, Poles and Jews, needed to create a unified society that was strong enough at the roots to resist tsarist rule. After the Second World War the positivist novels must have resonated with Poles who believed communism was just another form of Russian domination. Resistance to foreign control was buried between the novels' lines.

The editors of the Book publishing house in postwar Łódź were committed to their political ideology, and opposition to the new authorities was certainly not the message they would have wanted to send. Yet the plot lines of these nineteenth-century writers also had clear echoes of the problems that confronted Jews in early postwar Poland. In 1949, just three years after the Kielce pogrom and even after the Stalinist government's grip on power made the "Jewish issue" increasingly taboo, an editor at the publishing house, which was known as Book and Knowledge by then, sought the censor's permission to publish a positivist novel, *Mendel Gdański,* about a pogrom in Warsaw in 1881. The book, written in 1890 by the positivist author Maria Konopnicka, "presents the figure of the old Jew Mendel, who works hard and raises his young grandson, loving the country in which he lives and the city of Warsaw," a Book and Knowledge editor reported to the censor. "Antisemitic attacks break him, since the injustice greatly offends him. This novel comes to the strong defense of the underprivileged Jewish population, which works hard, dedicating itself to the common good, and in return for this encounters injustice and humiliation. The author presents the topic in a moving way, appealing to sentiments of the brotherhood of humanity."[11]

The censor approved *Mendel Gdański* and a second positivist novel about Jews, Eliza Orzeszkowa's *Mirtala: Powieść,* for publication, but the latter did not appear. And communist Poland would never succeed in untangling the knot of the "Jewish issue."[12]

—⁂—

Jewish editors at Book and Knowledge shared another belief with these nineteenth-century Polish positivist writers: that the shtetlekh were "fossilized in seventeenth-century rituals," as a report to the censor described one novel that was rejected for publication—"fairy-tales and myths," as Emil referred to those rituals in his 1959 letter for his son's twelfth birthday.[13]

Most of the parents at 16 Ujazdowskie Avenue had abandoned Jewish observance long before the war, but when they were young adults before the Holocaust, traces of Jewish tradition remained on the surface of their lives. At least nine lived in Warsaw's prewar Jewish neighborhoods for shorter or longer periods, surrounded by Jews and Jewish culture. Perhaps they visited childhood homes where extended families gathered for holidays, and where they might have spoken Yiddish with older relatives.

After the war the break with Jewish life was much deeper. Warsaw's Jewish quarters no longer existed. For most families of Jewish background, there were few grandparents or siblings to visit, no bris when boys were born and no kaddish on the anniversary of a parent's death. For all of the families of 16 Ujazdowskie Avenue, Jewish tradition was almost entirely absent from the life cycle. Sometimes May Day parades and other political rituals replaced old traditions. But Jewishness never disappeared entirely from the building's postwar homes and elsewhere in Warsaw, even when the parents cut themselves off entirely from that identity. Absence and hints of "otherness" preserved traces of the Jewish past. Only Luba Rudnicka remained in regular contact with Jewish institutions after the early postwar years, through her work as an editor at Yiddish newspapers and a leader of a Jewish scout troop.

Difference was most noticeable during holidays and celebrations rooted in Catholic tradition that was woven into everyday life in Poland. Children of Jewish background often had parties on their birthdays, but most of their non-Jewish peers celebrated name-days, marking the day connected with the Catholic saints after whom they were named. Even among secular Catholic families, relatives generally still celebrated with festive meals on Christmas and Easter. Some Jewish families gathered for dinner around Christmas time and put up Christmas trees, but most had few relatives to invite over, and religious tradition typically played no part in the evening.

Perhaps absence was felt most deeply on November 1, All Saints' Day, when most Poles paid respect to the dead, crowding narrow cemetery lanes and placing flowers and small candles on graves. Even if individuals of Jewish background considered visiting a cemetery on that day, most had few graves to visit; relatives were buried in pits in Poland's former eastern territories or had been killed in Nazi death camps.

The homes of Stefan and Aleksandra Bergman and Stefan's sister Luba Rudnicka were different in many ways from those of their Jewish neighbors. Language alone set them apart. The grandmother, Paulina Bergman, knew Polish, but she often spoke Yiddish with her children Stefan and Luba and her daughter-in-law Aleksandra. Yiddish was a native language for many of the neighboring parents of Jewish background as well, but their children rarely heard even a trace of Yiddish in their homes; for them, the Jewish past emerged only on the margins. Even for Nina Sztuczyńska, whose mother was Russian Orthodox and who had no contact with Jewish ritual before the war, Jewishness lingered in her home on the building's fourth floor. While Nina sometimes sang in French, a language she had learned in childhood when her family lived in France, she was dismayed when Samuel occasionally sang in Yiddish while shaving.[14]

Liliana Tyszelman, who lived with her parents and grandmother at 16 Ujazdowskie Avenue, recalled that her parents sometimes had matzah in their apartment around Easter,[15] but only in middle age, after the fall of communism, did Liliana fully understand the connection between Passover and her parents' ritual around Easter time. Without any knowledge of Jewish traditions or culture, the children of 16 Ujazdowskie Avenue could barely recognize traces of their Jewish background. Difference blended into the background, and the past echoed through absence.

As the children of 16 Ujazdowskie Avenue were beginning adolescence, the eruption of political turmoil throughout Eastern Europe in 1956 cast a shadow over the political ideas that defined many of their postwar homes. Politics began to expose the blank spots. On February 25, 1956, the Soviet premier Nikita Khrushchev secretly addressed a gathering of top Soviet party officials and described the false accusations, torture, and murders that took place under Stalin's watch.

Political change was inscribed on the streets of Warsaw once more. When the families of 16 Ujazdowskie Avenue began moving into the building eight years earlier, the political authorities had recently renamed the thoroughfare Stalin Avenue; in 1956, after Khrushchev's speech, new street signs rechristened it Ujazdowskie Avenue.

Soon afterward, security police who were secretly conducting surveillance from a family's apartment at 16 Ujazdowskie Avenue vacated the residence. The police had begun spying in the building nearly three years earlier in an operation known as "the Avenue." But in 1956 the family's relatives visited more regularly and the apartment became too crowded, the security police reported to their supervisors.[16] The neighbors were not aware of the surveillance, and the target is unclear. Perhaps the police were keeping an eye on embassies nearby or on one of the building's families. In those years, as one resident later commented, no one was beyond suspicion.

Even before Khrushchev's speech, Stalinist regimes were discredited throughout Eastern Europe. In 1954 a high official in Poland's security apparatus defected to West Germany and spoke on the radio of torture and other persecutions of Polish prisoners. By June 1956 Poles were in open rebellion. In the western city of Poznań, the military fired on protesters, killing four people. In October Soviet tanks approached Warsaw, and Soviet leaders appeared unexpectedly in the capital after the Polish party elected as its head Władysław Gomułka, a top communist leader in early postwar Poland whom the Stalinist government had imprisoned just five years earlier. Only in 1954 was he released. Now, in 1956, the Soviets feared that Gomułka's Poland would become too independent, withdraw from its military cooperation with the Soviets, and slip from their control. The two sides averted violence, and the Poles hoped Gomułka would usher in an independent "Polish road to socialism," the end of Soviet domination, the beginning of more freedom.

In 1981, twenty-five years after the turmoil of 1956, Stefan Bergman traveled to Poznań to mark the anniversary of the strikes there. By then he had given up on his old political faith and was helping the anticommunist opposition set up illegal presses—descendants of the crude contraptions he had created six decades earlier for the prewar communist party. The Bergmans' old friends Emil and Genia Adler were already living in Germany after their emigration in 1968, and Stefan sent them a postcard from the commemoration that read at the bottom: "1981, Solidarity."[17] Six months after that anniversary, when the Polish government declared martial law to rein in the anticommunist opposition, Stefan gave up his party membership entirely.

—⁂—

Aleksandra Bergman, a prewar communist, was never active in politics after the war. Perhaps she had seen enough during nearly a decade in the Gulag to strip away any political illusions. But Emil Adler and Stefan Bergman remained immersed in politics. Although neither one was a top politician or leading intellectual, Emil traveled to Moscow in 1950 with elite Marxist philosophers from Poland to study Marxist-Leninist doctrine, just as Stefan had done as a young man decades earlier. Emil saved wartime newspaper clippings with praise-filled poems of propaganda about Stalin, including one written in Yiddish by Itsik Fefer, a Soviet Jewish poet who was killed in 1948 together with the other most prominent Yiddish writers after a Soviet show trial. Even after the Adlers' departure from Poland in 1968, Emil kept Fefer's poem. By then those sentiments were relics of Emil's former self, not nostalgia for those years.

Emil, Stefan, and other communists of Jewish background who lived at 16 Ujazdowskie Avenue did not publicly voice disillusionment in the late 1950s. But Emil's letter to Marian on the son's twelfth birthday in 1959 offers a glimpse of the emotional turmoil many of the building's Jewish parents experienced as they began reconsidering what they had sacrificed for a party that was pushing them to the margins. It was already becoming clear to some communists that they had left behind Jewish identity in exchange for equality in vain. It was as if the bargain of Jewish emancipation had been made once again, and once more had not been kept.

The political changes of 1956 deeply affected all of Polish society. The authorities eased persecution of priests and released the Polish primate, Cardinal Stefan Wyszyński, from internment. Catholics could attend church and baptize their children with less fear of persecution, and the government allowed children to attend religious instruction in school. Writers began to voice opinions that did not agree with the party line.

But individuals of Jewish background experienced the turmoil of the 1950s differently. When the Polish government began scapegoating Jews for Stalinism and antisemitism increased, many wondered what the turmoil meant for them as individuals of Jewish background. In private apartments and during long walks in the 1950s friends and colleagues discussed the political upheavals, sometimes in hushed tones and at times openly. Emil's old friend Jakub Prawin, a prewar communist and top postwar diplomat, commented wryly during a visit to a friend's apartment, "We'll see whether they allow a Jew" to hold an important position for which he was being considered, his nephew, Daniel Passent, later recalled. Prawin raised Daniel in postwar Poland after the boy was orphaned during the Holocaust, and Daniel remembered spending evenings with his uncle at Emil and Genia's apartment, first at Ujazdowskie Avenue and later at the Adlers' new apartment elsewhere in Warsaw. Only after overhearing his uncle's comment in the late 1950s did Daniel, already in his teens, realize that Prawin was Jewish like himself.[18]

At the Book and Knowledge publishing house, the communists struggled to come to terms with Khrushchev's speech. Long before 1956 the editors and other communists must have known that the Stalinist regimes of the Soviet Union and Eastern Europe did not embody their political faith. Many communists from Poland, the Bergmans and Luba Rudnicka among them, were themselves survivors of the Gulag. One of Stefan and Luba's sisters was killed during the Stalinist purges. In 1956 they could no longer ignore what their ideology had wrought.

The communists at Book and Knowledge agonized over how to respond. Of the Jewish parents at 16 Ujazdowskie Avenue, only Stefan Bergman and Józef Tyszelman still held top publishing-house posts by then. Genia Adler was still working there as a translator, but her husband Emil was now a professor of Marxist philosophy at Warsaw University. Ignacy Kruc, its former director of finance, had also moved on to another employer. Their neighbor Barbara H., Book and Knowledge's first editor in chief, was an editor at a different publishing house, although two years after Khrushchev's speech Barbara returned briefly to Book and Knowledge, which became a refuge for Jewish intellectuals who were fired in the late 1950s.[19] Among the Jews who found work there was one of the government's highest officials, Jakub Berman, after he was forced out of the party's Central Committee. In 1957 the party expelled him entirely.

In the wake of Khrushchev's speech, Book and Knowledge's meetings were contentious and at times bitter. Józef Tyszelman often presided, and Stefan Bergman was deeply involved in the discussions. Poland's top leaders were keeping a close watch; the speakers had to be cautious about what they said aloud. The hollowness of the Stalinist authorities who controlled Poland was clear, and the government's grip on power was at risk.

Preserved records of those meetings at Book and Knowledge in 1956 and 1957 are dry and riddled with political jargon. Probably the minutes left out much of what was said. Between the lines, however, the records are a window onto the anger and disillusionment that a few dared to voice aloud.

One month after Khrushchev's speech, during one of the most tumultuous meetings, Book and Knowledge's top communists gathered in Warsaw's towering Palace of Culture and Science, which had been officially opened just eight months earlier. In this very symbol of Soviet dominance, the publishing-house leaders confronted political reality.

Józef Tyszelman and other Book and Knowledge leaders began by reading aloud the full text of Khrushchev's speech. One can only imagine the emotional reactions, probably outwardly subdued. The speech must have reminded them of friends and relatives who had been arrested and in some cases killed under Stalin's watch. Sitting in the hall, Stefan Bergman might have thought about his sister Róża, who was killed during the purges, and about the long years that he, his wife Aleksandra, and his sister Luba Rudnicka suffered in the Gulag. Now Khrushchev acknowledged the injustices they had endured. "Prominent party leaders and rank-and-file party workers, honest and dedicated to the cause of communism, fell victim to Stalin's despotism," Khrushchev had said. Many of those arrested "were actually never enemies, spies, wreckers.... [They] were always honest communists."[20]

The publishing-house communists then listened to Khrushchev's indirect acknowledgment of Stalinist-era antisemitism. Just before his death Stalin had accused sixteen Jewish doctors of conspiring to poison him; now Khrushchev admitted that the "doctors' plot" was entirely fabricated, though he did not mention that the doctors were Jewish.

Detailed minutes of Book and Knowledge's March gathering have not been preserved for history; the records are missing from the archive. Apparently their heated discussions went too far. Government leaders accused the publishing-house communists of being part of the threat to the political system they had helped to create, and the authorities demanded the meeting minutes. Book and Knowledge's leaders refused the government's demands; perhaps someone removed or destroyed the records. They submitted only a brief summary, according to a report from a later meeting.[21]

Book and Knowledge's communists had risked their futures as young adults in prewar Poland, when the party was illegal, and many had spent long years in prison. Now they wanted to know what had happened to the ideology for which they had made such sacrifices. With their open debates in 1956, they were risking their futures once again.

Despite the government's accusations in 1956 that the publishing house's discussions amounted to "enemy action," some at Book and Knowledge still refused to keep quiet. Mieczysław Orlański, an editor of Jewish background, was among them. "I want to speak calmly, even though I am shaken like everybody," he told the gathering before questioning a "certain tone" of a top government propaganda official who had come to deliver an oblique warning to the publishing-house colleagues about their criticism. Twelve years later, Mieczysław Orlański's son had been arrested as an enemy of the government during the antisemitic campaign in 1968, and Mieczysław himself left Poland.[22] By then communists of Jewish background at Book and Knowledge, including those from 16 Ujazdowskie Avenue, had been demoted or fired outright. In 1968 the institution they had established more than two decades earlier began printing antisemitic propaganda that questioned Jews' right to consider themselves Poles.[23]

—ᴍ—

If Stefan Bergman abandoned his political faith by 1956, he did not admit it openly then. Acknowledging the failure of a life's path is a devastating concession for anyone to make, and perhaps political passion still blinded communists to reality. Stefan insisted, at least publicly, that he was not ready to give up on his ideology.

At one of the publishing house's tense meetings that year, Stefan took the floor and proclaimed his continued political faith. He criticized the "distortions" of Stalinism but insisted that abandoning communism was not the solution. The party had to return to its ideological principles, he argued. Bergman urged his colleagues to study the classics of Marxist ideology, the ones he had pored over in prison as a young adult before the Second World War. His entire postwar life had been spent overseeing translations of those texts from Russian into Polish, reading over the translations repeatedly for any mistakes or improper grammar in a language that was not his first tongue.

After Stefan's speech, a Book and Knowledge translator named Igor Szczyrba rose to criticize the contradictions between government ideology and everyday life in Poland. Szczyrba spoke about the comfortable homes of top government officials compared with other Poles. Even into the 1950s the capital still suffered from a housing shortage, and differences in apartment conditions were the most glaring evidence that the government's egalitarian ideology was mere rhetoric.

Szczyrba did not mention 16 Ujazdowskie Avenue, and the building's comforts were far short of the privileges he described. Despite its elegant exterior most of the apartments were small, and leading intellectuals and top government authorities in Poland had far more luxurious homes. But editors and other leaders of Book and Knowledge, Jewish and non-Jewish, lived in greater comfort compared with the crowded rooms where many Varsovians still had to make their homes. Following immediately upon Stefan's exhortation to "return to the fundamentals" of Marxist ideology, Szczyrba's comments might have been directed at him.

"I am not so versed in theory in order to be able to engage in polemics as, for example, Comrade Bergman can," he began. Szczyrba wanted to speak instead about "practical matters." He recounted conversations with an "average worker" whose family lived in a basement and with another friend about a top official's widow who lived by herself in a three-room apartment. "We did not struggle for a Poland in which one person can live in three rooms . . . and a second in basements," Szczyrba declared. One friend, he said, cited the "wise words" of his father: "We will not achieve anything in 'large matters' as long as we do not pick up the trash in front of our own home. . . . These things are seemingly minor, but when neglected they grow into major issues."[24]

The meeting minutes did not record a response from Stefan Bergman. Immediately after Szczyrba spoke, Ozjasz Szechter, Stefan's good friend and old political comrade, who was also Jewish, publicly apologized to Stefan for using epithets in their polemics at an earlier meeting. Just over a decade later Ozjasz's son, Adam Michnik, became a leader in the opposition movement that eventually helped to bring down the communist government.[25]

"NUSEKH POYLN"—POLISH STYLE:
DEPARTURES AND RETURNS

As Stefan Bergman and his colleagues were heatedly arguing in March 1956 about Khrushchev's speech, elsewhere in Warsaw the chairman of the Jewish communal organization in Poland, Hersh Smolar, was absorbing the same revelations. But the information Smolar sought as he read the text was nowhere to be found. For eight years Smolar and Jewish leaders throughout the world had searched in vain for news about the fate of the most prominent Soviet Yiddish writers in the Soviet Union. Virtually no one had seen or heard from them since their arrests in late 1948 and early 1949. But Khrushchev made no mention of them.

Smolar and the rest of the Jewish leadership soon learned the truth: all but one of the Soviet Jewish intellectuals and leaders who had been arrested were executed in 1952, not long after their trial. He learned the news from the editor of the *Forverts,* the New York Yiddish newspaper, who was passing through Warsaw on his way home from a visit to Moscow. That night Smolar penned an article in Yiddish titled "Undzer veytik un undzer treyst [Our pain and our consolation]." The article lamented the persecution of Soviet Jewry but expressed hope that Poland would prove now that Jewish life could thrive under communism. It took more than a month for top Polish authorities to allow the *Folks-shtime,* Warsaw's Yiddish newspaper, to print the article, which was published without Smolar's name.[26]

Smolar, a communist since young adulthood and a wartime partisan leader in Minsk, was devastated. As longtime chairman of postwar Poland's Jewish communal organization, the Social-Cultural Association of Jews in Poland, Smolar and other Jewish leaders followed the party line in condemning "Jewish nationalism" and avoiding reference to the Jews as a nation. Yet they sought to sustain secular Jewish culture by organizing Jewish schools, a Yiddish theater, summer camps, and a Yiddish newspaper and literary journal—though not religious life, which was only nominally under their control. Their shade of communism was different from the ideology of comrades who distanced themselves from their Jewish identity, although friendships blurred the boundaries between the two groups.

Like the communists at Book and Knowledge, Smolar must have long known that Stalinism was not the political utopia he had envisioned. In the 1950s leaders of Eastern Europe's communist regimes were resorting to antisemitism, the most personal indication for Jews that the governments did not represent their ostensible ideology. Before Stalin's death in 1953, most of the fourteen defendants in a show trial of top communist officials in Czechoslovakia in 1952 were Jewish, most notably Rudolf Slansky. In Poland Smolar and other Jewish leaders were fearful for their own fate in those last years of Stalinism. In 1952 and 1953 the director of Poland's Yiddish publishing house, an Israeli diplomat, and Poland's former administrator for the American Jewish Joint Distribution Committee, which the government had kicked out of

Poland in 1949, were arrested as spies. Rumors that Polish Jews would soon be sent to concentration camps in the Soviet Union were rampant. No show trial took place in Poland, the three men were released after Stalin's death, and no evidence ever surfaced about plans to send Jews to camps. But news that the Soviet Yiddish writers had been killed confirmed the Jewish leaders' fears.

The late 1950s were a tumultuous time for all East Europeans, and in 1956 no one was quite certain what direction the Polish government would take. Poles expected that the new authorities would be freer from Soviet dominance and that persecution by the security police would cease. Many Jewish leaders also remained hopeful that the new freedoms would reinvigorate Jewish life. Poland's Yiddish newspaper, the *Folksshtime*, began printing articles in inside pages about Jewish religious life in Poland and cultural life in Israel, although articles supporting the party line continued to dominate the front page. The newspaper as well as the Yiddish literary journal, *Yidishe shriftn*, published literary criticism about the works of the murdered Soviet Yiddish writers. Jewish communal leaders even considered forming Hebrew classes in Jewish schools, a proposal that would have been unheard of in earlier years. The classes did not come to fruition, whether because of a government ruling or a decision by the Jewish communal leadership, who were divided over the proposal.[27] Yet Jewish life began to open up to the Jewish world outside of Poland and became relatively freer from the restrictions of the Stalinist years. Polish Jewish leaders would prove that Jewish life could thrive under communism, Smolar insisted, what he later referred to in Yiddish as "*nusekh Poyln*," or Polish style.

History quickly proved Smolar wrong. Some government leaders and segments of Polish society turned nationalist fervour into antisemitism, and reports trickled in about harassment of Jews throughout Poland. Most incidents were not violent: classmates taunted Jewish children in courtyards and at school, and Jews were sometimes forced to move out of desirable apartments. Jewish factory workers and managers, editors, journalists, and government officials at all levels were fired from jobs. Vandals broke windows of stores owned by Jews. One of the most alarming reports came from western Poland. In the coal-mining city of Wałbrzych hundreds of people menacingly surrounded a Jewish butcher's shop. The military initially rebuffed Jewish leaders who appealed for help, but eventually the police dispersed the crowd and headed off fears of violence.[28]

The year 1957 was especially tumultuous for Jews. It began with the arrest of a Jewish taxi driver, Ignacy Ekerling, in connection with the murder of Bohdan Piasecki, the seventeen-year-old son of an antisemitic, right-wing prewar nationalist. The father had morphed after the war into a pro-communist leader of a government-aligned Catholic organization. His son's body was found in the ruins of a cellar in Muranów, Warsaw's prewar Jewish district and the center of the wartime ghetto. Rumors spread that Bohdan had been nailed to the wall as if crucified and that "Jews murdered Piasecki's son."[29]

The Jewish leadership in Warsaw, fearful for Ekerling's fate, arranged for his legal defense. Later they helped Ekerling obtain permission to leave for Israel after he was released from prison, but the family was stopped at the border and prevented from emigrating. Two years later the police arrested Ignacy again. He continued to proclaim his innocence, and a trial was called off after Jewish leaders appealed to the Polish prime minister, Józef Cyrankiewicz. But for more than three decades, until the very end of communist rule in Poland, the investigation reached into all corners of Polish Jewish life.[30]

Ignacy Ekerling and his family were never allowed to leave Poland. He died in 1977 and was buried in the Warsaw Jewish cemetery. The murder of Bohdan Piasecki was never solved.

—∿—

Throughout the political upheavals, Jewish leaders appealed repeatedly to the Polish authorities to address anti-Jewish incidents. In the summer of 1957 their entreaties finally succeeded, and Cyrankiewicz, the prime minister, publicly condemned antisemitism. The moral leadership of Polish intellectuals, in particular, is credited with stemming the tide. But many Jews gave up hope that they could find a place in Poland, and they left to rebuild lives yet again in other countries. Some had been "sitting on suitcases," as the saying went, ready to leave at the first sign of danger. For them, that time seemed to have arrived in the late 1950s. But other émigrés to Israel were disillusioned communists who distanced themselves from their Jewish background and had not wanted to leave Poland until the antisemitic atmosphere took a toll on their political faith.

The Jewish leadership lamented the panicked atmosphere among the Jewish population. Jewish institutions were floundering: all of the linotypists of the *Folks-shtime,* the entire staff and all of the children at a government-run Jewish orphanage in Kraków, and nearly all of the teachers and students at Jewish schools in two western Polish cities were preparing to leave. In the Wrocław branch of the Jewish communal organization, all but one leader declared their intention to emigrate. Nearly all of the Yiddish writers and poets remaining in Poland, already only a handful, were packing their bags.[31] Before the turmoil of 1956 about 70,000 Jews lived in Poland; four years later, just over half remained. "People are asking who we are," lamented a Jewish leader from the western city of Wrocław who was intent on staying, addressing a meeting of the Jewish communal authorities in Warsaw. "Indeed what we are saying is the opposite from what the party declares. . . . In the elections to the [factory] cooperatives' leadership not one Jew was admitted. People do not want to be humiliated. . . . People are saying that the party does not want them. . . . A mood of uncertainty reigns. People do not want to leave, but they cannot stay."[32]

Poland was a blur of comings and goings then. Even as trains were carrying Jews away from Poland, Polish citizens were arriving in the country from the Soviet Union in the other direction. During the wartime occupation and annexation of eastern Poland, the Soviet government had deported hundreds of thousands of Poles to the desolate Soviet interior, while others found themselves in Soviet territory when eastern Poland became permanently part of the Soviet Union after the war. In 1955 the Soviet government agreed to allow those who remained in Soviet territory to return to Poland.

Only about 18,700 of the 267,000 repatriates were Jewish, and Poles were persecuted in the Soviet Union just as Jews were. But Jews were unlikely to have homes to return to as they confronted a country absent of old communities. Most Polish Jews had few surviving family members in Poland or none at all, and the Polish government relied on the Jewish communal authorities to assist them. The task was overwhelming. Housing was still short in Poland, so the Jewish leadership placed them in primitive, hastily built barracks until the repatriates found more permanent places to live. Some later moved into apartments in western Poland that recent Jewish émigrés had left behind. Many Jewish children among the repatriate families spoke only Russian, so the Jewish authorities organized Polish-language classes.

Hersh Smolar and other Polish Jewish leaders saw hope in the new arrivals. Repatriated children began replacing émigrés in Jewish schools, while their parents joined local Jewish communal boards and attended the Yiddish theater. But the Jewish leaders were again disappointed. Most repatriates saw Poland only as a stopover on their way to Israel, and they remained in Poland just long enough to receive visas. Four years later, only one-third remained.

Decades later the fate of one Jewish repatriate who came to Poland in those years, Naftali Herts Kon, stood out in Smolar's memory. Naftali Herts was a Yiddish poet who grew up in a traditional Jewish home in Bukovina, and he first came to Warsaw as a young man in 1929 to take part in the city's flourishing Jewish cultural life. He was quickly drawn to communism in the prewar capital and began publishing Yiddish poems espousing its ideology. Three arrests and sixteen years in the Gulag later, Naftali Herts arrived back in the Polish capital in 1959. He had long since abandoned communism, and in Poland he refused to dissent quietly. The Polish security police arrested him as a spy for Israel.

Those were trying years for all Polish intellectuals, and Kon's arrest was but one thread of the government's crackdown on Polish society as the authorities reestablished its grip on power. By 1957 the government was already signaling limits on dissent, dashing earlier hopes for greater freedom. The authorities shut down Polish newspapers, tightened censorship, and arrested Polish writers.

The Jewish communal leadership did not dare to utter political doubts aloud, as Naftali Herts did. They continued to proclaim loyalty to the party even after it had betrayed them. Perhaps for this reason, then, and despite his short stay in postwar Warsaw, several Jewish leaders later recalled Naftali Herts's imprisonment in Poland as emblematic of their disillusionment.

One Yiddish memoirist, the postwar Polish Jewish leader and writer David Sfard, later wrote about Kon:

> What did Naftali Herts Kon, in his eternal wanderings from land to land, from
> city to city and from prison to prison, search for in life, where was he constantly
> driven to, where did he get so much strength to resist everything and everyone?
>   Earlier it was the great truth that was supposed to free the world. . . . Later, after
> long years of prison and pain, it was the protest against strangled human dignity and
> the desire to tell the truth about extinguished dreams and lost hopes. . . . The words
> of Naftali Herts . . . are so laden with pain, with disappointment, with dejection and
> bitter introspection, that they contain in themselves the stamp of a generation.[33]

In 1961, four years before the Polish government finally allowed Naftali Herts and his family to leave Poland for Israel, he sat in a Warsaw
prison and feared that the Polish government was preparing to send him
back to the Soviet Union. He wrote a letter to his family as he awaited his
fate: "I wrote purely that which my heart and my conscience dictated,
and my motto in life was truth and once again truth and to do good for
people. Perhaps I should have been born one century later."[34]

He continued with advice to his children: "In the last minutes of life
do not speak what is not the truth. Remember that your father was an
honest person in everything—a person for whom God was humanism,
love for every human being who is worthy of this lofty word." His last
wish, he wrote, was to be buried at Warsaw's Jewish cemetery near the
grave of I. L. Peretz. He added in a postscript that he was writing from a
prison in the city's Mokotów section, "where I sat in 1932 as a revolutionary writer. Now the circle is closed. Every person has his circle. I have
reached the end of mine."[35]

THE PERSONAL AND POLITICAL AT 16 UJAZDOWSKIE AVENUE

In 1956 Tola Sławny packed up her family's belongings from their fourth-
floor apartment at 16 Ujazdowskie Avenue and boarded a train to Paris
with her teenage sons, Jan and Francis. Her elder son, Francis, never forgot the anti-Jewish slur he heard that year at Warsaw's May Day parade,
the annual political ritual when parents and children hoisted red flags
on poles and held placards with communist slogans for International
Workers' Day.[36]

Tola was never a communist, and her husband, Władysław, a party
sympathizer in his youth, never joined the postwar party. For six years
they lived through the repressions of Stalinist Poland. Now Tola was

convinced that her family's future belonged in France. Her husband Władysław remained in Poland for another year. After the political upheavals in 1956 Władysław retained his position as photography editor of a popular Polish magazine, and with the freer atmosphere he was able to travel abroad, bringing to readers images of life beyond Poland's borders. But in December 1957 Władysław received permission to travel to France for a one-year stay. The Sławnys refused to return to Poland.[37]

The emigration wave of the late 1950s changed life for many of the Jewish families at 16 Ujazdowskie Avenue. On the second floor Salomea Falk bid farewell to her surviving brother and his family, who immigrated to Australia in 1957. Their departure left Salomea, her husband, Ernest, and their teenage son, Feliks, without extended family in Poland. None of the Ujazdowskie Avenue neighbors who traveled to Israel stayed there permanently. Nearly half of the building's mothers packed bags to visit siblings and cousins, often taking their children with them. Sometimes the parents had only recently made contact with surviving relatives, after the end of Stalinism had eased severe restrictions on contact with the West and Israel; other times they felt free for the first time to admit they had relatives abroad. The mothers first had to plea for permission from the Polish authorities to visit. "I have not seen my brother since 1939 and recently I found him," Stanisława Kruc wrote in her application for a visa, which the government granted. "He is one of the only ones from my family who remained." Her neighbor Stefania Fedecka made the journey as well, taking her young son with her.[38]

In Israel the parents embraced relatives who had immigrated to Palestine in the 1920s and 1930s as well as those who arrived in the Holocaust's early aftermath. Some had not yet reached adulthood when they parted ways decades earlier, and now they were entering middle age. The children who grew up in postwar Poland often heard their parents speak Yiddish for the first time and visited aunts and uncles whom they had never met. For many children visiting from Poland, merely having extended family was a novelty.

Back at 16 Ujazdowskie Avenue, meanwhile, other reunions were taking place. The Jewish families arriving from the Soviet Union in the late 1950s included old friends and acquaintances of the building's residents, and some repatriates stayed in apartments there for several days or weeks until they found their own housing. Among them were Ester and Borys Rabinowicz and their teenage son and daughter, who arrived from Vilnius by train in 1957. Ester had been Luba Rudnicka's classmate in Vilnius decades earlier, but perhaps because Luba's second-floor apartment was cramped, the Rabinowiczes stayed downstairs in the home of a non-Jewish family, the Przewalskis.

The Rabinowiczes and Przewalskis were not entirely unknown to one another; during the Second World War the Przewalskis hid the young Jewish daughter of one of Luba and Ester's former classmates in Vilnius.[39] The connections shed light on the tangled web of acquaintances that connected neighbors and colleagues in the early postwar years, when informal connections were essential to finding apartments and jobs. That web sometimes included non-Jews; their networks were rooted not only in a common Jewish background, but also in wartime experiences and shared politics. Like the Przewalskis, Stefania Fedecka's husband, Edward, too, was involved with communist underground circles that helped Jews during the Holocaust, connecting him with Nina Sztuczyńska, who became his postwar neighbor.[40]

The Rabinowiczes stayed at 16 Ujazdowskie Avenue for only a few days until they were assigned a small room elsewhere in the city in a building for repatriates. But the parents regularly returned to visit Luba Rudnicka, sometimes bringing their daughter Lena along. The newly reunited friends were separated once more when the Rabinowicz family left for Israel the following year.

Three decades later, when Borys Rabinowicz and his daughter Lena visited Poland from Israel, they returned to 16 Ujazdowskie Avenue, where Lena spoke with Szymon Rudnicki, who still lived in the same second-floor apartment. By the 1990s Lena and Szymon lived together at 16 Ujazdowskie Avenue. They travel regularly between Tel Aviv and Warsaw, symbolic of the two poles not only of the physical geography of their lives, but also of their families' complicated identities.

—⁂—

In 1959 Paulina Bergman died. Her funeral took place at a tsarist-era military graveyard where communist dignitaries and other secular individuals were buried. Her simple gravestone read in Polish: "Mother. Grandmother. Comrade."

A half-century earlier, when Paulina's husband died and left her with five young children, his eldest son must have said kaddish for him. But as her children and grandchildren gathered around her grave in 1957, no one recited the Jewish memorial prayer. At home her children did not sit shiva. If Stefan said kaddish privately, his children did not know it.

Yet in those disorienting years of the late 1950s, as antisemitism and political turmoil cast doubt on political faith, Jewish identity gradually emerged from the shadows. Some Jewish intellectuals who had recently been fired from their positions had few other options. After being unable to find other jobs, some began working in a translation cooperative that the Jewish community established.

Emergence of Jewish identity was not only the result of antisemitism. Some who had distanced themselves entirely from their Jewish background during the Stalinist years, when personal expression was best kept to oneself, now began to reconnect with memory of the Jewish past. In December 1959, five months after Emil Adler wrote to Marian about the bar mitzvah rituals, Emil's wife, Genia, and their friend Aleksandra Bergman visited the Jewish theater in Warsaw for a performance of the Yiddish classic *Grine Felder* (Green fields). So taken were they by the play, with its romanticized scenes of the shtetl, that they returned the following night. It was just before Christmas, and other families were preparing to celebrate with aunts and uncles, grandparents and grandchildren. Perhaps Genia and Aleksandra longed for absent relatives even more so than usual then.[41]

Decades later Stefan Bergman reflected on the turmoil of those years. In 1956 he had insisted to his Book and Knowledge colleagues that there was still hope for "true communism" in Poland. But in 1992, after the fall of the communist government, he recalled that the start of his disillusionment began even before 1956.

Perhaps hindsight led to the disparity between his later recollections and his speeches in 1956. It is possible, however, that what he said openly at the Book and Knowledge meetings reflected the caution of an individual who spent six years in the Gulag, whose wife spent nearly a decade in the complex of camps, and who lost a sister and many friends to the Stalinist purges. Stefan understood the danger of criticism at times of political upheaval, and he knew how quickly political winds could shift.

In the 1992 interview, Stefan recalled that immediately after the Second World War:

> I still considered myself fundamentally a communist. I hoped that matters would develop differently in Poland. In the Polish communist party a popular myth was established beginning in 1920: We in Poland . . . will carry out socialism better than in the USSR. We wanted to believe that such deviations will not take place in Poland, that our Polish socialism will be in reality socialism.[42]

About his dedication to the communist party for almost all of his adult life, Bergman insisted:

> I did not regret it. Now a lot of things I cannot or do not want to fathom. But after all, we believed that we were fighting for the realization of the best hopes of humanity and that our road was the most just. The transformation of that which was called communism into something completely the opposite, into totalitarianism, and even into one of the worst incarnations of totalitarianism—this was a process, and those like me believed for many years that these were only temporary "distortions."[43]

—⁓—

Emil Adler's political disillusionment reached a climax during the government's antisemitic campaign of 1968. His wife, Genia, and their daughter, Halina, did not want to leave Poland, but Emil and their son, Marian, who was nearly twenty-one, were intent on emigrating. Marian was especially insistent. Although he did not understand the Jewish traditions that had shaped his parents' lives, his mother's survival of Auschwitz was always present in the number tattooed on her arm. Marian could not remain in a country where the government and parts of society were now openly expressing antisemitism. The entire family decided to emigrate.

Several months before the Adlers' departure, while they were shuttling from one government office to another for their emigration documents, Emil took the train alone to his hometown of Brody, which had been part of Poland before the Second World War but was now on the western edges of the Soviet Union after the postwar shift in borders. He did not tell his son and daughter the reason for his journey. As far as they knew, it was their father's first and last postwar trip to the Galician city of his childhood—a final visit to a past that had loomed in Emil's memory during more than two decades since the Holocaust.[44]

Emil had struggled through years of disillusionment with communism by then. In the nine years since he wrote to Marian on his twelfth birthday, it became increasingly clear that Emil's political ideology had failed, and by the early 1960s he began voicing his doubts in his scholarly writings. Emil's politics had always been intertwined with his personal identity as a Jew. In the nineteenth century the tumultuous process of Jewish emancipation in Germany led Jewish thinkers to grapple endlessly with the relationship between nation and state, state and religion, religion and nation; now the twentieth-century tribulations of Polish Jews left Emil struggling with the same preoccupations. He wrote about the humanist ideals of the German Enlightenment and the primacy of universal values over religion and nation, the lessons he sought to teach Marian in his letter several years earlier. And just as German Jews clung to liberalism even as other Germans began to take up a nationalist ideology that excluded them, Jewish communists in postwar Poland were more invested than their non-Jewish neighbors in a communist political system that was supposed to solve the "Jewish question."

In 1965, while still living in Poland, Emil published a book about Herder and the German Enlightenment that was perhaps as much about Emil's own life as a Jew in twentieth-century Poland as it was about the eighteenth-century German philosopher. Communist censorship made it difficult for Emil to voice his thoughts directly, so he buried them between the lines. He argued that Herder's embrace of the "national idea" did not necessarily exclude faith in universalism—an idea that Emil's younger self, still infatuated with internationalism, would probably not have supported. His writings in the early 1960s reflected the political questioning of a Jewish communist who was struggling with both continued discrimination against Jews in Poland and a flagging faith in internationalism. Later, as he entered old age in Germany, Emil penciled an entry "Jews" into the book's table of contents. It is possible that he made the addition around the time of the fall of communism in Poland in 1989, since that year was written in pencil elsewhere in the book. Perhaps Emil hoped to republish an uncensored version in post-communist Poland.

The added entry referred to a passage about Jewish emancipation. Herder, Emil wrote, argued that a state's treatment of Jews is a barometer for the country's broader ideals and that a state that discriminates against

Jews is discredited in the eyes of all its residents. The passage referred to Jewish philosophers of earlier centuries: Baruch Spinoza, the first "secular Jew," as some historians have referred to him; the "father" of the Jewish Enlightenment, Moses Mendelssohn; and one of Mendelssohn's students, Marcus Herz. For Emil they were his predecessors, Jews who sought equality in Christian society but refused to become Christians themselves. Emil wrote:

> The idea of humanity, despite its universal foundations, does not exclude, but rather establishes the simultaneous development of the national idea, whose foremost proponent in the German Enlightenment ... was Herder.
>
> ... Herder's final conclusion is this: Palestine should be for Jews the countries in which they live and work. "All laws that treat Jews worse than cattle do not encourage trust, and in this manner every day, every hour, violates the laws in everyone's eyes as testimony to the unremitting barbarism of this state, which tolerates such laws from barbaric times"—Herder writes, not leaving any doubt about what kind of state this is above all.... "Who, when reading the philosophical writings of Spinoza, Mendelssohn, Herz, would conclude that Jews wrote them?" The community of culture, Herder adds, unites people of all times, countries and nations.
>
> Let us remember that this was written at a time when discriminatory edicts toward Jews were still in place in Germany, and Mendelssohn ... as a young boy was helpless before the Rosenthal gate of Berlin (the only one through which Jews were allowed to enter the city), because he did not have money to pay the humiliating tax on Jews.[45]

The passage is a mirror of the personal struggle Emil began to confront six years earlier in his letter to Marian. As Emil wrote about Herder, he was still uncertain about how to integrate Jewishness into his political faith in universalism and attachment to Poland at a time when Jews were already feeling alienated from the party they had supported and from Polish society whose acceptance they sought. Emil's writings from the early 1960s reflect the stages of his identity: both the figurative cheder boy reading Spinoza for the first time, beginning to question his childhood faith, and a disillusioned Marxist who had placed his faith in man, only to be disappointed.[46]

CHAPTER FIVE

Ostriches in the Wilderness

Children and Parents

She believed above all in the weight of education. Only it could assure them a dignified place in Polish society. With her own parents and brothers she spoke in German or in Yiddish, and she spoke Polish with a distinct Yiddish accent. Her children she sent to Polish schools, where they learned flawless Polish, familiarity with Polish literature and history....

It would have been significantly more comfortable to raise all nine as cosmopolitans. To push them out from the tormented, enslaved country into the free, wide world.... But apparently Julia believed that people should belong to the place where they were born, and to carry the consequences, whatever they were.

—Joanna Olczak-Ronikier, *In the Garden of Memory*

GENIA ADLER SAW her native city for the last time through the window of a train on October 12, 1968. Dozens of people stood on the platform in the rain to see her and her family off. The train pulled out of the station and took her "away from my Warsaw, my life, and everything I knew," she later lamented.[1]

One evening several weeks earlier, Genia had walked with her husband Emil through the gateway of 16 Ujazdowskie Avenue for a final visit with their old friends, Stefan and Aleksandra Bergman. On the second floor, just down the hallway from a smaller apartment where the Adlers had lived before moving to a larger apartment elsewhere in the city, the two couples bid farewell.

The solemn dinner was likely one of reminiscences and discussions about an unknown future. In war's early aftermath, as young couples uprooted by dislocation and loss, they had hoped to build a new society even as they reconstructed their own lives and families. Now their paths were about to diverge. Since March that year, thousands of Jews had been fired from positions, kicked out of the party, and dismissed from universities as the government scapegoated Jews for student anticensorship protests, accusing them of disloyalty to Poland. Over the next two years, in the aftermath of what became known as the "anti-Zionist" campaign, about fifteen thousand Jews and those of Jewish background left the country.[2]

In the end the entire Bergman clan remained in Warsaw, but the Adlers had spent recent weeks visiting one bureaucratic office after another for the necessary emigration papers. They compiled the required lists of each book, each article of clothing, every belonging they would seek to take into emigration. Their son and daughter, Marian and Halina, were spending their last moments with their girlfriend and boyfriend. Before they were allowed to leave Poland, the Adlers were required to relinquish their Polish passports in exchange for permission to emigrate. As their train departed for Vienna, Genia and Emil were still uncertain of where and how they would rebuild their lives for the second time in just over two decades.

—⁀⁀—

As the Bergmans and Adlers gathered one last time at 16 Ujazdowskie Avenue, other families in the building also struggled through the turmoil of that year. Barbara H.'s daughter was forced out of her position as a professor at the Medical Academy in Warsaw. Samuel Neftalin on the fourth floor lost his job as director of an industrial architecture firm, and the communist party then expelled him after he accused the security police of antisemitism.[3] Samuel's son Jurek was debating whether to leave for Sweden. Stefania Fedecka, who had moved with her family from 16 Ujazdowskie Avenue to another building by then, was among dozens of individuals of Jewish background who were fired from the foreign ministry.

The emigration wave over the next two years left empty places in the Polish capital. New residents moved into apartments where Jewish families had lived, old friends were absent from social gatherings, and workplaces like the Book and Knowledge publishing house were missing longtime colleagues.

For children who grew up in the decades between the war's end and 1968, the turmoil of that year confronted them with an identity about which many of them knew little. But turning points are always rooted in more gradual developments, and the Jewish past had long shaped their generation, even among children whose parents sought to distance them from that identity. They grew up in homes where Jewish background left markers of difference from other families, sometimes through absence. Often they became friends with other children of Jewish background through scout troops and their parents' social circles and attended schools overseen by an organization whose secular ideology led to clusters of children from Jewish families among their classmates. Yet for many, the impact of their parents' Jewish identity on the children's lives remained largely in the background until 1968, when the government openly called into question their right to consider themselves Polish.

"SCHOOL OF THE GODLESS": AT HOME AND AT SCHOOL

When Włodek Paszyński was growing up at 16 Ujazdowskie Avenue with his mother and grandmother, he did not think much about his Jewish roots. He read about Jewish history in books—he was a voracious reader even as a boy—and he knew that his parents and grandparents were of Jewish background. But he felt that this history had little relevance to his own life. Jewish identity had been marginal to his grandmother's identity even in her childhood and young adulthood before the war, as far as Włodek was aware. His grandfather Leopold was killed during the Second World War not as a victim of the genocide of European Jewry, but in the Soviet massacre of Polish army officers at Katyń, an event inscribed in Polish memory of the past and as important in his family's history as the Holocaust was.[4]

Born in 1951, Włodek was the youngest of his generation among the Jewish families at 16 Ujazdowskie Avenue. He first became vaguely aware of difference from his non-Jewish peers when he was the only boy at a retreat who did not know the morning prayers. When the other boys teased him, he began joining in. Instead of praying, however, Włodek recited to himself the beginning of *Pan Tadeusz*, Adam Mickiewicz's epic poem, which his grandmother Barbara taught him. He did not have any concrete understanding of what it meant to be Jewish.[5]

Włodek's childhood home was an intellectual one, where conversations with his mother and grandmother were about the latest books they read. "The Jewish topic was not talked about among them. It did not have any meaning [for them]," he recalled. "They were internationalists. End of story." That outlook did not mean they did not feel connected to their country and Polish culture. Having a Christmas tree in their home every year was important for Włodek's mother as a Polish tradition, not a Christian one.[6]

In 1968 the question of who was a Jew was an entirely new topic for Włodek. "I never thought about this. This was my country, my language. Simply belonging to this country, and that was all," he commented years later. "There was nothing to discuss about all of this, who is a Pole, who is not a Pole, who has [Jewish] roots. This was new information. It was a shock."[7]

—※—

As life paths diverged among friends and family in 1968 and the following years, so, too, did memory of earlier decades. Recollections of childhood among those who remained in Poland frequently follow a different narrative than the memories of émigrés, who more often remembered encountering antisemitism in their youth. Perhaps those who experienced discrimination as children were more likely to leave Poland, or perhaps adulthood and the traumas of emigration shadowed memories of their early years, sifted through the lens of later life paths.

Even among those who remained after 1968, the feeling of otherness sometimes emerges in their recollections of childhood in postwar Poland. That awareness often developed at school, which was a perennial battleground in communist Poland in the struggle between state and society. Szymon Rudnicki remembered being confronted with difference from other students in his very first months in postwar Poland. When he arrived in Łódź from the Soviet Union with his family in 1947, he had never been in Poland before and spoke Russian. Szymon immersed himself in the sounds that surrounded him, just as his older cousin Zofia had done after her arrival in the city the previous year, and Szymon soon spoke Polish fluently. But language was not the only difference that separated him from most of his classmates. He was also one of the few Jewish children, and while the others attended Catholic religious instruction, Szymon waited alone in the hallway. Eventually he decided to attend religion classes, preferring not to be singled out.[8]

The experience lasted just a few months. When Szymon moved with his family to Ujazdowskie Avenue in Warsaw in early 1948, he began attending a school run by an organization called the Society for the Friends of Children, known by its Polish acronym TPD (Towarzystwo Przyjaciół Dzieci), which maintained a secular curriculum in its school network even when the government allowed religious instruction. The association had roots in the prewar Polish Socialist Party, and although some of its teachers caused skirmishes in the early postwar years and in the 1950s over restrictions on Catholic instruction and symbols in the schools, the society's ideology sought to imbue students with a view of patriotism and Polishness that was not rooted in ethnic background or Catholicism. Parents could send their children to the schools without having to choose between allowing their children to attend classes on Catholicism or having them singled out by waiting outside. By 1954 the organization operated hundreds of schools throughout Poland, including nearly fifty in Warsaw.[9]

All of the children from Jewish families who grew up at 16 Ujazdowskie Avenue attended the society's schools for at least part of their childhood, and most were students in one of its elite schools in the city center. Szymon's mother, Luba Rudnicka, a prewar communist from a working-class home in Vilnius, did not like the atmosphere of privilege at her son's school, but it was known as one of the best in Warsaw. Włodek Paszyński's mother was more insistent. She, too, was skeptical of the schools' association with communist elites, and she eventually sent her son to a different school instead.[10]

For another boy, Wilhelm Dichter, who was just a few years older than Szymon Rudnicki and grew up in a different building with a cluster of Jewish residents, education in one of the society's schools reinforced the political ideology he heard at home, as Dichter wrote in an autobiographical novel *Skoła Bezbożnoków* (School of the Godless).[11] Dichter survived the Holocaust as a boy, and when he endured antisemitic taunts from classmates and a school monitor at a regular public school in Warsaw just after the war, his mother switched him to one operated by the Society for the Friends of Children. Dichter was dumbfounded by two discoveries at his new school: among his classmates were other Jewish children, yet neither his non-Jewish classmates nor other Jewish students seemed to concern themselves with the "Jewish issue." "Why does the Jewish issue not exist on Feliński Street?" he asked himself, referring to the street where his school was located. "What is the cause?"[12]

Back home, Dichter came to a conclusion: his new school was "a drop of socialism." His stepfather, Michał, a communist party member and high official in the Ministry of Foreign Affairs, always spoke highly of the new government and its ideology. But Wilhelm's mother was vehemently opposed to communism, and political debates were heated at home. His mother and stepfather spoke endlessly about antisemitism. The stepfather was convinced: "They are changing," he insisted. Listening in, Dichter tried to make sense of this vague phrase. What his stepfather meant by "they are changing," Dichter concluded, was that attitudes toward Jews in Poland would change and that communism would eliminate antisemitism. So Dichter began to develop his own faith in the new system. The absence of the "Jewish issue" in his new school helped to convince him.

In Warsaw, the society's schools brought together youth from very different Jewish backgrounds. In other cities, parents could send their children to schools overseen by the Jewish communal organization, the Social-Cultural Association of Jews in Poland, if they wanted their sons and daughters to have a connection to Jewish identity and to grow up with others of similar background.[13] But the capital had no Jewish school by the end of the 1940s, and the Society for the Friends of Children's schools were the next-best option. As a result, children who were raised with little understanding of their family's Jewish past were sometimes classmates with youth who grew up with Jewish rituals and culture present in their homes and whose parents might have sent them to a Jewish school if one had existed in the capital. The clustering of children of

Jewish background at some Society for the Friends of Children schools, particularly those in the city center, distanced them, more so than in other schools, from the worldview that equated Polish identity with Catholicism. Yet the absence of Jewish identity on the surface of their lives often made them only vaguely aware that they shared a common Jewish background with many classmates.

Jurek Neftalin, who grew up at 16 Ujazdowskie Avenue, was about ten when he discovered that he was not the only Jewish child at his elementary school, which was part of the Society for the Friends of Children network. He was especially self-conscious about an unavoidable marker of difference from other children: his non-Slavic last name, Neftalin, and his father's first name, Samuel. Before he learned that many of his classmates were also Jewish, that identity was merely a topic that he felt other children seized on to tease and provoke him. He knew little else about what that identity meant. "In our home there were no Jewish traditions," Jurek recalled decades later. "And my father's Jewishness was like a very heavy suitcase. But I did not know what this suitcase was. I did not know about Jewish culture, about tradition, nothing."[14]

A half-century later, Jurek still remembered the day when he learned that among his classmates, he was not alone with that identity. When he was visiting another boy's apartment for a birthday party, his friend's mother took him into the dining room, sat him down at a large table, and told him, "I want to ask you why you have such bad grades. Jews cannot have bad grades." The information was a revelation for Jurek, who had not known that the classmate whose birthday party he was attending was Jewish. "I exhaled," he remembered. "I understood that there are Jews in this class and that nothing would hurt me. Finally I could be calm and I did not have to be careful about what will happen in a moment." Jewish background, which previously had been only a negative and isolating identity for Jurek, was now a bond of friendship.[15]

Children who attended the Society for the Friends of Children's schools were not immune from the feeling of otherness. Some of its schools had fewer Jewish children than others, and students sometimes encountered teasing and other incidents of discrimination. Particularly in the aftermath of the political turmoil of 1956, the schools became a focal point of skirmishes over religious instruction. But in the memory of many children, they did not feel like outsiders in their native country. "For me the problem of Jewishness and difference did not exist for a long time. Because no one around me was different! All of the children I knew were the same as me, nonbelievers and often Jewish like myself but without a deep consciousness of Jewishness," recalled the daughter of a woman of Jewish background who worked at the Medical Academy of Warsaw. Another former student of the society's schools commented to an interviewer when asked about her childhood, "Did I ever see a problem that I am a Jew and that I am raised in the Polish patriotism of Polish children? It did not even cross my mind that this could be some kind of problem!"[16]

The Society for the Friends of Children's postwar schools served as a carrier of the idea of Polishness as a secular identity that could include all citizens of the Polish state. That Polish opponents of secularization viewed these same schools as part of the communist threat to Polish national identity reflects the uneasy position of Jews between state and society in communist Poland.

The Jewish issue played such a prominent role in postwar politics despite the marginal number of Jews who remained in Poland for the very reason that the prewar debate over how to define Polish identity and the Polish state was never resolved. At the same time, memory of the Nazi genocide, worsening of Polish-Jewish relations during the Second World War, and the stereotype blaming Jews for communism made the Jewish issue more charged than debates over the position of other national minorities in postwar Poland. The Jew came to symbolize the "other" whose place in Polish society reflected the ways in which Polishness was being defined.[17]

Perhaps the most important issue in the struggle between state and society in communist Poland was the Catholic Church's role in Poland's national identity, and during heightened postwar tensions, that battle played out in part through shifting policies on religion in schools. In the early postwar years and right after the political turmoil of 1956, when restrictions on political expression were weakest, the government's more permissive policies on religious instruction helped to place the "Jewish issue" at the center of conflicts between church and state.

The Catholic Church's struggle against the secularization of schools was directed first and foremost not at Jewish families but against the communist regime. Yet the government's insistence on an entirely secular education for Polish children while occasionally backpedalling when political turmoil threatened the government's legitimacy affected Jewish families differently than most of their neighbors. While many Jewish parents did not accept the radical secularization embraced by communists, the absence of Catholic symbols and religious instruction at school protected their children from the image of Jews as the "other" regardless of the parents' politics. That difference reinforced stereotypes among much of Polish society that Jews were helping to motivate government efforts to suppress religious expression, which the Church and many Catholic Poles viewed as an assault on Polish identity. Any attempt to secularize the public sphere was seen as an attack on religion more generally. The "Jewish issue," while sometimes unspoken, was an undercurrent of debates over the role of the Catholic Church in the Polish state and national identity, so that Jews came to symbolize the very changes that the communist government sought to impose on a largely unwilling society.

—∾∾—

On October 27, 1956, the Polish primate, Cardinal Stefan Wyszyński, walked to freedom through the doors of a convent in a small mountain town in southeast Poland. The cardinal had been arrested for a second time more than three years earlier, in September 1953, and held under guard in numerous locations. Now he returned to his home in Warsaw's reconstructed medieval Old Town and greeted well-wishers.

Political unrest had engulfed the country for months before Wyszyński's release. Just a week earlier, Soviet tanks had menacingly approached the Polish capital before the newly elected party head, Władysław Gomułka, assured a Soviet delegation that Poland would remain loyal to the Soviet Union. But the struggle between state and society erupted during the turmoil that year, and even after the cardinal's release, Poland's communist authorities were still anxiously debating how to retain control.

At a rally in the city of Toruń in October a few weeks before Wyszyński's release, freedom of religion and Catholic instruction in schools were just behind the release of bishops and priests as well as Wyszyński in the protesters' list of demands, and the government sought to placate society in part by relaxing some of its policies. Authorities agreed not only to release Wyszyński, but also to allow Catholic instruction in schools where most students' parents were in favor.

As the severe repressions of the Stalinist years eased, church officials as well as other individuals began to voice their opinions. Parents and a high church official complained to the government's education ministry that local school administrators were still not allowing religious instruction even when most parents voted for it. Others wrote to newspapers or radio programs in late 1956 and 1957 about the issue, and the secular schools of the Society for the Friends of Children were one target of their grievances. Some complaints associated the schools' secular ideology with the children of Jewish background who were clustered among the students. One letter described an unidentified group that was "making many difficulties for children to study religion" in one of the society's schools in Katowice, referring parenthetically to one of the group's members, a parliamentarian's wife, as a Jew.[18]

Other parents complained from the opposite position: the debate over religious instruction, they wrote, was exposing their children to discrimination. "I am non-party. They say maliciously that this is supposed to be a virtue now, but this is not why I begin my letter this way," a woman who identified herself as Muslim wrote in a letter to a radio program in January 1957. "I begin this way so that no one will think that the problem which I raise is a burden only on party activists /true ones/ and on Jews." She knew of cases, she said, where "even Jews are sending their children to lectures on religion in order to protect them from moral terror. The same concerns party activists. The statistics of children of communist party secretaries would be very instructive in this regard. I spoke with several. All are sending their children for [instruction in] religion." A parent born in Germany complained that his children were called Jews and other names because they did not attend religion classes. "I am not a Jew, I am a Christian, though not Catholic, but it pains me in my heart when I see my children grumble that fists are shaken at them in school," he wrote.[19]

The Society for the Friends of Children schools fell victim to the political upheavals when the government removed the schools from the organization's oversight in late 1956 or early 1957. But the move seemed to be in name only: in January 1957 a new group, the Society for the Secular School, was established with government consent and oversaw many of the same schools. At a time when schools were once again allowed to hold classes in Catholicism, often taught by priests and nuns, some Jewish parents who wanted to protect their children from the politics of religion were relieved when they learned of the new organization. Poland's Yiddish newspaper, the *Folks-shtime,* reported the news in a front-page article in January 1957.[20] But the new organization infuriated Catholic Church leaders so much that Cardinal Wyszyński, newly released from house arrest, appealed to parents in a pastoral letter not to send their children to the new society's schools.[21]

The government did not take long to backpedal on its more permissive policies on religion. In 1958 it gradually began to limit Catholic instruction once again, eventually prompting Cardinal Wyszyński to write another pastoral letter in 1960 condemning the new restrictions and calling atheism "anti-state." By the following year the government had once again banned religious expression in schools. Priests and teachers were arrested and imprisoned when they resisted the change.[22]

Decades later, children from Jewish families sometimes recalled antisemitism from their non-Jewish classmates in those years and afterward, although they often did not connect those experiences with the political upheavals of the late 1950s.[23] For some, only the memory of standing in the hallway during religious instruction sometimes remained from those years. For parents, however, the charged political atmosphere and its impact on their children loomed large. Aleksander and Tosia Klugman, both journalists and communists, decided to leave for Israel in 1957 after their nine-year-old son was taunted about his Jewish background at school, and because they had begun to feel like "foreigners in their own country." Another communist of Jewish background, Roman Zambrowski, a high-ranking member of the party's central committee, was dismayed at the new atmosphere and lamented the troubles in the schools when he recalled the increased religiosity in Poland at that time. He did not mention the "Jewish issue" directly, but, he noted, the "situation among part of the teaching staff was especially painful."[24]

ON THE CUSP OF THE STORM IN THE 1960S:
JEWISH IDENTITY, POLISH POLITICS

In the late 1950s and 1960s, as political tensions continued to simmer, the generation of children who grew up in postwar Poland was coming of age. They were raised in a political system that glorified Stalin, and most were not yet in their teens in 1956 when Khrushchev openly acknowledged the extremity of Stalinism's crimes. Over the next decade, as circles of students in Warsaw turned from political questioning to rebellion, children of party officials who had become part of a privileged, intellectual class in communist Poland began challenging the system their parents had helped to establish. Among the most prominent student dissidents were young people who had Jewish roots.

Politics remained in the background in the 1960s for the sons and daughters of Jewish families who grew up at 16 Ujazdowskie Avenue, and they did not immerse themselves in circles of students who debated politics and protested in the streets against censorship in the coming years. As the decade began, the oldest among them were already embarking on careers. Zofia Zarębska was twenty-five at the start of 1960, studying to become a biochemist. Science was a relatively safe profession in communist Poland; Zofia was drawn to the written word, and perhaps she might have become a writer like her parents if cultural life was not so politically fraught. Zofia's younger cousin Szymon Rudnicki, meanwhile, was immersing himself in Polish history as a doctoral student and then as a faculty member at Warsaw University.

The youngest of the children's generation, Włodek Paszyński, was just nine years old in the first year of the new decade, while neighboring children who had been born during or just after the Second World War were in high school. As the decade began, they were preoccupied with the everyday concerns of young adulthood, from school and friends to dating and the newest music. Their parents rarely spoke with them about politics.

But the 1960s were a decade of youth rebellion and protests from Paris to Latin America to New York, and in Poland, as elsewhere, some young people were grappling with weighty political issues as they enjoyed the new music and fashions from the West. Even at the start of the decade, turmoil loomed in Poland. A handful of political philosophers had been gathering since the mid-1950s to debate reform, to the consternation of the political authorities, and by the early 1960s small circles of university and high school students were following their lead. Tension with the authorities mounted.

Among children of Jewish background, who were among the most active of the student dissidents, their politics were shaped above all by their identity as Poles. Many had little connection with their Jewish background. Yet their political dissent was influenced by their experiences as both insiders in intellectual circles and outsiders in much of Polish society. Their family's path to integration through intellectual life and politics, which gave them a view from inside the system, was shaped by the radically secularizing ideology of an unpopular government at a time when Catholicism remained a symbol of opposition to communism, casting them as outsiders.

"Our understanding of the world was exactly the opposite from what was the general Polish norm at that time," recalled one woman who was deeply involved in the student opposition.

> We were raised with the conviction that all intelligent people in Poland think in the same categories as us, that everyone was atheist just the same, believing in the regime just the same and Polish patriots just the same. . . . [We], the majority of us children of Jewish roots, we were absolutely Polish-patriots. We loved Polish literature, we identified with Mickiewicz, Słowacki, we wrote essays about the Chopin monument, we felt proud as Poles, since Chopin was a Pole. We were non-believing Poles, but we believed that modern patriotism depended on this—exactly on this. And on Polishness.[25]

—⁂—

Children from Jewish families were shaped by contradictory forces as they entered young adulthood in the 1960s, and as a generation, they did not follow any one path. Some continued to view their family's Jewish background as marginal to their own lives as they gradually became part of broader circles, while for others, Jewish identity became increasingly important. Even in the capital, where distance from Jewishness predominated, many young people remained connected with other youth of Jewish background as childhood friends and classmates. Jewish presence and absence often coexisted. But no single path leads from absence, and identity is often defined by contradictions. Common influences in their homes and at school helps to explain why children from Jewish families became friends and shared intellectual interests, but everyday life shaped identity differently in every individual. Worldviews were not uniform.

In the 1960s assimilation in the younger generation became central to the anxieties of Jewish communal leaders as they took stock of the communities that remained after the emigration wave from 1956 to 1960. The Jewish population had decreased by more than half since the mid-1950s, and the leaders worried about the future.[26] In the previous decade, schools overseen by the Social-Cultural Association of Jews in Poland had helped to preserve Jewish identity among a minority of Jewish children, though not in Warsaw, which did not have a Jewish school after the late 1940s. In the late 1950s, as many of the schools' students emigrated, the arrival of repatriate children from the Soviet Union in western Poland slowed the schools' decline.[27] Even repatriates who attended other schools seemed to have made a deep impression on some classmates who previously had little knowledge about Jewish life, and slowed down the decline. One boy in western Poland who befriended several repatriate children recalled that the new friendships prompted him to stop attending Catholic religion classes and then to switch to a Jewish school.[28]

But the number of children attending Jewish schools had been only a sliver of the country's Jewish population since the early 1950s, and by the 1960s the schools were hobbling along even more so than in previous years. Attendance had fallen exponentially, and the Jewish leadership's hopes that repatriate families who arrived in Poland from the Soviet Union in the second half of the 1950s would reinvigorate Jewish communal life were dampened when most repatriates emigrated. Teachers and students alike departed, forcing the leadership to close schools that were no longer needed. As children who remained in Poland into the 1960s advanced from elementary to secondary school, meanwhile, they often attended mainstream institutions that would prepare them best for university studies. In 1967, on the eve of the "anti-Zionist" campaign, 432 children attended just 8 Jewish schools at a time when about 36,000 Jews still lived in Poland.[29]

Even as schools became less central, summer camps overseen by the Jewish communal leadership were increasingly important for some youth as they became teenagers. In Poland as a whole, the number of young people who attended the association's summer camps was more than four times as many as the number of students at Jewish schools.[30] In Warsaw, some parents whose children might have attended a Jewish school if one existed in the capital, or if they lived away from the glare of central political authorities, sent their children to spend summers at camps with other Jewish youth. Other young people chose the camps on their own initiative, drawn there by classmates and friends.

Camp cemented friendships that were bound by shared Jewish background, an identity that became intertwined with nostalgia for the carefree rituals of summer and the melodies of Yiddish songs whose words they often could not understand. The Nowogrodzka Street offices of *Nasz Głos,* the *Folks-shtime's* Polish-language youth supplement, which the Jewish communal leadership established in 1957, became a gathering place for summer-camp friends during the rest of the year. Although Warsaw still had no Jewish school, and the number of Jewish schools throughout Poland was on the decline, the Social-Cultural Association ran after-school Yiddish classes in more than a dozen cities, including the capital.[31]

Leaders of Jewish communal institutions were not always happy with the ways that young people identified with their Jewish background. A Social-Cultural Association report from the mid-1960s took note of increased interest in Israel among small groups of youth in western Poland and at summer camps attended by Jewish children from throughout the country. The emigration wave from the second half of the 1950s continued as a trickle into the 1960s, and youth were among more than 1,000 Jews who emigrated each year in the 1960s, most of them to Israel.[32] Those views were never dominant at the camps or in the generation as a whole, but the political standpoint concerned the communal leaders.[33]

Even among youth who felt no connection to Israel and identified above all, and often exclusively, as Polish, their parents were sometimes dismayed at their children's interest in their Jewish background. One girl from Warsaw pleaded in vain with her father to be allowed to attend a Jewish camp where her friends spent summers, but he refused. "He was terribly upset, he said that we live in Poland and we are like everyone else, and we will not be separate and belong to a different group. And I will not go to any TSKŻ camp!" she later recalled.[34] At 16 Ujazdowskie Avenue, Liliana Tyszelman joined her neighbor Ela Kruc one summer at a Jewish camp even though they and their parents continued to keep their distance from Jewish institutions. Liliana did not recall any opposition from her father, but Jewish background remained almost entirely absent from the two girls' homes.

In the 1960s friends sometimes grappled together with how to define their identities, and decisions about whether to declare Polish or Jewish nationality on administrative forms became a heated topic of discussion for some at school and at camp.[35] Many encountered among their summer-camp friends an identity about which they knew little, one that was an open part of everyday life there. One former camper recalled decades later that bold, public displays of Jewishness sometimes made other youth of Jewish background at the camp uncomfortable even as they found comfort in an environment where they were not self-conscious about that identity. "At camp there were people whose parents had changed their names," Leon Rozenbaum ruminated years later to an interviewer, recalling fellow campers who, unlike him, had little connection to their Jewish background.

> Their children functioned as Jewish children at camp and in the [Jewish youth] club, but outside of the circle they did not want to be so uniformly identified. The majority of our camp circle even believed that they were not real Jews. And at camp there were those who generally did not want to have anything to do with Jewishness! They knew that they were Jews, but they were so assimilated, they appeared among us like ostriches in the wilderness. And I do not know why their parents sent them there: by mistake, or perhaps after all they wanted to awaken something Jewish in these children?[36]

Back in Warsaw, meanwhile, a Jewish youth club, the Babel Club, was becoming a trendy gathering place even among young people who did not attend the summer camps and had no involvement in Jewish communal life. The Jewish communal leadership established the group as well as other youth clubs throughout Poland in 1962 as a way to reach out to the younger generation, and the Warsaw club became especially popular.[37] One of its main attractions was the Saturday night dances where the house band, the Babel Quartet, performed. Young people who were active in Jewish communal life brought along friends and classmates who had little connection with Jewish identity as well as non-Jewish friends, and the dances quickly became a staple of social life. Just a few years earlier, one student later remembered, young people rarely discussed Jewish identity at home or among friends. Now it rose to the surface. "It became very trendy, and youth from all over Warsaw descended on the dances," she recalled. "At that time, some girls from my class began to worry that they were not Jews."[38]

Jurek Neftalin from 16 Ujazdowskie Avenue was still cautious about discussing his Jewish background with new acquaintances, but he sometimes mentioned Nowogrodzka Street, where the Babel Club was located, when he wanted to know whether a new friend might be Jewish. One of his Jewish neighbours sometimes joined her friends there as well—not because it was associated with a Jewish institution, but because she liked the music. The Babel Club also played a more serious role, sponsoring talks by writers, philosophers, and politicians who attracted an audience of intellectual youth, including some who were not among its estimated 150 club members or of Jewish background at all. Lecturers by prominent intellectuals and politicians drew dozens of students.

In the mid-1960s, meanwhile, as the Babel Club was establishing itself as part of Warsaw's social scene, politically involved students were becoming increasingly radicalized, and circles that frequented the Babel Club overlapped with those who were active in political dissent. Opposition networks were often rooted in social connections, and friends explored ideas about culture and politics together as they developed their worldviews. Students of Jewish background from intellectual homes became intertwined with the political networks of the student opposition. In 1967 and 1968, the competing factions in the government leadership seized on those overlapping circles, blaming Jewish background for political opposition.

Adam Michnik, the son of one of Stefan Bergman's publishing-house colleagues, became the most prominent of the young dissidents. Even in his early youth Michnik took an interest in politics, attending gatherings of philosophers and other intellectuals called the Club of the Crooked Circle, which began meeting in 1955 as the post-Stalinist thaw loosened restrictions on expression. After the government forced the club to dissolve, its former president met with the young student in 1962 at the popular Harenda bar near the university campus and suggested that he organize a discussion group with students from various secondary schools in Warsaw.[39] Forming a club with political discussion as its goal was not a simple matter in communist Poland, and Michnik, who was still in high school, sought out advice from other students and older intellectuals.

Among them was Aleksander Smolar, a son of the Jewish communal board chairman, Hersh Smolar. The two friends grew up in families that followed very different paths. Adam Michnik's father, a communist who was Stefan Bergman's good friend and publishing-house colleague, and Michnik's mother, who was raised in an assimilated Jewish family, were entirely distanced from postwar Jewish communal life. Aleksander Smolar, on the other hand, grew up in a world where not only his parents' communist ideology, but also the world of Yiddish culture, was a presence. If Hersh Smolar and his wife, Walentyna Najdus, a historian and long-time communist, had raised Aleksander and his younger brother Eugeniusz in western Poland or Łódź, they might have sent their sons to one of the Social-Cultural Association's Jewish schools. But Warsaw was the center of Polish political and intellectual life and the most logical place for Smolar as chairman of the countrywide Jewish communal board. Living in a city with no Jewish school was perhaps a difficult concession to make when it came to raising their sons.

The club that emerged after Adam Michnik's discussion with Aleksander Smolar and other friends became one of the foundations for student opposition circles. Called the Inter-School Discussion Club (Międzyszkolny Klub Dyskusyjny) and often known by the more intriguing name of the Club for Seekers of Contradictions (Klub Poszukiwaczy Sprzeczności), or simply Michnik's club, the group brought together students from four secondary schools in the city center, including the Society for the Friends of Children's Gottwald school, where many students were the children of prominent government officials and intellectuals of Jewish background. Other students and young academics formed another group at the university, called the Political Discussion Club.

Student dissident circles in Warsaw were influenced by older intellectuals who became increasingly critical of the communist authorities in the late 1950s and 1960s. The most important of the older dissidents, Leszek Kołakowski, a philosopher, was two decades older than most of the students, but two others, Jacek Kuroń and Karol Modzelewski, were closer in age to them—younger than the students' parents, but already established as intellectuals and critics of the government. Kuroń was particularly influential for many of the students in their childhoods. He was a scout leader in a troop known as the Walterites, nicknamed the "red scouts" because many of the children were the sons and daughters of top party officials. In 1961 the government forced the troop to dissolve, but when the former scouts became university students, they remained close with Kuroń at a time when he was a key figure of political dissent.

Kuroń imbued in his scouts a socialist ideology emphasizing a view of patriotism that could include every member of the Polish state, an outlook that made an impression on youth from Jewish families. "There were always a lot of games in the Walterites," one former scout, Marta Petrusewicz, recounted to an interviewer years later. "But at the same time it came with lessons: that if we were Apaches, then being an Apache depended on helping the weaker, that if we sang songs, then they were the songs of various nations—Polish, Russian, Jewish, and also revolutionary: Spanish from the Civil War, Chinese songs from the period of the revolution."[40]

The inclusive ethos of Kuroń's troop was a welcome relief for Marta. Her Society for the Friends of Children school had only a few Jewish students, and many of her classmates attended religion classes taught by a priest after school. She was distraught when they teased her about her Jewish background, and after a group of children attacked one of her Jewish classmates in a mock crucifixion, Kuroń's reaction comforted her. "As long as there are anti-Semites in the world, every decent person is a Jew," Marta remembered her scout leader telling her. Kuroń instilled in his former scouts a worldview that shaped their political outlooks as adults. He insisted, Petrusewicz recalled, that "being a minority is not a defect. . . . And we learned to be different with pride about our otherness."[41]

A few years later, when Kuroń's scouts entered the university and many became active in the student opposition, the political atmosphere in Poland was already tense as the government sought to suppress political criticism. Philosophers and students were not the only ones dissatisfied with the conditions of life in People's Poland, although everyday problems were more of a concern to many Poles than censorship was. Poland's economy was still struggling, and young people's prospects for the future were not promising. The authorities still had not solved the apartment shortage, so as the postwar generation began to marry, they often lived with their parents for years while waiting for a home of their own. There were long waiting lists for telephones, washing machines, and other conveniences. For many, everyday life was bleak.

At Warsaw University, meanwhile, the mid-1960s were a succession of dissent, protests, and arrests. As the older intellectuals became more vocal in their criticism of the political authorities, the students became more active as well. Crackdowns only united the student dissidents, who rallied around their intellectual mentors, Kuroń and Modzelewski, when they were imprisoned in 1965.

The students refused to be cowed. The government had forced the students' political discussion clubs to disband in 1963 and early 1964, so they began gathering privately instead, sometimes using a friend's birthday or other occasion as an excuse. The students shared books and journals from abroad that the government banned and spoke heatedly about the taboos of People's Poland: the Stalinist purges of the 1930s, the arrests and persecutions of the first decade of communist rule in Poland, the Soviet massacre of Polish officers in the forest at Katyń in 1940, the turmoil of 1956. Later, in the 1966–1967 school year, a handful of political discussion circles formed around different student leaders, crowding once more into private apartments to continue their discussions and opposition activities.[42]

Young dissidents formed a loosely connected group that were known as the *komandości* (commandos), which numbered between a few dozen and a hundred individuals but was connected with larger circles of students who joined them in their loud disruptions of party cell meetings and other dissent. Politics and friendship remained intertwined. Students were often old friends who had been classmates at a handful of the capital's best schools or former scouts in Kuroń's troop, and they were connected with one another, Kuroń later wrote, "by friendship, intimacy established in the same middle schools, and even in elementary school and in the Walterite scouts. They went to their first dances together, got into films not allowed for their age and conducted youthful political discussions."[43]

Many of the students at the heart of the opposition were the children of communist intellectuals, some from Jewish families, and they grew up in homes shaped by their parents' ideology and the privileges of their parents' positions, from trips abroad to access to books and newspapers unavailable to other Poles. The intellectual atmosphere in their homes, meanwhile, encouraged many of them to seek out new knowledge and explore political ideas together.[44] As students of Jewish background became involved in the political clubs, discussions with classmates from different backgrounds exposed them to new ideas even as their own worldviews influenced the student opposition. Some began to question their parents' rejection of religion and became interested in the ideas of Catholic intellectuals, challenging the secular worldviews they had learned at home and at school. Jewish identity sometimes took on a more positive meaning, not only for those whose parents sought to distance themselves from that identity, but also for students from non-Jewish backgrounds.

The students did not avoid confronting the role of the "Jewish issue" in communist politics. When Adam Michnik returned from a trip abroad in Paris for studies, he brought with him a newspaper article titled "Boars and Jews" (Chamy i Żydy), which was published in the Polish émigré newspaper *Kultura* in Paris and described the political groupings in Poland after 1956. Internal party politics was not to be spoken of openly in communist Poland, and one of the taboos was the "Jewish issue," which was intertwined with the political infighting that the article discussed. It did not help matters that the article's author was Witold Jedlicki, a Polish intellectual of Jewish background who had taken part in dissident circles in Warsaw before immigrating to Israel in 1962. The article made its way around opposition circles after Michnik brought it to Warsaw, and the university disciplined him.[45]

Most students from Jewish families in Poland were not at the center of political dissent, but contradictions in identity and upbringing that led some of them to the student opposition helped to shape their generation beyond dissident circles. For children whose parents were communists, the younger generation's view from inside and outside the political system gave them a sharp perspective on the chasm between political reality and the values that were central to their parents' worldviews. Communism had not created the utopian society that their parents envisioned, one in which nationalism and discrimination no longer existed. Even in some of their own homes, their families' privileges in everyday life, from cars to apartments that were often more comfortable than the homes of other Varsovians, underscored the emptiness of a system that purported to represent their parents' egalitarian ideology. As the children grew into adults in the 1960s, the impact of Jewish background in their homes, schools, and social circles became intertwined with the evolution of their worldviews, just as that identity had once helped to mold the outlooks of their parents.

"A TERRIBLE LONELINESS PREVAILS": PARENTS, 1963–1967

The parents at 16 Ujazdowskie Avenue had a hint of the political turmoil of 1968 several years earlier. In the previous decade, during the upheavals of the late 1950s, the Book and Knowledge publishing house was a refuge for intellectuals and political leaders of Jewish background who were fired from their positions, including the top party ideologue, Jakub Berman, after he was dismissed from his high-ranking position in the communist party. But in the mid-1960s individuals of Jewish background at Book and Knowledge found themselves in an entirely different situation.

The new climate already began to crystallize in 1963. That July Józef Tyszelman was dismissed as vice president of the governing board at Book and Knowledge, the publishing house he had helped to establish in war's early aftermath. Five months later Stefan Bergman was demoted from his position as the top editor of Marxist-Leninist literature, though he continued to work for the department. Juliusz Burgin, who also was of Jewish background, lost his job as the publishing house's president, and other dismissals and demotions followed.[46]

The following January, when Book and Knowledge's governing board formally approved the personnel changes from the previous year, it made a telling announcement: the new president was Stanisław Wroński, who was associated with a group at the center of political infighting in the communist party.[47] The marginalization of communists of Jewish background at the same time as Wroński became the publishing house's new president was not coincidental.

Wroński was one of the "partisans," an informal circle that was making a play for power in the party and government at the time. They were grouped around a wartime leader in Poland's communist underground named Mieczysław Moczar. Moczar built a power base among the legions of new communist party members who were too young to have been in the prewar party and who were starting to build their careers in the 1960s. For them party membership was obligatory and often a career move rather than an ideological statement. Moczar gained their support by playing on their ambitions, and he sought to place these "new" communists in positions of authority. Józef Tyszelman, Stefan Bergman, and other founders of the communist party publishing house were among the early victims of the subsequent political intrigues.

The year 1964, when Moczar became minister of internal affairs, was a turning point. In that year the government cracked down on writers who were openly challenging the government's ideological control of cultural life. Many of the intellectuals who were arrested were not Jewish, and antisemitism did not yet figure openly in the campaign against dissent.[48] Yet the "Jewish issue" was enmeshed in Moczar's play for power, and under his authority, Jews were among the security police's victims. Its agents cast a wide net, from leaders of Jewish institutions to those who were entirely unaffiliated with Jewish communal life. They made little distinction between them. The security agents compiled lists of genealogical histories, recipients of assistance from Jewish institutions and packages from Israel, individuals who were seen visiting the Israeli embassy—list after list, folder after folder.

The same year that Moczar took control of the Ministry of Internal Affairs, Ernest Falk from 16 Ujazdowskie Avenue also lost his job when he was accused of using official cars for private business as a top administrator in Poland's umbrella publishing institution. Ernest appealed his dismissal unsuccessfully to the courts.[49]

The parents at 16 Ujazdowskie Avenue who had been involved in Book and Knowledge and other publishing institutions since the first postwar years, even those who had moved on to other positions by then, were probably aware of the dismissals of Józef Tyszelman and Ernest Falk and the demotion of Stefan Bergman. Within the walls of their apartment building they might have discussed the implications. Yet most of the generation that grew up at 16 Ujazdowskie Avenue was in their late teens and twenties by then, busy with their own lives. The children were largely unaware of the politics behind their parents' change in jobs and their marginalization in the publishing institutions they had helped to found.

—⚹—

During the Christmas holidays in 1965, at the vacation home of the Social-Cultural Association of Jews in Poland in Śródborów in the forest just outside Warsaw, an atmosphere of despair prevailed. "Everyone around Śródborów is on edge, desperate and distressed," wrote Bernard Mark, director of the Jewish Historical Institute, who began keeping a diary in Yiddish that December while vacationing there. The main topic of conversation among the guests, Mark wrote, was a recent book by Adam Schaff, a Polish Politburo member and prominent Marxist philosopher of Jewish background who was director of Warsaw University's philosophy department, where Emil Adler was on the faculty. The book, *Marksizm a jednostka ludzka* (Marxism and the human individual), called for political reform and referred in a brief section to antisemitism by the communist authorities. Schaff put into words the disillusionment that pervaded circles of Jewish communists in Poland.[50]

"He develops a theory of alienation—the individual is even more alienated in socialism, even lonelier in socialism than before," Mark wrote in his diary about Schaff's book. "'Everyone dies in loneliness'— that is what a German writer wrote somewhere in Nazi times, and I, in my current situation, blind, feel this perhaps more than someone else. A terrible loneliness prevails—almost everyone feels this, and a Jew more than a Pole, who, after all, has a lot of family."[51]

In Śródborów, Mark's friends and colleagues came and went, and he ruminated in his journal about the fate of the ideology with which they had cast their lot. He went for a walk with Władysław Sławny's sister, Nina Sławny-Kac, a prewar communist whose family remained in Poland for more than a decade after Władysław, his wife, and two sons packed up their fourth-floor apartment at 16 Ujazdowskie Avenue and left for France. She, too, spoke of disillusionment, Mark recalled.[52] Hersh Smolar, the Social-Cultural Association head until 1962, had a long conversation with Mark about politics and the increasingly difficult situation of Jews in Poland. The two old communists discussed the travails of Jews who had been dismissed from their posts. In early January Adam Bromberg, director of the state Academic Publishing House, was dismissed from his position and expelled from the communist party after government officials seized on an entry in the *Wielka Encyklopedia Powszechna* (Great universal encyclopedia), whose publication he was overseeing. The entry distinguished between concentration camps and death camps and between the fate of Jews and Poles killed in the Holocaust, giving rise to accusations of separatism and "Jewish nationalism."[53]

Bernard Mark and Hersh Smolar were never particularly close, and decades later several former colleagues recalled that Mark kept his distance from Smolar. The relationship was so fraught, those colleagues insisted, that Mark left instructions before dying that Smolar should not speak at his funeral. But the two men shared similar life paths, and they ruminated on their fractured identities. Publicly they did not repudiate their political beliefs in the mid-1960s, but their innermost selves acknowledged the system's corruption of their ideology. Even during the political turmoil in 1956, when they learned of the murder of the Soviet Yiddish writers and other Stalinist-era crimes, Smolar insisted on his continued political faith. Now, as he and Mark lamented the fate of Jews in communist Poland in the mid-1960s, they found it difficult to convince themselves of that illusion. "Because this is the generation that was raised in the spirit of internationalism," Mark noted in his diary after speaking with Smolar, "Stalinism was a crime by crippling the soul, as Smolar says: 'Communists were raised as people of two souls, one for oneself, the other for the outside.'"[54]

Mark and Smolar were cautious as they spoke. They were aware that they were under security-police surveillance at home and at work and that some colleagues were informants. "It is not possible to speak openly about everything. To be public about everything," Mark wrote two days before Christmas in 1965 in the first entry of his diary. "But the day will come, and at that time let the most important things be noted, recorded."[55]

Back in Warsaw after the holidays, Mark's despondency did not lift. Just across a narrow passageway from the Jewish Historical Institute on Tłomackie Street, construction was taking place at the empty plot where the Great Synagogue stood before the Nazis destroyed it, and Mark found himself lost trying to make his way around the construction area to the entrance of the institute he headed. "And so Jewish Warsaw comes to an end," he wrote in his diary. "I had hoped that on the empty square a monument, a plaque would be erected, honoring a place of memory. Now the tall building will entirely block out our building, it will be barely visible, now it is no longer possible to drive up.... The new architecture does not have any feeling for history."[56]

Mark had not yet reached old age—he was only fifty-seven—but he was losing his eyesight, and he returned in his thoughts to childhood traditions that he had rejected decades earlier. At night he dreamt he was praying on the eve of Yom Kippur in a synagogue in Łomża, the northeastern Polish city where he had grown up; it was not long after New Year's Day, and perhaps the holiday of his Christian neighbors reminded him of the different marking of time in the calendar of his youth. Mark dreamt he was crying with an elderly, pious Jew and sitting with his own family around his parents' table for a Shabbat meal. "I long terribly for the times that have passed, how good it was to be among one's own," he recorded in his diary. "The Beit Midrash and its Jews with their eternal, fixed liturgy, which was like a rock." In his sleep he was in Israel, speaking fluent Hebrew and reciting poetry by the Hebrew bard Chaim Nachman Bialik. But even asleep, Mark did not abandon his politics entirely; in one dream, he met with leaders of Israel's communist party.[57] At night his ramblings about Israel woke his wife, Estera. "If I went to Israel now, I would kiss the ground," he wrote. "A lot of Jews feel this way as well, many Jews in Poland, the USSR, Czechoslovakia. If I die here in Poland, I will demand earlier that I be buried in Israel. Israeli Jews are, despite everything, the avant-garde of the Jewish nation. More and more, I understand the feeling of generations of Jews toward their historical homeland."[58]

Less than six months later, Mark died and was buried in the Warsaw Jewish cemetery. When his wife, Estera, left Poland during the emigration wave of the late 1960s, she brought with her his diary and other papers. But Mark's grave remained in Warsaw. In 1969, when hooligans ruined a section of graves, his tombstone, too, was vandalized.[59]

"EVERY POLISH CITIZEN SHOULD HAVE ONLY ONE FATHERLAND"

On June 5, 1967, war broke out in the Middle East between Israel and the surrounding countries of Egypt, Syria, and Jordan. The conflict lasted only six days, and two weeks later, Poles gathered around their radios as the head of Poland's communist party and government, Władysław Gomułka, addressed the country about the conflict. The Soviet Union supported the Arab countries and broke off diplomatic relations with Israel; the communist governments of Eastern Europe were expected to follow suit.

Gomułka's speech was as much about the political intrigues in Poland as it was about the Middle East, however, and he took up the weapon of antisemitism that his political rival, Mieczysław Moczar, was employing. Gomułka claimed that some Polish Jews rejoiced when Israel won and that their support signaled disloyalty to Poland. "We maintain that every Polish citizen should have only one fatherland," he told his audience. "Every citizen of our country has the same rights, but also the same responsibilities of a citizen toward People's Poland. But we do not want a fifth column to be created in our country." Afterward, a top party official, Edward Ochab, protested privately to Gomułka. When the speech was printed in Polish newspapers the following day, the warning about a "fifth column" was missing, but many Poles, including Jews, had already heard the accusation on the radio.

Young adults of Jewish background who never questioned their identity as Poles were shocked by Gomułka's accusation of disloyalty. "I did not believe my own ears!" recalled a young man with a similar background as those who grew up at 16 Ujazdowskie Avenue after the war, with little knowledge about his family's Jewish past. He was in his late teens when he gathered with his family in their home to listen to Gomułka's speech. "My parents yelled, 'You hear! They most clearly do not want us here!'" In the following months he discovered that many of his closest childhood friends were Jewish and that their parents were also struggling with dismissals from work as well as other tribulations. They and other young people of Jewish background became closer, he recalled.[60]

Antisemitic propaganda intensified quickly. Jews were pressured at party cell meetings and at work to sign declarations condemning Israel, and at mass meetings in workplaces, colleagues voiced accusations of disloyalty. The formality and stilted language of political meetings in communist Poland masked the emotions and tensions that reigned. The security police collected dozens of folders with reports from informants who denounced colleagues and neighbors, and it compiled lists of the number of Jews in key jobs in government and cultural institutions, whose positions "in institutions on the ideological front and in the national economy," the police alleged, "could comprise a source of danger and unease."[61] Most of the 1,100 individuals it counted were in press institutions, including 790 "Polish citizens of Jewish nationality" among 3,300 employees in radio and television. Widespread dismissals from work began, and that fall, newspapers and other press institutions became a primary target of the purge. But at the communist party's ideological publishing house, Book and Knowledge, only five Jews still held key positions in June 1967, the security police reported. The marginalization of its founders and other top employees who were Jewish had taken place years earlier.[62]

Young people were also subject to surveillance. Just two days after the Six-Day War began, Warsaw's Jewish youth group, the Babel Club, sponsored a political lecture by a prominent newspaper editor, and the security police latched on to the meeting as proof of "disloyalty" among Jews. The talk had been scheduled weeks earlier and was not intended to focus on the conflict in the Middle East, but heated discussions about the war and about the communist countries' denunciation of Israel dominated the gathering. The meeting turned chaotic and emotional. Many older Jews in the packed hall were concerned about family in Israel, while younger ones were indignant at the accusation of disloyalty. Jurek Neftalin from 16 Ujazdowskie Avenue recalled being in the audience as Natan Tenenbaum, an editor at the Jewish youth newspaper, *Nasz Głos*, angrily compared the antisemitic propaganda to articles in Nazi newspapers. But the security police's confidential report about the gathering insisted that euphoria at Israel's victory dominated the meeting, and Tenenbaum was fired from his newspaper position.[63]

Less than a year later, after students' anticensorship protests began, the security police and government propaganda made the Babel Club a main target of the "anti-Zionist" campaign, denouncing the group as a conspiratorial hotbed of Zionism. By then, the antisemitic atmosphere had already been established.

—⁓—

The turmoil that came to be known as the "March events" was set in motion weeks before March. It began with that most beloved of Polish bards, Adam Mickiewicz, the one whose verses Włodek Paszyński's grandmother taught him as a child and whose play *Dziady* Genia Adler remembered performing at summer camp decades earlier, in the last months before the outbreak of the Second World War. In January 1968, when *Dziady* was staged at the National Theater in Warsaw, audiences were especially receptive to verses with anti-Russian overtones. The government decided the play could not continue.

For years, students and their intellectual mentors had been defying censorship with their discussions about political taboos in clubs and private gatherings, and now the students' challenge to the government's control over cultural life was even more forthright. After the last performance of *Dziady* at the end of January, three hundred students marched in protest to the statue of Mickiewicz that stood just down the street from the iron gates of Warsaw University's campus. The demonstration was brief, but it marked the beginning of months of turmoil that altered Poland and, with it, the fate of its Jewish population.

Prominent Polish intellectuals threw their support behind the students. At the end of February the Polish Writers' Union publicly expressed support for the students' opposition to censorship. The arrests of the protest's student organizers came weeks later. Antisemitic flyers at Warsaw University began to appear. The propaganda singled out Adam Michnik and Henryk Szlajfer, both of Jewish background, whose non-Slavic last names made the message clear: "Michnik and Szlajfer cannot and will not teach us the tradition of patriotism of our nation," read one flyer. When the two students were disciplined, a student petition protesting the action led to even more demonstrations.

On March 8, when about two thousand students took to the streets on a Friday afternoon, the government decided it could not let the demonstrations continue. Military personnel wearing civilian clothes waded into the crowd and began striking the students, some of whom were seriously injured and hospitalized. Even students who experienced the turmoil at a distance recalled the moments when their lives crossed paths with what became known as the "March events." Piotr Sztuczyński from 16 Ujazdowskie Avenue remembers walking around campus that Friday afternoon, although he did not take part in the protests, while his brother Jurek Neftalin recalls receiving news of a friend's arrest. Their downstairs neighbor Włodek Paszyński, who was in high school and helped to lead a scout troop, led his charges through blockaded streets that month, insisting to a policeman that they be allowed to continue on their way. Halina Adler-Bramley, who lived with her family elsewhere in Warsaw by then and was in her second year at Warsaw University, joined the protesting students and was chased away by a policeman with his baton as other students were being beaten.

The protests quickly spread to universities and high schools throughout Poland, but by the end of the month the students were defeated. In Warsaw nearly six hundred protesters were detained by the fifth day of protests, and in the following months thousands of people throughout Poland met the same fate. Dozens remained in prison for months. The government shut down several university departments, and students were expelled. Hundreds were sent to the military.[64]

The spirit of youth rebellion was everywhere in the world that year. At the end of January, police broke up raucous student protests at French universities, and in April, students in New York took over university buildings at Columbia University. For students in the West, the Vietnam War was often at the center of students' ire. Youth in Eastern Europe protested the war as well, but many of their concerns were different: they were challenging a system that criminalized the very act of protest. Here, students were fed up with censorship and the hypocrisy of regimes that brought oppression instead of the just society they had promised. Just to the south of Poland, discontent in Czechoslovakia prompted a new, reforming government to ease censorship in the first months of that tumultuous year, and what became known as the "Prague Spring" brought the citizens of Czechoslovakia uncensored news from around the world. In March they read about the demonstrations and the violent crackdown in Warsaw. Five months later, when Soviet tanks and militaries from four other countries in the Warsaw Pact invaded Czechoslovakia, among them Poland, the violence in Prague was far more severe.

In Poland, the government made clear that the antisemitism of the previous year would now be part of its clampdown on student dissent, and the "anti-Zionist" propaganda accelerated. The authorities found a scapegoat in the students of Jewish background who were prominent among the protest leaders. Many of them were the children of top communist officials, the so-called banana children who grew up with privileges (such as bananas, hard to come by in communist Poland) that came with their parents' high positions. For decades, Jews were blamed for "imposing" communism on Poland; now the government accused their children of opposition and disloyalty to that system. Articles in the official party organ blamed the demonstrations explicitly on Jews. The publications listed student leaders of Jewish background and the names of parents who were communists in top government positions, drawing attention to the parents' non-Slavic names. For those who had changed their names after the war, some articles made sure to include prewar, "Jewish-sounding" names in parentheses.[65]

The authorities zeroed in on the Babel Club. They accused the group of being a cover for a "Zionist conspiracy," the mastermind of the student protests, and security agents compiled lists of members and informants' reports about meetings. They manipulated the overlapping networks of young people of Jewish background who frequented the Babel Club and circles involved in the student opposition. Among the students whom the government accused of being "Zionists" were not only the sons of Hersh Smolar and David Sfard, longtime leaders of the Social-Cultural Association of Jews in Poland, but also young people from families entirely distanced from Jewish institutions, those who occasionally attended its political discussions but never joined the group.

The Babel Club's leaders were indignant and met to formulate a reaction. "We are a normal youth club," they asserted in a resolution. "Among our most important activities are meetings with interesting people, working with amateur artistic groups, travel, dance evenings,

bridge tournaments. . . . We live, like all Polish youth, immersed in the
matters of our country of People's Poland. We are not Zionists and we
have expressed this repeatedly."[66]

—ʍ—

The struggling Jewish communities of postwar Poland barely survived the turmoil of 1968. Government pressure on Jewish institutions
had been mounting for almost a year by then, threatening Yiddish cultural life. After the Six-Day War in 1967 the censorship department
stopped recognizing Yiddish as a language native to Poland, treating
it as a foreign language like any other and therefore requiring Yiddish
publications to translate works into Polish before submitting them to
the censor. Time and resources made it impossible to comply, and the
communal leadership received a reprieve, allowing it to continue publishing in 1967. But for David Sfard, the editor of the Yiddish literary
journal, the ill will of the authorities signaled the end of all illusions.
"I knew that this was the last day of what until then was called *nusekh
Poyln,* that what is happening now will be a shameful farce to the world
. . . and my heart aches all the time because the wonderful work which
all of us carried out over the course of twenty-odd years had such a
disgraceful end."[67]

The Jewish leaders were at odds with one another after the Six-Day
War in 1967. The government pressured them to condemn Israel in the
Folks-shtime, and some of the leaders were furious when an article signed
by the Social-Cultural Association's governing board appeared in the
newspaper that July proclaiming "solidarity with the position of the
party and the government of our Fatherland—People's Poland." They
accused Hersh Smolar, the newspaper's editor, of giving in to the government's demands.[68]

Now, after March 1968, government pressure became an outright
assault on the old comrades in Poland's Jewish communal leadership.
Hersh Smolar and David Sfard worried about their sons, who were in
prison for their involvement in the student protests. Within weeks of
the March events, Smolar was fired as editor of the *Folks-shtime,* and
he and Sfard were kicked out of the party to which they had belonged
since youth. The Yiddish publishing house stopped functioning after the
government followed through on its order from the previous year that

Yiddish articles and books must be translated into Polish for the censor. The publishing house closed down entirely the following year.[69]

That June of 1968, the most important historian of Polish Jewry who remained in Poland, Artur Eisenbach, resigned from his short-lived role as director of the Jewish Historical Institute. The party committee at the Polish Academy of Sciences had already suspended Eisenbach's rights as a party member. In explaining his decision to resign, Eisenbach cited false accusations that the institute had helped to publish what government authorities referred to as anti-Polish ideas in a German edition of materials from the underground archive of the Warsaw ghetto, which was the Jewish Historical Institute's prized collection. Even more painful for Eisenbach was the government's removal of some materials from the institute's museum and its archive. Some collections were deposited in other institutions or retained by the security police. "In this situation," Eisenbach wrote, "when I cannot defend the Jewish Historical Institute and the collective of employees against baseless accusations, or to protect the Institute against the dismemberment and dispersal of the materials it possesses which were collected with such great difficulty, I resign as of today from the position of director as well as from my other functions in the Jewish Historical Institute."[70] By 1970 most of the institute's scholars had left Poland.

"THEY STOLE FROM ME MY HOLY TOPIC": BOOK AND KNOWLEDGE IN 1968

As the "anti-Zionist campaign" reached a boiling point, Poland's leaders celebrated the fiftieth anniversary of the Communist Party of Poland. In 1918 the newly founded communist party had established its illegal press, Book, and Book and Knowledge considered itself to be the prewar press's inheritor. In 1968, in the midst of the betrayal of the ideology that Book and Knowledge had been responsible for spreading, the publishing house celebrated its own birth.

Book and Knowledge was not the same institution it had been just a decade earlier, and the anniversary volume it published that year made the new climate clear. Jews were prominent among the editors who established the postwar publishing house, but not one was mentioned in the commemorative book. Stefan Bergman must have felt betrayed. In the copy he kept on the shelf in his home, he added the names of his colleagues in the margins.

Just after the March protests, Book and Knowledge began taking part in the dissemination of anti-Jewish propaganda. One young Jewish woman whose mother was on the board of a society associated with publishing institutions recalled that in 1968, two Book and Knowledge editors who served on the same board followed instructions from higher-ups to fire her mother. "She always spoke well of them," the daughter recalled about her mother's colleagues, "but when they received instructions, they did what was expected of them. Mother was broken."[71]

Later that year, Book and Knowledge's new leaders had an angry exchange of letters with Artur Eisenbach during his brief stint as director of the Jewish Historical Institute. The institute's scholars had worked for years on a series of books about the role of Jews in the history of the communist party in Poland and elsewhere, but Book and Knowledge's leadership insisted they never received Eisenbach's proposal to publish the tomes.[72] A month after the March events in 1968, Eisenbach took his complaints about Book and Knowledge to the Center for the History of the Party. The volumes still were not published.

The climate at Book and Knowledge was more ambiguous than at other publishing institutions and newspapers, however. Stanisław Wroński, who took over Book and Knowledge's leadership in 1964, had never been at the very center of circles around Mieczysław Moczar in the interior ministry, and Stefan Bergman was not dismissed from the publishing house entirely when he lost his position as department head several years earlier. Nor was he fired in 1968. Some younger employees of Jewish background also remained. Even in 1968, one young editor, Feliks Cieszyński, recalled his experience at Book and Knowledge that year with an ambiguous description. Wroński and another top editor, he recalled, "tried to convince me that my future is here, in Poland. It was a brief conversation. It lasted fifteen minutes, maybe twenty. I said that no, I had already decided. I would not be a 'show Jew' in the publishing house."[73]

There were other indications that Book and Knowledge's editors and other publishing-house leaders did not fully support the "anti-Zionist" campaign. In 1968 a new volume of Polish translations of the works of Marx, Lenin, and Engels listed Stefan Bergman's name as its translator and editor, Bergman's elder daughter, Zofia, later recalled, which she took as a sign of support among some of the publishing house's employees and a protest against the anti-Jewish propaganda.[74] Even the commemorative volume included hints of opposition. The last essay, written by a prewar communist named Zygmunt Trawiński, cited a poem that was largely unrelated to the rest of the piece, probably as a statement about 1968 rather than about the prewar publishing house, which was the focus of the essay. The verses were written by a communist who helped to lead Book and Knowledge's prewar predecessor. Trawiński cited a few lines of the poem, which seemed to refer to a book titled "Are the Jews a Race?" by the Marxist thinker Karl Kautsky:

> I am a Polish freethinker.
> I know—as the Lord our Savior taught.
> I would write about Christianity,
> Which arose in a Jewish state,
> I would publish it in a book.
> I would write—I give you my word of honor,
> But Karl Kautsky beat me to it,
> The cursed Germans beat me to it,
> They stole from me my holy topic,
> In its thick volume.[75]

DEPARTURES

On March 19, 1968, hundreds of communist party members crowded into a cavernous hall in the Palace of Culture and Science, the towering building in the heart of Warsaw that represented Stalinism for many Poles. In the midst of the crackdown on student protests and "anti-Zionist" propaganda in March 1968, Gomułka addressed the hall about the recent turmoil. Only toward the end did he raise the topic of "Zionists," and his speech was tempered, intended to ease the antisemitic atmosphere, according to one historian.[76] But in the previous year the words "Jew" and "Zionist" had become interchangeable in party propaganda, and in 1968 the message Gomułka conveyed was clear: "We are ready to give emigration passports to those who consider Israel their fatherland," he declared.

Gomułka concluded with a more moderate message: "We will firmly oppose every manifestation of antisemitism." Yet many young people were again shaken, as they had been the previous year, at being so openly targeted for an identity about which they knew little. Their family's Jewish background often emerged unexpectedly in their homes, and reactions from parents and non-Jewish friends had a particular impact. "Suddenly I saw that [my mother] was speaking to me in a way that she never did before," one émigré later recalled. "That antisemitism is everywhere in Poland—that this is antisemitism, and that is antisemitism—that antisemitism is how many people relate to us (because there were people in our section of the building who knew me my whole life and did not even say goodbye to us when we left!)." But she recalled reassuring experiences as well. A few non-Jewish friends invited her over to say goodbye, and several professors lamented the antisemitic atmosphere. "Some neighbors from our section of the building whom we barely knew came to us especially to say how badly they feel that we have to leave, how ashamed they are of this," she recounted.[77]

Some families decided quickly to emigrate. Friends and family began gathering regularly at the Gdańsk train station in Warsaw, from which trains left for Vienna before continuing on to other countries. Parents parted with sons and daughters, and childhood friends lingered on the platform, bidding farewell for what might be the last time. Before leaving, the émigrés had to relinquish their Polish passports in order to receive travel documents. They became citizens of nowhere. Government regulations for their emigration forced them to accept, at least on paper, an identity that the antisemitic propaganda imposed on them. Émigrés had to identify themselves as Jewish by nationality, a label many would not have chosen for themselves.[78]

The Polish government gave exit permits only to those who declared Israel as their destination, but most émigrés traveled elsewhere once they left Poland, and for years afterward the security police compiled reports about the activities of émigrés in other countries.[79] Not all were allowed to depart. The authorities refused to permit some scientists and others who worked at Poland's nuclear institute to emigrate. Ignacy Ekerling, who had tried for more than a decade to leave Poland after he was accused in the 1957 murder of the son of a prewar right-wing nationalist leader, again failed to receive permission to leave. Others were forced to wait months or years before the Polish authorities granted them exit permits.

In Denmark and Sweden some émigrés found their bearings relatively quickly, living for a time in temporary apartments and rooms before finding jobs. Others remained in limbo in Vienna and Italy until they received visas to the United States, Canada, and elsewhere. Foreign Jewish aid agencies and other organizations helped them find apartments, but many spent months looking for work.

From Austria and Germany, Sweden and Israel, the émigrés sent letters back to friends and family in Poland, and the Polish security police dutifully read the émigrés' letters and copied them for their files. The police made lists of who sent letters, what countries they lived in, and the recipients in Poland. Some notes never reached the intended recipients, lying instead for decades in the Interior Ministry's archive. Certainly the émigrés knew their correspondence would likely pass through the censors, so few wrote about politics, either in Israel or back in Poland, and even less so about the antisemitic atmosphere in which they had left.

Instead they wrote of the daily struggles to begin anew, filling pages with the travails of their early days as refugees and the minutiae of everyday life. They described the details of their modest rooms or apartments, their search for a job, the plays and movies they had just seen. Often they wrote of loneliness. Occasionally the émigrés ruminated on their confusion of identities as Poles who were forced to leave as Jews and on life in exile from their native country. A few wrote about longing for Poland and regrets about leaving. One émigré who wrote to her former colleague in Wałbrzych, a city in western Poland, described the struggles to adjust and her dismay at having to leave Poland. In the middle of the letter the émigré began addressing her former colleague as Pan Tadeusz, the title of Adam Mickiewicz's epic poem, which portrays a Jewish tavern keeper, Jankiel, as a Polish patriot during a nineteenth-century Polish uprising. Jankiel was a literary symbol of Jewish belonging to Poland, and the letter's author, too, seemed to convey that message, perhaps not only to her former colleague but also to the censor who might read her words:

> They say, Pan Tadeusz, that Jews, like Gypsies, do not value their country, like the
> Latin expression: *ubi bene ibi patria* /wherever it is good—that is my country/.
> But that is not how it is. We, people of the older generation, born and raised in
> Polish culture, among Polish people and nature, we cannot come to terms with
> this and everyone finds tearing oneself away from this environment very painful.
> Upon leaving Poland we were forced to "freely" renounce our Polish citizenship,
> closing forever the path of return to the country in which we spent our lives,
> where we left behind our dearest ones. . . . I believe that the day will come when
> the authorities who were responsible will want to correct this terrible mistake, yet
> will it not be too late? Because our children adapt quickly to the new conditions
> and forget that they were born on Polish soil.[80]

Learning a new language was often one of the first challenges. Polish was for many a symbol of their very identity as Poles, not only to
themselves but also to new friends and acquaintances in their adopted
country. Living in a new language was often the first step in the transformation from émigré and refugee to a new identity, a mix of old and new. A
young émigré in France ruminated in a letter to a friend in Poland about
the complications of language and identity, writing in his native tongue,
Polish, about the new language of his everyday life:

> Most intriguing is the conversion in language. Everything depends on this—in
> the course of the last few weeks I have spiritually become French, to such a degree
> that I prefer to speak in French than in Polish. It suits me better. And although I
> do not have such fluency as in Polish, somehow I identify with it. And I already
> write directly in French. . . . And I think to myself that my emigration has already
> ended. Because I already know entirely for certain, from elsewhere as well: Father-
> land is language.[81]

The security police kept close tabs on the émigrés. The previous year
it had compiled lists of those whom they identified as Jews in influential
positions and government offices, and as the emigration wave accelerated in 1968, they counted how many were leaving. Almost a year after
the March events, security police officials sent a report to Władyslaw
Gomułka, head of Poland's communist party and government, titled
"List of data of people of Jewish nationality employed in essential economic departments and other institutions." Once again it estimated the
total number of "individuals of Jewish nationality" employed in government ministries, publishing houses, and other media institutions, and it
gave an update on who left from each profession: government officials,
doctors, engineers, professors, physicists, writers, and editors.[82]

The emigration wave accelerated in the summer of 1968. Among those departing were the only five individuals who, until they declared their intention to emigrate, had managed to retain important positions at Book and Knowledge, which had once been known for its large number of Jewish employees. Yiddish publications lost editors, writers, and typesetters. Ida Kamińska, the highly respected director of Warsaw's Yiddish theater, settled in the United States.

The departures left holes in Polish cultural life as well. Intellectuals who spent their entire careers immersed in Polish culture left for new countries. Alexander Ford, one of Poland's most prominent filmmakers, departed for Israel before traveling on to Denmark and then settling in the United States. The sociologist Zygmunt Bauman, who was fired from his position at Warsaw University after the March protests, immigrated to Israel as well before moving to England. Young scientists and intellectuals made their homes in new countries and new cultures.

At the top of the security police's alphabetical list of intellectuals who departed in October 1968 was Emil Adler. After taking the train across Poland's eastern border with Ukraine in the Soviet Union to visit his hometown of Brody for the last time, he returned to Warsaw and prepared to board another train, this time to Vienna. He left behind a home once more.

—⁓—

Włodek Paszyński, the youngest of the children from Jewish families who grew up at 16 Ujazdowskie Avenue after the Second World War, never seriously considered leaving Poland even as childhood friends prepared to emigrate. In early 1968 he was still in high school, not yet seventeen years old, when students began demonstrating in Warsaw's streets and the government's antisemitic propaganda intensified. Perhaps Włodek's grandmother, Barbara H., recalled the atmosphere in which she had come of age in the 1930s, when she and other Jewish students were forced to sit on "ghetto benches" at the back of classrooms and the numerus clausus kept other Jews out of the university altogether. But even after Włodek's mother was fired as a professor at the Medical Academy, his family still did not talk about the "Jewish topic" at home, and his mother's income as a doctor as well as his grandmother's pension allowed the family to avoid the financial struggles that many other families faced.

Only after the turmoil of that year did Włodek learn that many child-hood friends were also of Jewish background. His internal debate over whether to emigrate was a brief one. He remembered asking himself at the time, "Am I from here or from somewhere else? I decided that I am from here, my world is here, my books are here." He was intent on staying.[83]

—⁓—

Samuel Neftalin, who lived at 16 Ujazdowskie Avenue, was indignant at the antisemitism that surrounded him and his family in 1968. A few months after the turmoil of March, one of his employees told Samuel that a security police agent had questioned him several times, looking for incriminating information about Samuel. The employee told Samuel of the pressure.

Samuel took his complaint directly to the Polish prime minister, Józef Cyrankiewicz. The police agent was motivated by the "antisemitic diversion in the state apparatus" and was therefore breaking the law, he wrote in a letter to Cyrankiewicz on June 13, 1968. It was the prime min-ister's obligation, Samuel asserted, to bring his letter to the attention of Władysław Gomułka. Instead, Samuel was fired from his job and kicked out of the party.[84]

Samuel and his wife, Nina Sztuczyńska, debated briefly whether to pack their belongings on the fourth floor of 16 Ujazdowskie Avenue and leave Poland. Their son Jurek was making plans to follow friends to Sweden, and Samuel and Nina weighed whether they, too, could build a future there. They decided to stay behind. The following year Jurek boarded a train bound for Gdańsk, where a ship took him across the Baltic Sea. Waiting for him at the station in Göteberg, Sweden, were his childhood friends, with whom he had felt an immediate sense of comfort years earlier as elementary school classmates after learning that they, too, were from Jewish families. If his friends had remained in Poland, Jurek later ruminated, he, too, might not have left.[85]

Jurek's older brother, Piotr Sztuczyński, was not part of his brother's same circle of friends, who also came from Jewish families and went to dances together at the Babel Club. But a few of Piotr's fellow scouts and classmates with whom he was close were also of Jewish background, and their departure from Poland only deepened the melancholy that began to overtake Piotr. He had never before considered his identity to be fragmented. The Polish aristocratic background of a father he never knew, the Jewish background of his stepfather Samuel and his mother's father, the Russian background of his mother's mother—they were never in tension with one another. He was not a cosmopolitan, he later commented; he was a Pole.[86]

After all, Piotr was not so different from many other families he knew: the friends at the Society for the Friends of Children school he attended, many of whom were also of Jewish background; the Sławny brothers from France who lived down the hall when he was a boy and whose parents were from Poland, even as they sometimes spoke French with Piotr's mother, who lived in France as a girl; the children from other neighboring families with whom he played when he was growing up. The Hebrew Bible that Piotr gave to his stepfather with his brother and mother one Christmas when they were boys, and which stood on a bookshelf in their apartment, was not unlike the melodies from the Russian Orthodox Church to which Piotr's mother had once taken him: remnants of a culture that was part of his family's past. He later thought of those years after 1968 as a kind of "internal emigration," when he began to develop a consciousness about his varied roots. But he remained resolute in his sense of belonging to the country of his birth.

—⁓—

Emigration scattered families across countries and continents. Stefania Fedecka's son, who moved with his parents from 16 Ujazdowskie Avenue to another apartment in Warsaw in the late 1950s, had already left Poland by the time of the "anti-Zionist campaign" in 1968. He settled in France, where his mother's brother, her only surviving family, had resided since before the Second World War. Stefania remained in Warsaw and lived out her years in a large apartment, bereft of any relatives at all in her native country. Ryszard Kaczyński from the fourth floor of 16 Ujazdowskie Avenue also emigrated before 1968, studying first in Switzerland before making his way to Canada. After the March turmoil, his parents and two younger sisters were dispersed around the world. Halina Adler, whose parents and brother moved to Germany, settled in the United States.

Bolek and Ela Kruc did not take long to decide whether to leave Poland in 1968. The Jewish past was only marginal to the identities of most children who grew up at 16 Ujazdowskie Avenue, but for the Kruc children, that identity was deeply ingrained in their psyches. They were part of the "in-between" generation, those who were born just before or during the Second World War. As children who had survived in hiding in L'viv, the adoptive siblings were keenly aware of the obvious way in which the Holocaust and Jewish background shaped their postwar family. But their parents, who had adopted them separately after the war, did not talk about that past, and Bolek struggled with his identity as a Jew. "With all of those years that I was in Poland I was not ashamed but I was always trying to cover my Jewishness . . . with friends, with people. I knew all my life that I am Jewish and that these are my adopted parents. [But] we never talked about it. Not even once did they mention it to me. From what I observed from all those years, my parents did not want to talk about being Jews. Never did the subject come up, what are we doing here in Poland? . . . Never ever."[87]

In 1968 the antisemitism that labeled Jews as outsiders was reminiscent of the traumas of their earliest years. As they prepared to emigrate, the Kruc family's path in postwar Poland was about to end. "I said to my parents, 'I'm leaving,' and they were very disappointed at first because they realized that if I leave that they could lose their jobs," Bolek recounted decades later. "They were secure, they were well-established in Warsaw and they had a nice apartment. People like my parents, there were many friends that they had that were in the same situation. And I and my wife said we are going."

His parents were disappointed. "But then when they started to harass my father and my mother," he recalled, "they found out that there was no other way but to leave."[88] Bolek and his wife found their way to the United States in 1968, while his sister Ela settled in Australia, living out her days in Melbourne until her death in 2007. Their parents settled in Sweden. In emigration, the Kruc family of postwar Warsaw, which had been patched together from the remnants of Polish Jewry, was once again dispersed into the three parts from which they had come together just over two decades earlier.

CHAPTER SIX

Finding the Obliterated Traces of the Path

Seeds of Revival

Perhaps the time has finally come to shake off this feeling of fear and shame, coded in one's genes, hidden deep in the soul. It is high time to find the obliterated traces of the path. To restore the existence of names of people long dead.

—Joanna Olczak-Ronikier, *In the Garden of Memory*

JEWS WHO EMIGRATED after March 1968 remembered that time as one of severed roots and exile from their country. The atmosphere that surrounded their departure cast a shadow over earlier years. For those who stayed behind, however, the antisemitic campaign of the late 1960s also became part of the longer drama of life in communist Poland after 1968: the long lines at stores with empty shelves, the hope of the first Solidarity years, despair and defiance under martial law, and euphoria when the communist government fell in 1989.

The government's attack on their identity as Poles in that year influenced not only how they related to their individual histories. Some began exploring their Jewish roots, seeking not only to fill in the blank spots in memory within their own families, but also to assert their very identification with Poland. As the anticommunist opposition sought to create a civil society beyond the reach of government authorities, meanwhile, interest in the Jewish past became an expression of political dissent among Jews and non-Jews alike, challenging the antisemitism that the government manipulated in 1968 to quash dissent and emphasizing a definition of Polishness that could include all residents of the state.

—⁓—

More than a decade after the turmoil of 1968, Marek Edelman, a survivor of the Warsaw ghetto uprising, addressed a group of young people who gathered in a private Warsaw apartment to discuss and learn about their Jewish background. In the Warsaw ghetto during the Second World War Edelman, a Bundist, helped to found the Jewish Fighting Organization, which led the ghetto uprising in 1943. He lived in Poland until his death in 2009.

In the late 1970s, as the anticommunist opposition in Poland was gaining ground, Edelman stood facing members of the younger generation, who knew the Jewish world of Edelman's youth mainly through absence. These "children" were Polonized intellectuals of Jewish background and some non-Jews, who were mostly in their thirties by then. Several were children of communists.

In 1971, a New York publication by an organization calling itself the Committee for Jews in Poland had declared the exodus of 1968 to 1970 "the end of a thousand years."[1] And yet, as Polish intellectuals and workers were uniting in opposition to the communist government, here was an apartment full of young people who called themselves the "Jewish Flying University" and sought to learn from Edelman and other Jews of his generation about an identity that had been thrust upon the younger generation a decade earlier but about which most of them knew little.

The Jewish Flying University began meeting informally in the fall of 1979 after a summer retreat for followers of the humanist psychologist Carl Rogers. In a country where Jews were estimated at the time to be less than one-third of one percent of the population, approximately 10 of the estimated 120 intellectuals at the retreat discovered they had Jewish roots.[2]

One participant in a session on Jewish identity at the retreat, Konstanty Gebert, recalled walking into the room that night and finding several of his friends seated. "That was how many of my friends found out I was Jewish, and how I found out they were Jewish," he recalled. The first speaker recalled the wooden crates of oranges that had arrived periodically at his home in Szczecin, in western Poland, when he was a child. The crate was marked "Haifa," sent from family in Israel, but his parents told him Haifa was in Egypt. The group soon realized that many of their memories were variations of similar stories. They continued talking into the night. Ryszarda Zachariasz, who had grown up with stronger connections to her family's Jewish background than the other participants and whose father was a prominent communist in the Jewish communal leadership, taught her peers a few Hebrew songs. At the end of the retreat, as the group walked together to the train station, a few participants began singing one of the Hebrew songs. Residents of the small town looked on, bewildered.[3]

Back in Warsaw, these young intellectuals and some members of the Club for Catholic Intelligentsia began meeting in private apartments, discussing their Jewish roots while changing their locations regularly to avoid restrictions on large gatherings. The group took its name from the Flying University of the Polish democracy movement of that period —itself named after a nineteenth-century movement challenging tsarist rule.[4] Helena Datner, who attended the Jewish Flying University gatherings only occasionally, recalled that her father, who had served for a period as director of the Jewish Historical Institute, was worried about the gatherings of the Jewish Flying University. "That was the way of the older people. They were cautious," Datner recalled. "We were not. That was the point."[5]

A main obstacle for the Jewish Flying University was obtaining written material from which to learn; foreign visitors sometimes found their way to this group and later provided them with books. Informal lecturers included the writer Hanna Krall, who had survived the Holocaust as a hidden child, and the writer Julian Stryjkowski, who was also Jewish. The group met every few weeks for more than two years until the declaration of martial law in December 1981.[6]

When Marek Edelman, the Bundist survivor of the Warsaw ghetto uprising, addressed the gathering, however, he told them that a new generation of Jews in Poland was a "literary fiction," frustrating many of those who had come to learn from him. Gebert, one of the group's organizers, recalled that in 1980 the young people viewed their own generation in some ways as Poland's "last Jews,"[7] although for many of them their identity as Jews was not clear even to themselves at that time.

At the time an organized Jewish community in Poland still existed. Roughly 5,000 to 10,000 Jews were estimated at the time to be living in Poland after the emigration wave that followed March 1968. The Jewish Historical Institute continued to operate, although with difficulty, since the institute was isolated from Jewish research outside Poland and much of its former staff had left Poland after March 1968. A small group of mostly elderly Jews worshipped in the basement of a community building in Warsaw, next to the Nożyk synagogue. Similar groups prayed together in small rooms in Łódź and a handful of other cities. The sprawling Jewish cemetery in Warsaw still operated.

Those who established the Jewish Flying University in 1979 often had little intention at first of becoming observant Jews, establishing new Jewish organizations, or even taking part in the small Jewish religious and cultural institutions that had limped along after 1968. Little could most of them imagine raising their own children as Jewish in a way that would create a new generation of Polish Jews.[8] Their interest in their Jewish background was in large part driven not by a desire for Jewish continuity or religious belief but by their opposition to the communist regime. Discussing their Jewish roots was part of their protest against a government whose anti-Jewish campaign a decade earlier had strengthened the stigma associated with that identity, in the process underscoring the bankruptcy of a political system whose official ideology proclaimed religion to be irrelevant and ethnic differences a problem to overcome.

—⁂—

In April 1983 Jews in Poland and elsewhere commemorated the fortieth anniversary of the ghetto uprising. The anniversary took place at a politically tense time. Poland was still under martial law, which the government had declared sixteen months earlier in an attempt to rein in the political opposition. In 1968 the twenty-fifth anniversary of the uprising had fallen just a month after the students' anticensorship protests and the culmination of the "anti-Zionist" propaganda campaign. Now, in 1983, the adults for whom 1968 had been a watershed in their coming of age protested the government's manipulation of the uprising's commemoration at a time when the rights of Polish citizens had been curtailed even more than before.

The 1983 commemoration made clear the divide between the older and younger generations, between the official Jewish communities and the democracy activists who sought to explore their Jewish roots outside of communist-dominated communal institutions. Jewish dignitaries from Israel and the West attended the commemoration along with government officials and community leaders, but Marek Edelman, the only surviving uprising leader who still lived in Poland, declined to attend. He wrote in an open letter dated February 2, 1983: "Forty years ago we fought not only for life, but for a life of dignity and freedom. Commemorating our anniversary here, where today degradation and coercion weigh upon the whole of society, where words and gestures have been utterly falsified, is to be disloyal to our struggle, to participate in something entirely the opposite, it is an act of cynicism and contempt."[9]

The younger group, including some who had participated in the Jewish Flying University before the declaration of martial law, boycotted the commemoration. Instead they organized ceremonies at the ghetto monument a few days before the official observance and at the Umschlagplatz a day before the official events. The group also sought to lay flowers at a marker for the ghetto fighters in Warsaw's Jewish cemetery, but when they arrived, the gate, which typically was open at that time of day, was locked. Just as they placed the flowers at the gate, a line of cars passed carrying Jewish visitors from abroad. A passenger in one of the cars snapped a picture of the group. "At that moment I felt how lonesome we were," one participant recalled.[10]

The "Jewish issue" never disappeared from the political arena in Poland, even after the fall of communism. But when Marek Edelman died more than a quarter of a century after the 1983 commemoration, a military honor guard accompanied his coffin to the Jewish cemetery through the formerly Jewish neighborhoods that had been the Warsaw ghetto. As Poland's chief rabbi, Michael Schudrich, led the prayers, the Polish president stood nearby.

"I CANNOT BE IN SUCH A PARTY"

The Adler and Bergman families lost contact for more than five years after the Adlers left Poland in 1968. But in 1973 Stefan began corresponding with their old friends in Germany. "I know that it was above all <u>my</u> fault that our correspondence was cut off," Stefan wrote to Genia. "Not because I objected to corresponding with good friends living in the Federal Republic of Germany [West Germany]. Perhaps you will not consider me to be such a prig. It was above all a matter of a certain mood. It is difficult for me to explain in a letter. In any case it dwelled in me—and not otherwise. I did not have any resentment toward you that you do not write, because for my entire life I have remembered the principle: if you want to receive letters—write yourself."[11]

For the next two decades, Stefan Bergman and occasionally his wife, Aleksandra, continued to write to the Adlers, sometimes in letters mailed from abroad to avoid the Polish censor. Stefan reported about his and Aleksandra's publications, about the lives of their daughters and nephew Szymon, about common friends. He recorded the mundane facts of daily life as well as important events in Polish political and cultural life, either openly or indirectly. Stefan's letters to the Adlers comprise not only a story of the two couples' friendship, but also fragments of a kind of memoir or diary of Stefan's life and that of his country in the last decades of the twentieth century.

Stefan never wrote openly to the Adlers about the "Jewish issue" in Poland. But occasionally he seemed to refer wryly to the topic. In 1976, when he wrote to the Adlers after attending the funeral of the Polish poet Antoni Słonimski, the antisemitic campaign of 1968 was clearly on his mind. In 1968, after the students' anticensorship protests at Warsaw University began, Słonimski stood up at a meeting of the Polish Writers' Union to condemn censorship and the government's treatment of the students. He was at the forefront of writers who defended the students. In response, the government banned Słonimski and nearly thirty other authors from publication.

Słonimski was one of the most prominent Polish writers between the world wars. His grandfather, Chaim Zelig Słonimski, had been a Hebrew writer and newspaper publisher; Antoni's father converted to Catholicism, and his mother was Catholic. Before the Second World War Antoni Słonimski wrote extremely critically of "unassimilated" Polish Jews, but by the second half of the 1930s he began ridiculing Nazi antisemitism and "stood in solidarity with Jews."[12] Gomułka's speech in

March 1968 had singled out Słonimski as a "cosmopolitan" who did not feel rooted in Poland.

Słonimski's life and death resonated with Stefan Bergman. Immediately after the funeral, he returned to 16 Ujazdowskie Avenue and typed a letter to the Adlers. Nowhere in the letter did Stefan write about Słonimski's Jewish background, but his recounting seems to refer to it:

> I am writing this right after returning from Słonimski's funeral. . . . I do not know the name of the priest who gave the homily.[13] He spoke intelligently and at least he did not try to present the dead as a pious Catholic. He called him a rationalist of great conscience, a person of a Christian soul. . . . The casket was carried by church literati, but among them was also Ozjasz's son [referring to Adam Michnik, a leader in the student protests in 1968 and the son of Stefan's longtime Book and Knowledge colleague, Ozjasz Szechter]. It surprised me that apparently few young people were in the church. . . . At the opening of the grave, prayers were said, religious songs were sung, after which it was announced: At the request of the deceased, there will not be any eulogies. They began to lower the casket, someone intoned "Jeszcze Polska nie zginęła" ["Poland has not yet perished," from Poland's national anthem]. All of those gathered sang. And then an incident occurred: it turned out that the space that was prepared in the grave was too narrow and there was no way to fit the casket in, so after several attempts it had to be pulled back up to the top. . . . People began to disperse. But then some lady stood above the grave (none of my acquaintances knew who it was, and I have a feeling that the organizers also did not know her) and she gave a short eulogy—perhaps 5–7 minutes. What I heard of it was: "Ladies and gentleman, Mr. Antoni was a man with a great sense of humor. Perhaps it will be better if we treat this incident with the casket, which did not want to go into the grave, as one last, final, post-mortem joke of Mr. Antoni. He always was atypical, and here it turned out to be atypical."
>
> In [the newspaper] Tygodnik Powszechny, aside from a death announcement, a feuilleton of the deceased has also been printed in the traditional place. Very good. But in general our weeklies reacted to his death with extraordinary reticence, worse than perfunctory. What shame (and at the same time: what lack of shame!)
>
> . . . Perhaps it can be expected that in the next issues, "serious," "weighty" articles about this great but "controversial" writer, and so on, will begin to appear. But the fact that right after his death they could not overcome their petty-mindedness—this will not change.[14]

—⚭—

By the 1980s, Stefan began to lament in his letters to the Adlers the frailties of old age and the deteriorating health of his wife Aleksandra. He became nostalgic. Even in one of his first letters resuming correspondence with the Adlers in 1973, Stefan reminisced about the early postwar years as he recounted a story about their lives "on Piotrkowska," the main street in Łódź where the offices of the Book and Knowledge publishing house had been located.[15]

A month later he wrote to Genia:

> I am already in my seventies.... I am terribly tired from life and from everything. ... I do not regret in the least all of the years that have passed that were spent at this work, but recently I have been thinking sometimes that I should have left [work] 2–3 years ago and dedicated these last years to writing something "of one's own" (only, god forbid, not memoirs). I had certain plans for this, but now I already doubt that I will be able to stand for this in a year, perhaps it is already too late.

Aleksandra, he noted, continued to drag herself from archive to archive and write despite illness. Seven years later, Stefan wrote to Genia that he had begun working at the Jewish Historical Institute but was uncertain about what topic to take up there.[16]

Genia Adler never saw the Bergmans again after her emigration in 1968. But nearly a decade after the Adlers left Poland, Emil visited Warsaw and returned to the Bergmans' apartment at 16 Ujazdowskie Avenue. Stefan later ruminated about the visit in a letter to the Adlers back in Germany:

> When we parted ten years ago, none of us would have suspected that we would meet again after so many years and, what is more, that we could hope it would not be the last meeting.... I feel a certain sense of dissatisfaction with my conversations with Emil. You, Emil, certainly feel the same. We live in two different worlds, but this should not be such a great obstacle. Each of us is, in a certain sense, in the role of an observer of the transformations and events taking place in the world, but perhaps I am an observer somewhat more involved and perhaps this is felt.[17]

Three months later, Stefan wrote to the Adlers:

> I will not succeed in hiding (anyhow, what for?) that today I turned 75. Various thoughts have been going through my head about this. Looking back, I see that the time we spent together in Łódź and Warsaw is among the best times in my life (and I believe in your lives as well). More and more now the feeling of loneliness deepens, a kind of nostalgia for the years that have passed, that is, for what was good in them, and I consider you to be part of this.[18]

—⁂—

In the early 1980s, Stefan began writing about the "Jewish issue" that he had spent so long trying to separate from his politics. He took up research on the history of the Bund, the Jewish socialist movement that had been founded in his native city of Vilnius nearly a century earlier, and he wrote letters to the Bund's Yiddish journal in New York, *Undzer Tsayt.*

As Stefan was exploring Jewish history in his research, however, he was completing a different project: a Polish translation of the Russian-language memoirs of a Polish revolutionary, Józef Łukaszewicz, who was sentenced to death for his part in the attempted assassination of Tsar Alexander III in 1887. Translations of other writers' works were among the safest undertakings for writers and scholars in communist Poland. If the topic was not obviously critical of the government's positions, the censor might not pick up on more subtle nuances, and a Polish revolutionary who tried to assassinate the tsar was certainly not a theme that would obviously challenge the communist authorities. But between the lines of his writing about Łukaszewicz, Stefan ruminated on the problem of identity that had challenged the internationalism of political ideology in his own life. He seemed to persist in his political faith despite the disillusionment that political reality had caused.

"Józef Łukaszewicz—revolutionary, assassin, prisoner of the tsar, eminent Polish scholar, author of works encompassing various fields of knowledge, ardent Polish patriot. Who today knows anything about him?" Bergman began the introduction. "During more than eighteen years spent in prison, he was not broken—he read a lot, deepened the knowledge he had acquired at the university, researched, contemplated."[19] Łukaszewicz and his fellow revolutionaries, Stefan wrote, were a diverse group of "Russians, Poles, Ukrainians, Jews. The idea did not figure in any of their heads that differences of opinion could exist among them because of nationality. That does not mean at all that the national question was insignificant for them."[20]

One of Łukaszewicz's fellow revolutionaries, Stefan noted, wrote about Łukaszewicz's motivations for his politics: "It would be possible to present the entire matter as a 'Polish intrigue' . . . and challenging this kind of interpretation would be difficult. On top of this, Łukaszewicz spoke with a strong Polish accent. Whether or not one wants to, I would have to agree."[21] Stefan then cited a different view, this time from one of Łukaszewicz's school friends: "Society will wait for an explanation from history how it happened that at that time, our youth . . . was prepared, with the thought of Poland, with one's sights set on Poland, to give his life for a matter which was essentially non-Polish."[22]

But Stefan had a different interpretation, one that seemed to recall the tensions within his own identity as a Jewish communist in twentieth-century Poland. Non-Russians such as Łukaszewicz who were active in Russian revolutionary politics, Stefan commented, were motivated both by their role as national minorities subject to repressions and by their dedication to the country's universal good. Writing at a time when Poles of Jewish background continued to play a central role in the political opposition in Poland, his words contained echoes not only of his own life, but also of the tumultuous times that he was then witnessing. Stefan continued, pondering the interpretation of Łukaszewicz's school friend:

> It is difficult to agree with the author of this reminiscence that the struggle to overthrow the tsar, in which Łukaszewicz and so many other Polish revolution-aries were involved together with Russian revolutionaries, was a matter that was "essentially non-Polish." History demonstrates that independent of any later positions, this was also a struggle for Poland. . . . For Łukaszewicz it was an obvi-ous thing that he must join the struggle in the place where it was under way and where he found himself in the given moment.[23]

Stefan concluded by citing a different Polish revolutionary in Tsarist Rus-sia, who wrote: "In Petersburg I am a national adherent [narodowoliec], in Warsaw—a member of the Proletariat."[24]

He submitted his translation of Łukaszewicz's memoirs to the pub-lisher in September 1980 just after the wave of strikes throughout Poland that summer. A year later, a group of intellectuals that supported the workers in their protests announced its dissolution with the following vision for Poland's future: "We were guided by an ideal of a Poland which could once be proud of its tolerance and freedom, of a Poland which could be a common fatherland for Poles, Belorussians, Lithuanians, Ukrainians and Jews, a fatherland for all its citizens, regardless of their language, religion, or national origin."[25]

—〰—

On December 13, 1981, the Polish government declared martial law as it sought to rein in the opposition. Ten days later Stefan Bergman final-ized his break with the party of which he had been a member since his youth. In a letter addressed to the party cell of the Book and Knowledge publishing house, he returned his party membership card and asked to be removed from the list of communist party members, even as he continued to maintain faith in the political thought which had motivated him since youth. The reality of the communist system in Poland, he wrote, had nothing in common with the ideals that system purported to follow.

Stefan sent a copy of the letter to Emil and Genia Adler in Göttingen, writing at the bottom in pencil: "In the end I was removed [from the party list]." He reported to them that two of his publishing-house comrades "demanded that aside from this I be 'expelled,' as was practiced in 1968."

In the letter to the party cell, Stefan wrote:

> I have been connected with the communist movement from age 15. I joined the Communist Union of Youth in 1919, I was a member of the Communist Party of Poland beginning in 1923. As long as I live I will maintain faith in this idea to which I dedicated the entirety of my conscious life. But the Polish United Workers' Party no longer has anything in common either with socialism or with communism. The party today represents and supports violence. . . . I cannot be in such a party.[26]

THE JEWISH FAMILIES OF 16 UJAZDOWSKIE AVENUE, 1981–2011

A half-century after Stefan Bergman traveled around Poland setting up clandestine presses and printing propaganda for the illegal communist party, a hidden typewriter drew him into conspiratorial politics.

The incident was a very minor skirmish in the political wars in Poland that followed the government's declaration of martial law. A younger neighbor who had moved to 16 Ujazdowskie Avenue in the 1970s, Andrzej Friedman, who was also Jewish, was arrested in February 1982 after police found his briefcase on a street with antigovernment fliers. As the security police began inspecting typewriters to find the one on which the fliers had been printed, Andrzej brought his machine downstairs to Szymon Rudnicki's apartment. Szymon was then interrogated. But the investigators did not find the typewriter; Szymon had brought it down the hall to his Uncle Stefan.[27]

Szymon, an historian who taught at Warsaw University, had been scared during his first encounter with the security police in the early 1960s, when the police were investigating Karol Modzelewski, the young scholar who had challenged the government's policies in 1964 and whom Szymon knew through the history department. Later, in 1971 and 1972, Szymon was the official host in Poland for Jan Karski, a courier for the wartime Polish underground who brought a report about the Warsaw ghetto to the Polish government-in-exile in London and world leaders during the Second World War. The security police again sought to interrogate Szymon. He refused to give them information, as he had refused during his first encounter with them.[28]

Now, in the early 1980s, with some departments at Warsaw University closed during martial law, Szymon took similar risks as the ones his mother, uncle, and aunt had faced six decades earlier as members of the communist party. Szymon held classes in the small apartment he shared with his mother at 16 Ujazdowskie Avenue, and when one of his university colleagues was arrested, he taught those classes as well. He sat in courtrooms during his students' trials and sought permission, in vain, to visit one student who was imprisoned.[29]

Włodek Paszyński became active in the opposition movement, organizing self-education circles and, after the declaration of martial law, coediting an underground newspaper.[30] During martial law, neighbors at 16 Ujazdowskie Avenue—Andrzej Friedman and Szymon Rudnicki, together with Włodek Paszyński and Lena Bergman—sometimes gathered in one another's apartments after the government-imposed curfew, drinking vodka and sharing whatever information they learned that day.

—⁂—

By the 1980s, seven of the Jewish children who grew up at 16 Ujazdowskie Avenue remained in Poland, and most had moved to their own apartments elsewhere in the city. Many of their childhood friends were Jewish and had emigrated during and after 1968, but during their university studies and adulthoods they became increasingly part of non-Jewish social circles as they made new friends. All who were married by then had non-Jewish spouses, and all who had children raised them as Catholic or without any religion. Yet nearly all of their generation from 16 Ujazdowskie Avenue who remained in Poland took some interest in their Jewish background, even though for most of them, Jewish culture and religion never became central to their lives.

Jewishness became most central in the lives of two members of the Bergman family. Lena Bergman became a scholar of synagogue architecture and served as director of the Jewish Historical Institute, while her cousin Szymon Rudnicki is a prominent historian of twentieth-century Poland and Polish Jewish history. Szymon's spouse is Lena Rabinowicz, the woman from the repatriate family who moved to Israel after a brief stay in Poland in the late 1950s. After the deaths of Stefan and Aleksandra Bergman, Lena Bergman moved back into her childhood home, and she and Szymon now live at opposite ends of the hall on the second floor of 16 Ujazdowskie Avenue.

Lena's older sister, Zosia Zarębska, whose first husband was of Jewish background and left Poland during the emigration wave of the late 1950s, married a Catholic man and attended church regularly even after his death, although she never converted to Catholicism. But she, too, became interested in Jewish culture, occasionally attending lectures about Jewish history and taking up the history of her family.

In the 1990s the Jewish past became significant in Liliana Tyszelman's life as well, as she became a guide for Jewish groups and other tourists visiting Poland from abroad. Liliana's younger sister Krysia immigrated to Alabama in the 1980s with her husband, who is also of Jewish background. His uncle is Hilary Minc, a top party official in the first postwar decade before he was dismissed from his position in 1956 and kicked out of the party as a scapegoat for Stalinism.

For the other members of the children's generation from 16 Ujazdowskie Avenue, Jewish identity was marginal to their lives. Włodek Paszyński, Barbara H.'s grandson, does not attribute much significance to the role of Jewish background in his identity. The Jewish past is not entirely absent in his life, though. He has taken part in a Polish-Jewish friendship society, and as vice mayor of Warsaw in the first decade of the twenty-first century, he has been involved on the city's behalf in the establishment of the Museum of the History of Polish Jews in the heart of what was the Warsaw ghetto.

Piotr Sztuczyński works at a Polish ethnographic museum and has little connection to his Jewish background, but he occasionally visited a café-bar in the basement of the Jewish community building, and his hobby is making paper cuts using motifs of Hebrew letters that he cannot read. Feliks Falk, who became a prominent Polish film director, has no formal association with Jewish communal life and remains distanced from his parents' Jewish background, although in 2007 he gave a talk at a meeting of the Social-Cultural Association of Jews in Poland, which had provided his mother, Salomea, with a community in her old age. Feliks's wife, who is Catholic, has visited Israel and is a "philo-Semite," as he describes her. They are raising their children in the Catholic faith.[31]

Some of the émigrés, too, developed a connection to their Jewish background. For most, that connection is informal. In France, the Sławny brothers do not feel connected with their Jewish background; they described themselves, with some irony, as "cosmopolitans."[32] Living in France is another former neighbor of 16 Ujazdowskie Avenue, Stefania Fedecka's son. His Jewish background, he said, is a complete puzzle to him; he has no knowledge of Jewish holidays, no understanding of Jewish traditions. Even after living in France for four decades, he ruminated, he does not consider himself connected with any particular country, but then his thoughts became ambivalent. "I don't feel Polish, I don't feel French," he said. "But if there was a war in Israel I would go there as a volunteer [soldier]. Although I have no connection to any of that, there is still something that remains. The same with Poland. If there was a war in Poland I would go there as a volunteer."[33]

Marian Adler lives with his German wife in Göttingen, while his sister Halina married a non-Jewish man in the United States and lives outside of Boston. For Halina, emigration was both a trauma and an adventure, from waiting in Rome for a visa to finding her first job in the United States. Halina became interested in kabbalah, and her daughter attended a Jewish summer camp as a teenager, but Halina and her husband raised her without a specific religious identification.

The Jewish past reemerged most fully in the life of Bernard Krutz, for whom that identity had always remained on the surface of his life despite its suppression in his parents' home in Warsaw. Bernard lives in New Jersey with his wife and is involved with the local Jewish community.

In Sweden, Jurek Neftalin remains close with the Jewish friends with whom he emigrated and whom he has known since childhood, and over the years he learned about the religion and culture that had been a blank spot in his childhood. When he read biblical stories, he was surprised to find that some were already familiar: his father had told him about Joseph and his brothers, the exodus of Jews from Egypt, and other tales during their long walks together in a Warsaw park when he was a boy. He never realized the fables were more than stories his father had made up. Every Yom Kippur Jurek attends services at the local synagogue. But his connection to Jewish identity is still mainly through his friendships and the informal community of fellow Polish-Jewish émigrés in Sweden. Since the end of communism he has returned to Poland regularly for business and to visit friends who remained.

In the 1990s Jurek's former neighbor at 16 Ujazdowskie Avenue, Ryszard Kaczyński, began returning to Poland regularly as well and making Polish film documentaries. He split his time between his native country and Canada, his adopted one. One of Ryszard's films chronicled the search for the missing part of the underground archive of the Warsaw ghetto.

Andrzej Friedman did not grow up at 16 Ujazdowskie Avenue, but he moved there with his family in the 1970s and became friendly with neighbors of Jewish background in the building. In the 1990s, as Andrzej and his wife were raising their children, Jewish observance became increasingly present in their home. After decades in which Jewish background was nearly invisible on the surface of life at 16 Ujazdowskie Avenue, the informal networks at the root of the building's cluster of Jewish families preserved Jewish identification in a way that now allowed it to emerge into the open, in the form of a sukkah during the holiday of Sukkoth on the rooftop extension that the Friedmans had built onto their top-floor apartment.

—〰—

Nineteen sixty-eight was a defining year not only for young people from Jewish families who had grown up after the war, and they were not the only ones who began reconsidering their family's distance from Jewish identity. Some of their parents followed a parallel path. It was a year when the failure of their ideals could no longer be denied. At

16 Ujazdowskie Avenue and elsewhere in Poland, Jewish background began to rise to the surface as they reconnected with the Jewish community from which they had long separated themselves.

After 1968 Barbara H.'s daughter never reconsidered her distance from her family's Jewish background. But in the other six Jewish families of 16 Ujazdowskie Avenue from which parents remained in Poland after the emigration wave, at least one parent in each family become involved with Jewish communal life in the 1980s and 1990s. Józef Tyszelman became active in the Jewish Historical Institute, where he was vice director for a brief period in the 1980s, while Salomea Falk attended gatherings of the Warsaw branch of the Social-Cultural Association of Jews in Poland. Samuel Neftalin and Nina Sztuczyńska spent summer vacations at the Social-Cultural Association's retreats just outside Warsaw, where their grandchildren sometimes joined them.

Stefania Fedecka also became active in the Social-Cultural Association and helped with the Jewish community's outreach to elderly Jews in Poland. She had never been a communist by ideology; her distance from her Jewish background was rooted instead in her prewar identification with Polish culture and her wartime survival on "Aryan" papers. Her renewed connection to Jewish communal life came after four decades of marriage to a non-Jew, during which time she had no association formally or informally with Jewish institutions. In old age, the same Jewish agency that Stefania had helped with assistance to elderly Jews began caring for her as she herself became infirm.

When Stefania was asked by an interviewer for the Shoah Foundation in 1996 whether she had any reflections on her long life, she first responded with a question: "As a person or as a Jew?" Then she continued: "I would like to say that it is not possible to hide one's Jewishness. That [although] I was terribly assimilated, I didn't know how to speak Yiddish … there comes a time when something happens in one's soul, something deeply, deeply hidden returns, either with tears or with a smile, but it returns and this is not to be hidden and I don't see any reason to hide."[34]

—∞—

Among the Jewish parents of 16 Ujazdowskie Avenue, the Bergman and Adler families became most strongly connected to their Jewish background in their old age. Emil and Genia Adler were leaders in their local synagogue in Germany. In Warsaw Stefan Bergman became deeply involved in the Jewish Historical Institute. As his wife, Aleksandra, suffered from Alzheimer's, she sometimes cried out from pain in Yiddish, returning to her native tongue as the elderly sometimes instinctually do. Stefan's sister Luba died in 1986, living in the same apartment with her son at 16 Ujazdowskie Avenue until her death. She had never been entirely distanced from Jewish communal life; in the early postwar years she had worked at a Yiddish newspaper, and later on she led a Jewish scout troop.

Aleksandra and Stefan Bergman lived at 16 Ujazdowskie Avenue until their deaths, as did parents in three other Jewish families. The Bergmans were buried in the Warsaw Jewish cemetery, in a section of new graves. A few rows away are the graves of Stefan Bergman's sister Luba and their mother, Paulina. Although Paulina Bergman had initially been buried in a nondenominational cemetery where communist dignitaries are among those buried, her grandchildren decided to move her grave to the Jewish cemetery upon Luba's death. The decision, as Luba's son Szymon explained it, was partly for pragmatic reasons, since otherwise there was no room to bury Luba next to her mother.

The result is that the entire Bergman and Rudnicka family, who survived Gulag and war, is buried in Warsaw's Jewish cemetery. Next to Stefan and Aleksandra Bergman's graves were plots reserved for their daughters, Lena and Zosia. Zosia was buried there when she died in 2013. The descendants of Paulina Bergman are the only ones of the ten Jewish families from 16 Ujazdowskie Avenue that remained in Poland whose final resting place is a Jewish cemetery.

Epilogue

Present and Past

WHEN I VISITED WARSAW for the first time in February 1997, I wandered around looking for a trace of the familiar. My grandmother had grown up in the city, and after her death ten months earlier, I became curious about where she was from. I wanted to walk the streets she had left behind for New York in 1923 and see the images she had in her head. I had only a vague idea of what I was seeking.

My trip to Warsaw was not unusual at the time. After the fall of the communist government in 1989, the children and grandchildren of Polish Jews who emigrated long before the Second World War or who survived the Holocaust were increasingly visiting Poland in search of the past. They wandered around the formerly Jewish neighborhoods of Warsaw and Kraków, visited death camps, and walked through small towns where their parents and grandparents once lived. Often they came in search of a connection with ancestors, perhaps the roots of their identity as Jews. Holocaust survivors came, too, confronting traumatic memories and a landscape they had left behind.

During that first visit I landed in the snowy city of Warsaw in the middle of February for a two-week stay. Not long after I arrived I ended up at the Jewish community center, a three-story white building next to the Nożyk synagogue at 6 Twarda Street in the city center. The door was locked, and I waited outside in the cold for what felt like a very long time before a Polish-Jewish woman in her late twenties, Miriam Gonczarska, approached. She opened the door and led me up a dark, narrow staircase into a small office. I told Gonczarska I was searching for some trace of my grandmother's family, perhaps the cousin who wrote to them in New York during the first years of the Second World War asking for help. "Do you know how many Jews survived in Warsaw?" she responded. "One half of one half of one percent. I don't think you will find any trace of your family here."

Gonczarska sent me to the Jewish Historical Institute two tram stops away. Towering over me as I stepped off the tram was a bluish glass skyscraper. Behind it, across a narrow pathway, was a prewar building with pilasters decorating the length of each side. I pulled open the heavy door and began a long journey through Poland's present and past.

—⚬—

On a Friday evening during that visit, just before Shabbat, I sat in the women's balcony of the Nożyk synagogue as two elderly men prayed downstairs. I did not expect to find Jews still living in Poland, and as a journalist at the time, I was curious about their stories.

Eighteen months after that first trip, I moved to Warsaw to write about contemporary Jewish life there. I immersed myself in the life of the community, sitting in the women's balcony at synagogue on Shabbat and standing on bitterly cold winter days at the Jewish cemetery for funerals. I sat with an elderly Jewish man in his apartment in Lublin overlooking the sixteenth-century cemetery to whose gate he held the key, and I spoke over coffee with a young woman of Jewish background who was organizing an exhibition on the city's ghetto.

One Friday evening that year I sat with a group of young people around a narrow table for dinner in a brightly lit room of Warsaw's Jewish community building. About a dozen Jews from Poland and others visiting from the United States and Israel were talking and singing, taking turns bringing out dishes from the adjacent kitchen.

At the end of the table was Natan Cywiak, one of the men I had encountered at the synagogue during that first visit to Poland. He was the only elderly person in the room that night. Cywiak had been in the hospital lately, and he looked rather shrunken, wobbling as he walked and leaning on his cane. Despite his failing health, he still attended services every day, hobbling from his apartment in the Jewish community building to the Nożyk synagogue next door. He stopped every time he passed through a doorway, struggled with his cane, and reached up to touch the mezuzah as he leaned on his good leg.

On this evening he sat back in his chair, listening to the conversations around him. At one point during dinner he was sitting separately from most other people, and as he spat out his prayers in rapid Hebrew, I imagined the others who might have surrounded him once, before the war. In my mind I saw both a room filled with ghosts and Cywiak sitting there alone, reciting the prayers.

Until he died the following month at eighty-one, Cywiak lived in the Jewish world that remained in Warsaw after the Second World War, a world infused with tragedy and loss but also with life and, in recent decades, with reconstruction. For nearly fifty years Cywiak made his home in a small upstairs apartment in the Jewish community building. Though he lived largely in the background, his death left a hole in the community of Warsaw Jews.

Cywiak was a pious Jew, a connection to a time when Warsaw streets teamed with Jewish life, when religion and prayer blended into everyday routine. His life spanned the various incarnations of Warsaw's Jewish world in the past century: the thriving Jewish capital of Europe before the Holocaust and the suffering Jewish population of the Warsaw ghetto during the Second World War; then, under the communist government, a sharply restricted world that was barely an echo of the one destroyed during the Holocaust; and now a slowly growing and hopeful community with increasing numbers of young people. Cywiak was a vestige of the shadows that hover over Jewish Warsaw.

In describing at the time what Cywiak meant to the city's current Jewish community, Paweł Wildstein, a retired Polish army colonel in his seventies who headed the Jewish community for many years, pointed to a painting of a Jewish man with a long beard. "A picture is on the wall for fifty years, and it is not noticed until it is gone," he said. "That was Natan."

Cywiak was an ordinary man with no known occupation. He was short and always spoke in a scream, and often when I saw him walking, I was reminded of a boxer or fighter. "He was not afraid of anyone or anything," said Maria Tkaczyk, Cywiak's ex-wife, who took care of him in his old age. Like Cywiak, she was a mainstay of Warsaw's postwar Jewish life. "I asked him one time, 'Natan, why do you scream?' He said, 'Because I'm short and no one can see me, so I have to scream.'"

Cywiak's screaming often took the form of admonitions at the Nożyk synagogue, where he spent much of his time in old age. When something was awry, or not to his liking, he protested loudly in his scratchy, high-pitched half-shout. In the December before he died, on the sixth night of Chanukah, Cywiak loudly admonished a tourist who tried to take a picture of the lit menorah on a table under a window. A few minutes later, another man stood in front of the menorah, mesmerized. Again Cywiak yelled until another man came over to quiet him down.

On most Friday nights Cywiak arrived early at the synagogue and began to pray while the sanctuary was still empty. He always sat on the right side, on the far left corner of the front bench. Cywiak liked to argue, and the other men in the synagogue often had to ask him to quiet down as they did that night on Chanukah. In deference to his long history in Warsaw and to his piety, he always recited certain parts of the Sabbath service as well as the kiddush, the prayer over the wine.

On the first Shabbat after Cywiak died, his customary seat in the sanctuary remained empty. The men seemed more reserved than usual. Just before the kiddush they conferred quickly among themselves before motioning to an older man who often attended services, asking him to recite the prayer. He declined. So Jakub, a young, newly observant Polish Jew, stepped forward and said the kiddush somberly. Only about fifteen people attended services that night, but all thoughts were clearly with Cywiak.

His funeral was on Easter Sunday, just after Passover. At the Jewish cemetery on Okopowa Street, about thirty people gathered around an empty grave. It was an unusually hot day, and some of the elderly mourners leaned on tombstones as the sun beat down. Many looked confusedly at the black plastic marker stuck into the dirt, a temporary marker until a gravestone was placed. "Naftule Cywiak, 76," the marker said. Several people commented that Cywiak looked much older than seventy-six. "Why does it say Naftule? His name was not Naftule," said one elderly woman who had known Cywiak since the war.

The name on the plastic marker was not Cywiak's identity at all, I later learned, but that of his younger brother, whom the Nazis had killed in the early war years along with his parents and younger sister. Cywiak's own identity papers were lost during the war, according to Marysia, and Cywiak assumed his younger brother's identity on all official documents ever since.

Two of Cywiak's older brothers survived the Holocaust, including one, Leib, who became a rabbi in New York. (When I contacted Leib by phone, he refused to speak with me as a reporter for the secular *Forward*.) Cywiak also had family in Israel and other countries, and he had opportunities to leave Warsaw for a place where Jewish observance would have been easier. Cywiak decided to leave once, in the late 1940s. After waiting for several months in France for a visa, however, he turned back at the last minute and returned to Poland.

In the days after the funeral, I discovered that while everyone in the Jewish community knew Cywiak, no one knew much about him. It was commonly known that he survived the war years in the Soviet Union, but nobody seemed to be certain of much more than that.

Marysia, Cywiak's ex-wife, sat down with me a few weeks after the funeral. Through her, his life unfolded, although some details conflicted with other versions of his story. Many mysteries of his past remained uncertain.

"He was born on Chanukah and died on Passover. Providence looked on him," she told me. His father had been a schoolteacher, his mother a shopkeeper. When the Second World War broke out and the Germans entered Wyszków, a small town near Warsaw where Cywiak lived with his family, his parents and younger siblings jumped into a cart and started to wheel away. They called after Cywiak, but he would not join them, riding off on his own instead on a bicycle. He had with him a suitcase in which he had hastily packed some items from his mother's store.

Cywiak made his way east by foot and other means. After he crossed the border into Soviet-occupied eastern Poland, soldiers accused him of carrying contraband and he was sent to Siberia, where he worked for four years chopping wood. Cywiak traded his ration of cigarettes for bread, a move he believed had saved his life, he later recounted to Marysia.

When Cywiak returned to Poland after the war, he was alone. His two older brothers emigrated; his parents and younger siblings were dead. Most people he knew had also been killed. The reconstruction of Jewish life was limited in Warsaw, but the city's small Jewish community was centered on the Nożyk synagogue and the community building at 6 Twarda Street. In the late 1940s, a few weeks after returning to Poland from France, Cywiak moved into an upstairs apartment in the building and began life anew. He worked for a short time in a factory polishing furniture. But for most of his life Cywiak earned money through vague means, trading illegally in goods and selling Polish currency for dollars to Jewish visitors from abroad. "That's why we had problems with the police," Marysia said.

Ever since the war Cywiak had one bout of trouble after another, she recounted in a lively narrative that might have been as much lore as a life history. There were periodic prison terms for private trade. He was often sick; he could not walk for three years, from 1968 to 1971—difficult years for Jews in Poland, during the aftermath of the government's antisemitic campaign. Cywiak's condition persisted until he survived a risky operation to remove a lump from his spine. Once he was hit by a police truck as he crossed a street near the Jewish cemetery, where he had just attended a funeral. Another time, he nearly electrocuted himself.

He fended off trouble when he could—he was tough and not afraid to fight—and he was occasionally assisted by shadowy characters with whom he associated over the years. Marysia described one incident in which a thug tried to rob Cywiak at knifepoint in the street late one night. Out of nowhere came a burly man who knew Cywiak and shooed away the thief before escorting Cywiak back to 6 Twarda Street.

Cywiak's toughness seemed to mock him in his old age. He could no longer climb unassisted up the narrow stairway to his apartment, relying on Marysia or whoever was nearby to help him.

But Cywiak continued to fight, even when he was taken to the hospital at the beginning of Passover. As he drifted in and out of consciousness, he repeatedly asked to be taken back to 6 Twarda Street.

At the time of Cywiak's death, the Jewish community of postwar Poland was undergoing a transition associated with political changes and the passing of generations. In 1999 the generation of parents, those who survived the Second World War as adults, handed off the religious leadership to the generation of children. The two generations' paths in the previous decades were parallel in some ways. The leaders of the parents' generation included former communists who had "returned" to the Jewish community in the 1970s and 1980s, following decades in which they were distanced from Jewish life. The new generation of middle-aged leaders, meanwhile, included those who began exploring their Jewish background as part of the anticommunist opposition in the late 1970s. Despite their opposing political views, the Polish government's antisemitic campaign in 1968 was a turning point for both generations in their relationship to their Jewish background.

Cywiak never left behind his connection to Jewish identity. But his funeral was a marker of the passing of his generation. The burial also highlighted a peculiar feature of Jewish life in contemporary Poland. Cywiak, who died during Passover, was buried on Easter Sunday. Although a group of about thirty mourners gathered around the grave, few young members of the Jewish community were present at the burial. Some were attending Easter Mass with their families.

The previous fall Menachem Joskowicz, Poland's chief rabbi at the time, spoke to a young girl, Ruta, from the *bimah* of the Nożyk synagogue: It is the children who guarantee that the traditions of the Torah will be carried on, he told her in Polish.

On this fall night, Ruta was becoming a bat mitzvah—a daughter of Jewish tradition—and the benches of the synagogue were overflowing. Michael Schudrich, an American rabbi who has been Polish Jewry's spiritual leader since the early 1990s and by the early twenty-first century was the chief rabbi of Poland, told her, "In life, for individuals and for communities, there are new beginnings."

A month later the sanctuary was full again, first for another bat mitzvah, then for a bar mitzvah the following week. The future, it seemed, was bright for Warsaw's Jewish community. Many Jews here saw the change of leadership from the older generation to the younger one as a sign of continuity. At a time when funerals were still more frequent than bar or bat mitzvahs, the hope was that the young people would form a new generation of Jewish leaders.

These efforts proved effective. In the late 1990s several dozen young people became active in Poland's Jewish communities each year. Some developed strong connections to their Jewish identity, joining communal organizations and, in some cases, attending synagogue regularly. But the renewal of Jewish life in Poland was still a struggle. Young people exploring their Jewish roots sometimes drifted away from the community even as new individuals became active. The departures complicated efforts to rejuvenate Jewish life, and while Jews in Poland celebrated rites of passage with bar and bat mitzvahs, they were also saying goodbye. Two young Jewish women left Poland that fall: one for the United States, the other for studies in Israel and then New York. Almost simultaneously, a Jewish family from a town near Wrocław in western Poland left for Israel. Another young woman from Warsaw left a few months later.

Often those who became serious about studying Judaism and observing religious strictures, including the dietary laws of kashrut, left for Israel or other countries where leading an observant Jewish life is easier. Some sought formal Jewish education that was not available in Poland at the time. A few wanted to observe Jewish law less stringently than what was required by Orthodox Judaism, the only option at the time in Poland's Jewish communities and its synagogues. Between twelve and twenty Polish Jews left each year for Israel in the late 1990s through the Jewish Agency, the Israeli government's immigration arm. About half were in their late teens or twenties, while the rest were families. Others immigrated on their own to other countries.

A decade later, the newest generation began to join the leadership, and a small kosher store by the Warsaw synagogue made it more feasible to observe dietary laws, while a young Polish-born rabbi joined Michael Schudrich as a religious authority in Warsaw. A small Conservative congregation was founded in the capital in 2011, and Beit Warszawa, a group associated with Progressive Judaism, became established as part of religious and cultural life with its own rabbi. In Kraków, where Jewish culture had been a domain mainly of non-Jews despite the presence of a Jewish congregation, the founding of a Jewish Community Center drew an increasing number of young people into communal life.

The community's character will change when the survivors' generation passes on, Andrzej Zozula, a Jewish communal leader, had predicted in the 1990s. Because the younger members do not have firsthand memories of the war, the Holocaust will not dominate Jewish identity, Andrzej predicted. "It will be a big part, of course, but not the only thing," he said. "You cannot build a future on the Holocaust."

—ᴍᴍ—

Irmina Pasieczna became a bat mitzvah not long after Ruta did. In an ankle-length skirt, her long brown hair tied back at the nape of her neck, the twelve-year-old girl stood in the women's balcony of the synagogue and prayed before she was called to the bimah. "Today people from all over the world, and especially from Israel, celebrate with you," Rabbi Schudrich said to her the previous night, as Israeli schoolchildren and American tourists filled the synagogue's benches. Irmina had studied for months for this day, and she smiled with quiet confidence. Born at the end of the communist period to a Jewish father and a Catholic mother, Irmina, who converted to Judaism with her mother two years before her bat mitzvah, was among the first of a handful of Polish children raised since the early 1990s in traditional Jewish homes. Jewish prayer and tradition seemed to come naturally to her.

Yet Irmina's family was not certain of their future in Poland. Her parents were considering moving to Israel, where keeping kosher would be easier and where Irmina's mother would not have to worry about leaving her job early on Friday to observe Shabbat. In the meantime Irmina's parents did what they could to raise her in a Jewish home. She attended a Jewish school run by the Ronald S. Lauder Foundation in Warsaw, where she studied Hebrew and learned about Jewish traditions in addition to her regular subjects. When friends visited the United States or Israel, they brought back kosher food for the family. Irmina said she might like to move to the United States one day.

In the same month as Irmina's bat mitzvah, Miriam Gonczarska, who had taken me in from the cold at the Jewish community building during my first visit to Warsaw, left Poland for Minsk to teach in the Jewish community there for a year. She was not certain at the time whether she would return to Poland, although by the early twenty-first century she was living in Warsaw once more.

The night before Gonczarska's departure from Warsaw, her friends gathered for a farewell dinner in a restaurant near Warsaw University.

Later in the night the group dwindled to just four, and Miriam's mood turned serious. "Will you visit my father's grave?" she asked Michael Brous, an American Jew who was a volunteer for the American Jewish Joint Distribution Committee in Poland. Gonczarska drew a map of the cemetery. "Past the graves of the Chasidim, near the forest. There is a hill up here," she said as she sketched. "Good," she concluded. "Now there will be someone here with my father. . . . It is because he decided right before he died to be buried in a Jewish cemetery that I am on this path."

—⁂—

During my first trip to Poland, I came in search of my grandmother. Instead I found other people's grandparents, their children, and their grandchildren. I moved to Poland to write about the young people who attended synagogue, the elderly Jews, the Shabbat dinners where they gathered on Friday evenings in the Jewish communal building or in their homes.

But again I found a different story. During extended stays in Warsaw, I happened upon Poles with Jewish roots in my everyday life, far from Jewish communal life: on a local bus from the northeastern city of Białystok through the surrounding towns and countryside, in a cafe in Warsaw, at the party of a Polish friend who had no connection with the Jewish community. Often they knew enough about their Jewish identity only to say that they or their family was of Jewish descent.

Because I was a foreigner who was only beginning to learn Polish at the time, the circles with which I had contact in my everyday life were mainly educated Poles in Warsaw. Even with those limits, however, it became clear that the story of contemporary Polish Jewish life was more complex than the narrative of Jewish communal revival. The history of middle-aged Poles and young people who were active in Jewish institutions was easier to access, because they could be found at the Jewish communal building and the synagogue or at Jewish cultural events. Some were prominent intellectuals who became the public face of Polish Jewish communal life. Yet it became increasingly evident that the reversal of assimilation was not entirely representative of the descendants of Jewish families who remained in Poland. The story of Jewish life in contemporary Poland included not only those such as Miriam and Irmina, whose family's narrative was one of assimilation, to return after decades of absence, but also those who identified with their family's Jewish background or were curious about that past without becoming religiously observant or involved in Jewish communal life.

—⁓—

In early January in 1999, in a dimly lit basement pub with brick walls and a maze of rooms, nineteen-year-old Paweł Skorupka played keyboard in a small alcove with a three-man blues band. The bar was called simply Piwnica—"cellar" in Polish—and it had no sign out front, only the name of a hat shop on the ground floor.

Most Sundays a group of amateur photographers met in the pub to share pictures of their recent trips. One of them, Ola, wanted to introduce me to Skorupka, who is Jewish and was the keyboardist in the bar's house band. Although Ola was interested in the stories I was writing about Jewish life, neither she nor the mutual acquaintance who introduced us was Jewish, and they were not connected in any way with Poland's Jewish institutions or cultural life.

I began joining the photography group on Sundays and speaking with Skorupka. On my first Sunday we sat at a long corner table and listened to the band as his lanky body swayed, his fingers moving quickly over the keyboard, elbows pushed outward, feet tapping the floor. During a break he sat with us and talked of going to Israel to study music. He would live on a kibbutz and learn Hebrew, Skorupka said. From the neck of his shirt he pulled out a chain with a Star of David. He did not hesitate to speak about being Jewish.

Skorupka identifies himself as Jewish, but his father is Catholic, and for many years he attended church on Sundays. "Everyone I knew went to church," he said by way of explanation. In his early teens, when he was old enough to make his own decisions, he stopped attending. But otherwise, that Jewish identity had little concrete impact on his life. He had never been to synagogue, and his Jewish background was a connection with his family's past rather than identification with Judaism or Jewish culture. Two years later he married a woman from a Catholic family, and they raised their children without religion in their home. Skorupka remained in Warsaw, and by 2011 he had established himself as a professional musician.

Another evening at the pub, sitting on the small stage in the alcove, Skorupka recounted what he knew about his mother's parents. Her mother—Skorupka's grandmother—had grown up in a religious home in Kraków, the daughter of a prominent businessman, but as a young adult she lost her faith. His grandmother lived her entire life in Warsaw except for the war years. She was sick in 1999 and could not communicate much.

Skorupka's band had its last performance at Piwnica six months later. He improvised with a slow rhythm on the bass guitar, which he occasionally played when he was not on the keyboard. One of the photographers brought along a friend, Bartek, who was visiting from Gdynia on the Baltic Sea. When he asked why I was in Poland, I told him I was writing about Jewish life here. "You are a Jew?" he asked. When I responded yes, he paused. "I am a Jew too," he said.

Bartek had learned of his Jewish background only a few years earlier. "I found documents, my grandparents' passports from before the war," he recounted. The names on the documents were not the ones by which Bartek had known them. When he asked his mother about the names, she responded that they were Jewish and had survived the Second World War in the Soviet Union. They were communists before the war, Bartek's mother told him, and they had been to prison because of their illegal politics. The grandparents lived in Warsaw before the Holocaust, but afterward, when they returned as their families' only survivors, memories were too painful. They settled instead in Szczecin, a formerly German city in western Poland.

Bartek spoke quietly. He wanted to learn more about his Jewish background, he said. "I do not believe in God, but I wanted to find out, only to find out," he explained. Officials at a local government office he called did not know where to find a synagogue or a Jewish communal group in Gdynia. Other than Bartek's girlfriend, not many friends knew he was Jewish. He does not bring it up often, he said.

The next morning I went with Bartek to Warsaw's Nożyk synagogue, where a member of the Jewish youth group gave him the phone number for its counterpart in Gdańsk. Along the way Bartek spoke about his mother's kitchen growing up. She used to cook dishes that were slightly different from the ones his friends' mothers made: carp prepared in her own way, or a meal with matzah. Only when Bartek discovered that his mother's parents were Jewish did her cooking make sense to him.

—m—

More than four years later, on Yom Kippur in 2003, the benches of the Nożyk synagogue were overflowing. On other holidays and on Shabbat, unless Israeli school groups were visiting, the congregation struggled to gather a minyan, the quorum of ten men needed for communal prayer, because many of the young people who attended regularly were not considered Jewish according to Jewish law. But on this night the synagogue was so full that women stood behind the balcony's benches and others crowded onto window ledges. Rabbi Schudrich addressed the congregation. Although the holiday is one of contemplation, it is also one of celebration here, he said, for when do so many Jews in our community gather to pray? An Orthodox Jew and an atheist Jew, he added later, have the same obligation to understand their history. "It is the same history," he said.

I had moved back to Poland that year to attempt once more to peel away the layers of Polish Jewish history. My academic home was the Jewish Historical Institute, where my path in Warsaw had begun six years earlier. On my first day there in 2003 I walked back through its heavy wooden doors and across a floor that was charred in places. The building had been renovated in recent years, but the faded burn marks remained as a reminder of the past. When the Nazis put down the ghetto uprising in 1943 and dynamited the Great Synagogue, the fire that destroyed the synagogue also damaged the adjacent building where the institute is now housed. Before the Second World War it had been home to the synagogue's Judaica library and the Institute for Jewish Studies, where scholars wrote early versions of Polish Jewish history.

Visitors entering the Jewish Historical Institute pause at a large map, its tiny lights marking the towns and cities where Jews once lived, before climbing the expansive steps to the upper floors. On the third floor, behind a door, is a room crowded with the desks of archivists who try to make order out of hundreds of shelves of boxes with documents that found their way to the institute in the years since the war. Among those documents are records of Jewish life in Poland after the Holocaust. On a shelf in the front room are registration books with the names of every survivor who registered with the Central Jewish Historical Commission in the first months and years after the Second World War, helping those who were searching for family members. Behind a closed door in that office, on metal shelves in the storage room, are boxes of more than seven thousand testimonies, mostly handwritten, which the Central Jewish Historical Commission collected from survivors, beginning in the earliest years after war's end. Others were recorded in later decades. Holocaust survivors and their descendants arrive here in search of an address, a photograph, any trace of their murdered families and sometimes of their own life in Poland.

During one of my first days back in Warsaw, as I sat in a café in the old town translating a Yiddish testimony for the institute, a middle-aged man stopped in front of my table and looked at the dictionaries. At first he said only that he was from Israel, before inviting me to his table, where he sat with his father, a white-haired man named Jan.

The son left Poland in the late 1950s with his mother after his parents divorced, and he was eager to talk. His father was mostly quiet. He told me only a few details: that he was a lawyer and lived his entire life in the Warsaw region except for the wartime years, when he survived in the Soviet Union, as did most surviving Polish Jews. The father stayed in Poland after the postwar emigration waves because he had a comfortable life, he said. He agreed to let his son give me his address and phone numbers, but the father crossed out his work number. The father's colleagues did not know he was Jewish, his son explained.

When I called the father a few days later, I left a message. He did not return my call.

—◊—

I was not certain how to find the history of Jewish families whose lives were invisible on the surface of contemporary Poland. Few traces of assimilating Jews could be found in the archive of the Jewish Historical Institute or other Jewish organizations, since they had distanced themselves from postwar Jewish communal life. For Jan, the lawyer who did not respond to my attempt to contact him, only with his son's departure in the late 1950s did his family emerge onto the surface of the narrative of postwar Jewish life. Émigrés were a significant element of postwar Polish Jewish life, but departures, too, were only part of a much more complicated story.

In November 2003 I walked for the first time through the gates of an apartment building at 16 Ujazdowskie Avenue. I wandered through the arched entranceway into a courtyard in the back, which was surrounded by crumbling brick structures. Lena Bergman, an assistant director of the Jewish Historical Institute at the time and later its director, grew up in an apartment in the building's elegant front section overlooking the avenue. She pointed up at the balcony where she had looked out onto the courtyard from the back room of her home as a young girl. Lena's mother, Aleksandra, still lived there, but her mind had long been lost to Alzheimer's. Sometimes when Aleksandra tried to speak, the words that came out were in Yiddish, Aleksandra's elder daughter, Zofia, recalled. Only after her mother's death two years later did Lena move back into her childhood home.

The apartment building at 16 Ujazdowskie Avenue became a focus of my research, but initially I did not expect to find a history of assimilating Jews there. Lena Bergman and her cousin Szymon Rudnicki, whose apartments are at opposite ends of the second floor, both live in the Jewish world of contemporary Warsaw. But as I spoke with Lena and Szymon, I learned of Jewish children, now adults, who grew up in neighboring apartments at 16 Ujazdowskie Avenue and still lived in Poland: a well-known filmmaker, a tour guide, a pedagogue who later became Warsaw's vice mayor. They stayed behind even after many other Jewish friends emigrated.

I had already spent time in a different building that had been allocated to Jewish communal authorities just after the Second World War, but I was curious about the history that had brought together Jewish families at 16 Ujazdowskie Avenue, which had no connection to Jewish institutions. As I began to ask others of Jewish background about their friends and neighbors, I discovered that among those who had grown up in communist Poland in families distanced from Jewishness but who had reconnected with their Jewish background in recent years, many had Jewish friends in childhood, and some had grown up in buildings with Jewish neighbors. Their friends, extended family members, and former neighbors provided access to a broader cross-section of Poles of Jewish descent than those I found at the Jewish community building.

At 16 Ujazdowskie Avenue, the postwar emigration waves had scattered the building's Jewish residents to the United States, Australia, Scandinavia, and Western Europe, and members of only two of the original families still lived in the building by the time I began my research. Parents in two other families had died just a few years earlier, and a Jewish resident on the top floor had moved into the building in the 1970s.

Virtually none of the former or current residents of 16 Ujazdowskie Avenue who remained in Poland maintained contact with any of their childhood neighbors who had emigrated, but a few details of Jewish residents remained a vague memory for at least one of their former neighbors: the country to which they had emigrated, their names, the profession a child had taken up as an adult. One resident led to another. Each one was aware that a few of their childhood neighbors in the other twenty-two apartments were Jewish, but none was aware that nearly half of them were.

I found Marian Adler in Göttingen, Germany. In the first postwar years he and his sister lived with their parents, Genia and Emil, just down the hallway from the Bergmans at 16 Ujazdowskie Avenue, and the Adlers were among the Bergmans' closest friends. Lena's sister, Zofia Zarębska, recalled the city to which the Adlers had emigrated in 1968, and when I located the correct Adler in Göttingen—calling him from the Ujazdowskie apartment just down the hallway from where he once lived—I made plans to visit. Marian was taken aback when we first spoke, and we forgot to exchange descriptions of one another, so I was unsure how I would find him at the station. But when I emerged outside in Göttingen, I immediately recognized Marian, to his surprise; he looked exactly like his father, whom I had seen in a photograph Zofia had shown me.

Marian longed for Poland and read Polish newspapers online, and he turned melancholy as we talked in that language over two days about his parents and his childhood. Memories of the Holocaust had haunted his mother, Genia, in nightmares throughout her adult life, he recalled. But after the family's emigration in 1968, during the government's anti-semitic campaign, the young Germans with whom Genia worked at a publishing house looked after her and became her friends.

In the room where I slept in Marian and his wife's house, just down the street from the city's university, were several boxes with Emil and Genia's personal papers: the letters they wrote to one another for decades after the war, government forms with details of their lives, and Emil's scholarly articles. Marian wavered about whether to allow me to read them, but on my second day he agreed. He had never read his parents' papers, and that evening he poked his head into the room occasionally, asking whether I had found anything interesting.

The morning of my departure, while Marian was at his job teaching immigrants, I left a letter nearly a half-decade old on his kitchen table with a note. "This is your bar mitzvah letter," I wrote. He called me a few weeks later, saying I had made a mistake; nothing in the letter had been about a bar mitzvah. The letter never used those words, and the rituals it described were unrecognizable to him.

I tracked down Stefania Fedecka's son by phone in Paris through his architectural firm. Initially he was guarded and did not agree to speak with me, suggesting instead that I contact his mother, who still lived in Warsaw and was terribly lonely. In Stefania's spacious apartment two avenues away from 16 Ujazdowskie Avenue, to which she and her family had moved in the early 1960s, she and I sat in her kitchen as she narrated the story of her life before and during the Holocaust. Stefania's apartment was spacious and immaculate, with a large wooden credenza and heavy wooden table dominating the living area.

Stefania recalled the streets of her hometown of Lublin, details of her wartime survival, and the names of childhood friends, but her memory seemed to end in 1945. She was frail, though her beautiful younger self was still visible in her face. Elections to municipal and nationwide offices were being held that day, and Stefania asked me to join her to vote at a nearby school. The internal passport she showed as her identification still had the Slavic last name with which she had survived the Holocaust on the "Aryan" side in L'viv.

Two brothers in another Jewish family from 16 Ujazdowskie Avenue lived in France, to which they and their parents had moved from Poland in the late 1950s. We met in a small, noisy café in the heart of Paris, and over tea they recounted their lives in Polish, a language they had spoken rarely in recent decades. That evening I called Stefania's son again, and this time he agreed to meet. The following day we sat at a sidewalk café on the Champs- Élysées. He did not want me to record our conversation, but we spoke for hours about his parents and childhood, his emigration to Paris in the mid-1960s, and his architectural firm.

Back in Warsaw I spoke with Włodek Paszyński, with whom Lena Bergman had kept in touch occasionally over the years. In the 1980s he was active in the Solidarity anticommunist opposition, and as we spoke in his home on the outskirts of Warsaw, he played a few recordings of songs that other activists had written and recorded in those years. Włodek spoke openly about his life and Jewish background. He grew up with his grandmother Barbara H., who lived with him and his mother at 16 Ujazdowskie Avenue, but he did not know much about Barbara's past. Włodek's mother still lived at 16 Ujazdowskie Avenue. She had been fired from her job as a professor at the medical academy during the "anti-Zionist" campaign in 1968. When I called, she spoke for barely a few minutes: Jewish identity, she said, has nothing to do with her life.

At 16 Ujazdowskie Avenue I met several times with Szymon Rudnicki, Lena Bergman's cousin, in the small front room of his apartment. He was in his sixties at the time, and his whole life has taken place in the building other than his early childhood. Szymon is a historian of twentieth-century Poland, and initially he was hesitant to accept aspects of the building's history that he himself did not know. Eventually, however, he became curious about the setting of his life. "You could write the entire twentieth-century history of Poland through this building," he said.

If there is one place in Warsaw where the pulse of the city's past Jewish life is still visible, it is in the main Jewish cemetery, a vast graveyard on the edge of Warsaw's ruined Jewish neighborhoods. A low brick wall hides the gravestones from busy Okopowa Street in the middle of the city, but the burial ground remains on the surface of city life through the tram stop that bears the name "Jewish cemetery."

The graveyard stretches far back into the woods, and the sections of postwar graves are relatively small, with only about four hundred tombstones. The fresh dirt of new burials reveals a quiet transition: the remaining Jews who remember the prewar world of Polish Jewry are dying.

The narrative of Jewish life in Warsaw after the Holocaust is written on the postwar gravestones. Only a few are from the 1950s and 1960s, and all but a handful are inscribed in Polish, sometimes mixed with Hebrew and at other times with Yiddish. The names of the dead are Polonized more often than not, but sometimes Jewish names that many had buried beneath the surface of their postwar lives returned to them in death: "Mieczysław (Mordechaj) Wajnryb"; "Henryk Majewski (Dawid Wajsbard)." There are the names of those whose existence has no marker anywhere else, inscribed on the tombstones of relatives who survived and never left Poland: "For the memory of parents Eliasz and Chana Bieżumska and 21 members of her closest family who were murdered in 1942–1943"; "For the memory of her grandparents, whose grave is unknown, Amalia and Maksymilian Grünberg."

There are symbolic graves for those killed in wartime and a few for those who left Poland during postwar waves of emigration but never lost their connection with the country of their birth. Adam Rutkowski, a historian at the Jewish Historical Institute, and his wife, Regina Rutkowska, were buried in Paris after their emigration from Poland in 1968, but in the Warsaw Jewish cemetery is a symbolic gravestone for them. Regina is identified not only as a bookseller, but also as an "emigrant of 1968."

On many graves is the story of return to Jewish life by communists who had distanced themselves from Jewish identity until they lost their positions during the political turmoil in 1968 and earlier in the 1960s. In the 1970s and 1980s some elderly Jews who had lost their political faith chose to be buried there—"new-old Jews," as a Polish sociologist described them, "disillusioned ex-Communists and ex-fellow travelers, longing for the lost warmth of their childhood after their whole world collapsed in 1968."[1] Among them is Paweł Wildstein, who had spoken with me about Natan Cywiak after the latter's death in 1999; the two men are buried not far from one another. Wildstein became involved in Jewish communal life only after he lost his military position as a colonel in 1968. When he died in 2008, his roles in both Polish and Jewish life were inscribed on his gravestone: "Chairman of the Union of Religious Communities of Jews in the Republic of Poland and corporal in the Polish military." His Slavic first name and his Jewish last name, which he refused to change after the war despite pressure to do so, are themselves a marker of his dual identities.

Further back in the cemetery, in a larger section of postwar graves, is the tombstone of Michał Friedman. Like Wildstein, he was a communist and a colonel in the Polish military until his dismissal in 1968, and like Wildstein, Friedman reconnected with the Jewish world of his youth. For decades after 1968 until his death in 2006, Friedman was a writer and translator for Poland's Yiddish publications, and beginning in the 1990s he taught a young generation of Yiddishists in Poland who are now helping to reconstruct the history of the Polish Jewish past.

Nearby is the grave of Chone Shmeruk, another Yiddish scholar but one with an entirely different life path from Friedman's. After surviving the Second World War in the Soviet Union and returning to Poland after war's end, Shmeruk left for Israel in 1949 and rose to become one of the world's foremost Yiddish literary historians. Yet as a widower in the 1990s, Shmeruk met and married a Polish woman, and he lived in Warsaw before his death in 1997.

In this postwar section a visitor can wander among seventeen rows of postwar graves. One of the tallest is that of Julian Stryjkowski, a Polish poet and author who was beloved by Poles and Jews alike. Inscribed in parentheses on the gravestone, next to "Julian," is "Pesach," the first name with which he was born. Beneath are verses from the lament of the poet Julian Tuwim, "We, Polish Jews," in Polish and in Yiddish: "We, Polish Jews . . . We, the legend dripping with tears and blood . . . With pride, mournful pride, that we should count ourselves of that glorious rank which will outshine all others—the rank of the Polish Jew."[2]

When Stryjkowski died in 1996 at the age of ninety-one, the Polish writer Andrzej Braun gave a eulogy as hundreds of people gathered over his grave: "With great sadness we say farewell today to a great writer. A great Polish writer. Because although Julian Stryjkowski introduced himself . . . with the words 'I am a Jewish writer,' he is and he will be a great Polish writer," Braun intoned. "Julian Stryjkowski was a master of the Polish language, and through this language he enriched Polish culture forever. At the same time he was in his soul a Jewish writer, through his experiences from childhood to death as a Jew in Poland."[3]

A few rows away are the graves of Stefan and Aleksandra Bergman and nearby the tombstones of Stefan's sister Luba Rudnicka and their mother, Paulina Bergman. Stefan's and Aleksandra's tombstones, created by a sculptor, stand out with their artistic design and rounded shape, with a jagged line cutting diagonally across the front of the stone. Below their postwar names are the ones with which they had been born, inscribed in Yiddish: "Chawa born Kuczkowska" for Aleksandra, and "Beniamin Epsztejn" for Stefan. On Stefan's grave the names of murdered family members are listed beneath his own name, "to the memory of his sisters who were killed": Róża, murdered in 1937 in Homel during the Soviet purges, and Chana, killed in 1943 in the Otwock ghetto during the Holocaust.

—∾∾—

As I researched the families at 16 Ujazdowskie Avenue and the city where they rebuilt after the Holocaust, I often returned in my memory to a walk I took through Warsaw on the day before New Year's Eve in 1998 with a Holocaust survivor named Jakub Gutenbaum. As a child in the 1930s Gutenbaum lived with his parents and younger brother in the Polish capital. He grew old a few city districts away, in another Warsaw apartment.

Gutenbaum and I walked through the city as he narrated his life. As a boy he witnessed and survived the destruction of Polish Jewry and a war that nearly wiped out the Polish capital. He saw the starvation of the Warsaw ghetto during the Second World War and the daily struggles to live. He hid in an attic as the Jews of Warsaw were sent to Treblinka in July and August 1942; he crouched in a crowded cellar bunker during the ghetto uprising in April 1943 before the Nazis put down the ghetto uprising and then burned down the building above him. He was found and deported to slave labor and concentration camps, where he escaped death only to find out later that his mother and brother did not.

And Gutenbaum returned to this city to watch it rise from rubble; he saw it fall under more than four decades of communist rule and then emerge into democracy. He built a successful career as a mathematician; he married, raised a son, and fawned over his grandson. As Gutenbaum aged, he watched Warsaw remake itself again in the 1990s as skyscrapers rose next to the gray, drab, communist-era buildings that had been built on the rubble of prewar Warsaw.

"After the war, the city planners had two choices. They could build the city again in another location, or they could build it in the same place. They decided to build it in the same place," Gutenbaum commented as he walked toward his childhood street. His words might just as well describe a similar decision in his own life, which paralleled the life of his city.

—∾∾—

As a boy before the war, Gutenbaum lived in an apartment at 42 Żelazna Street in the middle-class, predominantly Jewish neighborhood of Grzybów, not far from Genia Adler's childhood home. Gutenbaum's apartment house is gone now, destroyed during the war. Walking through Warsaw six decades later, he took me first to a weed-covered lot as his eyes scanned the ground, looking for a clue to the past. "My home was right here," he said. He looked around, disoriented. Although Gutenbaum was almost seventy, he seemed a decade younger, and his memory was still good. But there were no markers of his childhood here. Enough remained, however, that Gutenbaum was able to find the plot of ground that was his childhood home.

We entered the courtyard of a nearby brick building, a rare survivor of wartime. "It was something like this. Here there was a toilet for people who did not have one," he said, pointing to the center of the courtyard. His own building had been full of young boys like himself, mostly Jews but also some non-Jews, including the two brothers who lived upstairs. They played together in the building's courtyard.

Gutenbaum continued down Żelazna Street, scurried across an intersection, and looked up at a freshly painted building that houses a coin mint. "I went to school here," he recalled. His parents did not attend synagogue, though they lived close to one, and they spoke mostly Polish at home. Still, every year for Passover, the family gathered at his uncle's house for a Seder.

Gutenbaum moved back and forth in time as he talked, from childhood to adulthood, from before the war to the ghetto and afterward. At the outbreak of war with Germany, his father, who had been active in labor unions and feared persecution by the Nazis, fled east to Soviet-occupied Poland and left his wife to take care of Gutenbaum and his brother. The family received a postcard from him in the summer of 1940. They never heard from him again.

People turned their heads as Gutenbaum hurried down the street, talking about the war. As we walked further north, he spoke of the weeks he spent in a cellar bunker during the ghetto uprising. Soon their building was burning, and the smoke was filtering into the cellar. They were forced to emerge onto the street.[4] The family was taken at gunpoint down Zamenhof Street to the Umschlagplatz, the platform from which Jews were forced to board trains to the Nazi camps. Buildings were burning on either side of them. When they arrived at

Majdanek, Gutenbaum was selected to work. His mother and brother were sent to the gas chambers, and over the next two years Gutenbaum was a prisoner in five different camps. In May 1945, the Terezin camp, where he was a prisoner, was liberated. He had survived.

As Gutenbaum spoke of the war, there was little trace of bitterness in his words. Perhaps the city gave him strength; it was his only witness. In all his life, Gutenbaum spent just a handful of years outside of Warsaw. Unlike many Jews who remained in Poland, he never changed his name. "It was not a decision not to change it," he said. "It was a decision only if you changed it."

As an adult he rarely spoke about his wartime experiences with his friends or colleagues at the Polish Academy of Sciences, where he was a mathematics professor and department head. He did not encounter problems with antisemitism at work or among friends, he said. Only after he took part decades later in a group for child Holocaust survivors in Poland did he discover that some of his acquaintances were also Jewish. A half century after war's end, following the fall of the communist government, they began to talk about the past, some of them for the first time.

Several hours after Gutenbaum stood on the street where he lived before the Second World War, he walked back and forth across an intersection elsewhere in the city, at Franciszkanska Street, where he lived with his aunt in the ghetto before the borders were redrawn and they had to move elsewhere. Her building was near an intersection, but the street layout and street numbers are not the same, and Gutenbaum could not figure out where the apartment was located. Frustrated, he gave up and talked instead about his current life as he walked along the rebuilt streets of his city.

NOTES

1. The postwar communist party's ideological publishing house was known as Book (Książka) until the fall of 1948, when it absorbed the Polish Socialist Party publishing house, Knowledge (Wiedza), to become Book and Knowledge (Książka i Wiedza). That change followed the dissolution and absorption of the Polish Socialist Party into Poland's communist party, called the Polish Workers' Party, to form the Polish United Workers' Party.

2. Interview with Andrzej Friedman by the author, Warsaw, Dec. 1, 2004, and Nov. 20, 2006.

3. Interviews and documents in the Ministry of Interior Affairs archive confirmed the presence of clusters of Jewish residents in at least five other buildings aside from the one at 16 Ujazdowskie Avenue, while informal conversations indicated a higher number. A building on Jagiellońska Street in right-bank Praga was assigned to Jewish communal authorities after the war for the allocation of apartments, while residents of another apartment house, on Konopnicka Street, included numerous employees and members of Jewish institutions. The latter was home to Ignacy Ekerling, a former driver for Jewish institutions who was accused of the 1957 murder of the son of a Polish nationalist leader, and in 1972, the security police counted thirty-five Jewish families who were residents of the building before their emigration in the 1950s and late 1960s. Other apartment houses were not associated with Jewish communal life and point to informal networks that connected Jewish families. A building on Puławska Street was home to party officials, among them at least four Jewish families, while at least three Jewish families lived in a prewar apartment house on Litewska Street. Informal conversations pointed to the presence of clusters of Jewish residents in a handful of other buildings as well, including in the Żoliborz and Mokotów neighborhoods and on Ordynacka Street in the city center.

See archives of the Instytut Pamięci Narodowej (Institute for National Remembrance, IPN), collection of the Ministerstwo Spraw Wewnętrznych (Ministry of Internal Affairs, MSW), archival no. MSW SGO 0747/30, folder 21; and interviews by the author with Helena Datner, Warsaw, May 16, 2004; and May 20, 2004; Stanislaw Krajewski, Warsaw, July 11, 2004; and Aleksander Bilewicz, Warsaw, May 27, 2004, and June 3, 2004. On the Ekerling case, see chapter 4.

4. See chapter 5, footnote 2, for a range of estimates of the number of émigrés. The emigration wave continued through 1971, when about 1,100 individuals left Poland.

5. Moshe Shklar [Szkliar], "Nishto mer [No more] . . . ," in *Poshete verter* [Simple words] (Warsaw: Yidish Bukh, 1962), trans. by Magdalena Ruta.

6. This study assumes a definition of assimilation by Milton Gordon, a sociologist of American society who studied various ethnic groups, as a process distinct from ideological implications of the term in popular contemporary usage. According to Gordon, assimilation begins with acculturation and can, but does not necessarily, continue to social integration, intermarriage, and adoption of the host society's sense of peoplehood. This microhistory of 16 Ujazdowskie Avenue views assimilation as a process that can take place within an individual's lifetime or over the course of generations within one family. See Milton M. Gordon, *Assimilation in American Life: The Role of Race, Religion, and National Origins* (New York: Oxford University Press, 1964).

7. See Clifford Geertz, *The Interpretation of Cultures: Selected Essays* (New York: Basic Books, 1973).

8. Roger Chartier, "Intellectual History of Sociocultural History? The French Trajectories," in *Modern European Intellectual History: Reappraisals and New Perspectives*, ed. Dominick LaCapra and Steven L. Kaplan (Ithaca, N.Y.: 1982) 32, cited in Carlo Ginzburg, "Microhistory: Two or Three Things That I Know about It," *Critical Inquiry* 20 (1993): 22. Chartier's comment refers to Ginzburg's *The Cheese and the Worms*, his study of a sixteenth-century miller in Italy who was condemned by the Inquisition.

9. The families that registered were the Adlers, the Bergman and Rudnicka family, the Kaczyńskis, Ignacy Kruc, Samuel Neftalin, and the Tyszelmans. Not listed are the Falks; Stefania Fedecka; Barbara H. and her daughter; Ignacy Kruc's wife Stanisława; Samuel Neftalin's wife Nina Sztuczyńska; and the Sławnys, who had not yet arrived in Poland from France when the registry was compiled. Bolesław Kruc is registered, but Ignacy and Stanisława Kruc had not yet adopted him, so he is listed as Bernard Strzycki, the name with which he survived the Holocaust as a child.

10. In addition, two interviews were conducted with non-Jewish postwar residents of 16 Ujazdowskie Avenue.

1. HISTORY BRUSHED AGAINST US

1. Interview with Genia [Eugenia] Adler by Marek Pelc, Survivors of the Shoah Visual History Foundation, Göttingen, Germany, Aug. 19, 1996. Translated from Polish by Genia's and Emil's daughter, Halina Adler-Bramley.

2. Ibid.

3. Yuri Slezkine, *The Jewish Century* (Princeton, N.J.: Princeton University Press, 2004), 3.

4. Interview with Genia Adler by Marek Pelc, Survivors of the Shoah Visual History Foundation, Göttingen, Germany, Aug. 19, 1996.

5. Antisemitic campaigns in the 1920s and 1930s to introduce a government-sanctioned *numerus clausus* and later a *numerus nullus* were not successful. However, as Ezra Mendelsohn and Emanuel Melzer noted, the percentage of Jewish students at Polish universities declined from 24.6 percent in 1921–1922, to 8.2 percent in 1938–1939. See Monika Natkowska, *Numerus clausus, getto ławkowe, numerus nullus, paragraf aryjski. Antysemityzm na Uniwersytecie Warszawskim, 1931–1939* [Numerus clausus, ghetto benches, numerus nullus, Aryan paragraph. Antisemitism at Warsaw University, 1931–1939] (Warsaw: Żydowski Instytut Historyczny, 1999); Szymon Rudnicki, "From 'Numerus Clausus' to 'Numerus Nullus,'" in *From Shtetl to Socialism: Studies from Polin,* ed. Antony Polonsky (London: Littman Library of Jewish Civilization, 1993), 359–381; Ezra Mendelsohn, *The Jews of East Central Europe between the World Wars* (Bloomington: Indiana University Press, 1983), 42; and Emanuel Melzer, *No Way Out: The Politics of Polish Jewry, 1935–1939* (Cincinnati: Hebrew Union College Press, 1997), 71–72.

6. Interview with Genia Adler by Marek Pelc, Survivors of the Shoah Visual History Foundation, Göttingen, Germany, Aug. 19, 1996.

7. Ibid. This recollection is confirmed by a notice in *Gazeta Żydowska* [Jewish gazette] in October 1940 on the anniversary of Cesia's death. *Gazeta Żydowska* was the Polish-language newspaper sanctioned by Nazi authorities in the General Government.

8. Interviews with Marian Adler by the author, Dec. 2–3, 2006, and Halina Adler-Bramley, Sharon, Mass., Jan. 7, 2007.

9. Interview with Genia Adler by Marek Pelc, Survivors of the Shoah Visual History Foundation, Göttingen, Germany, Aug. 19, 1996.

10. Details of Emil Adler's biography draw on his personal papers in the possession of his son, Marian Adler, in Göttingen, Germany, as well as party and personal records in Poland, including the file of Emil Adler, "Ankieta" [Questionnaire], 1–2, and "Życiorys" [Biography], 3, in the Central Committee of the Polish United Workers' Party [KC PZPR] collection in the Central Archives of Modern Records [Archiwum Akt Nowych, AAN], Zbiór akt osobowych działaczy ruchu robotniczego [Collection of personal records of activists of the workers' movement], 61.

11. File of Mendel Adler, Archive of Warsaw University, archival no. 25.854, unpaginated.

12. In L'viv between September 1939 and June 1941, the Polish communist and socialist intelligentsia who had fled from the Nazis was centered around the newspaper *Czerwony Sztandar* (Red banner), among them party leaders whom Adler knew from Warsaw. Emil was connected with this group but was on its margins. See Barbara Fijałkowska, *Borejsza i Różański: przyczynek do dziejów Stalinizmu w Polsce* [Borejsza and Różański: Contribution to the history of Stalinism in Poland] (Olsztyn, Poland: Wyższa Szkoła Pedagogiczna, 1995), 72.

13. Jakub Prawin to Emil Adler, April 4, 1942, personal papers of Emil and Genia Adler, Göttingen, Germany.

14. Emil Adler, "O przyjacielu [About a friend] . . . ," in *Jakub Prawin (Wspomnienia)* [Jakub Prawin (Recollections)] (Warsaw: Książka i Wiedza, 1959), 45.

15. Details of Stefan Bergman's life are compiled from his personnel file at Book and Knowledge; his file in AAN, KC PZPR, Zbiór akt osobowych działaczy ruchu robotniczego, archival no. 7711; an interview in Russian on Deutsche Welle radio conducted by Borys Weil in Copenhagen on August 17, 1992, and translated by his nephew Szymon Rudnicki and daughter Zofia Zarębska into Polish in Szymon Rudnicki, "Wspomnienia:

Stefan Bergman" [Recollections: Stefan Bergman], *Kwartalnik Historii Żydow*, no. 211 (2004): 414–415; an interview published in 1992 by Barbara Hołub, "Stefan Bergman: Jerozolima Północy" [Stefan Bergman: Jerusalem of the North], in *Przy wileńskim stole* [At a Wilno table] (Warsaw: Książka i Wiedza, 1992), 191–205; and interviews with Zarębska and Rudnicki.

16. Iris Parush argued that Jewish women's exposure to secular education, which was often off-limits to many Jewish boys in religious families, facilitated secularization among Jews in Eastern Europe. See Iris Parush, *Reading Jewish Women: Marginality and Modernization in Nineteenth Century Eastern European Jewish Society*, trans. Saadya Sternberg (Hanover: University Press of New England for Brandeis University Press, 2004).

17. Hołub, "Stefan Bergman: Jerozolima Północy," 197.

18. Ibid.

19. "Drukarnia KC KPZB w białymstoku przy ul. Stołecznej nr. 19 [Printing press of the Central Committee of the Communist Party of Western Belorussia in Białystok at 19 Stołeczna Street]." AAN, KC PZPR, Zbiór akt osobowych działaczy ruchu robotniczego, archival no. 7711, file of Stefan Bergman, subfolder 2, 8.

20. Aleksandra Bergman's biography is reconstructed from an interview by Aleksander Barszczewski, chairman of the Belorussian Social-Cultural Association, Feb. 21, 1985, Warsaw, recorded in Russian and Belorussian and translated into Polish by Zofia Zarębska; and interviews with Zofia Zarębska by the author, July 12, 2004, and August 2, 2004.

21. "Życiorys" [Biography], November 16, 1949. AAN, Zbiór akt osobowych działaczy ruchu robotniczego, archival no. 5057, file of Luba Rudnicka.

22. Interview with Zofia Zarębska by the author, July 12, 2004, and Aug. 2, 2004.

2. THE FAMILIES OF 16 UJAZDOWSKIE AVENUE, 1900–1948

1. The reconstruction of Barbara H.'s history is based on records in the Archive of Warsaw University, archival no. 33.809, unpaginated; her personnel file at Book and Knowledge, unpaginated; and interviews with her grandson, Włodek Paszyński, Warsaw, Nov. 4, 2004, and Nov. 30, 2006. Prewar and postwar documents provided divergent details about her birthdate, birthplace, and other aspects of her biography. For her life before the Second World War, therefore, I have relied mainly on her prewar university files. Although she wrote in postwar files that she was born in 1899 or 1900, her birth certificate, of which there is a Polish translation from Russian in her prewar university records, indicates she was born in 1907.

2. In a 1932 document Barbara referred to herself as an orphan and cites the death of her father, leaving her dependent on one or both of her brothers, while in a 1935 record she refers to herself as "without parents." Archive of Warsaw University, file of Bina H., file 33.809, unpaginated. According to her Book and Knowledge personnel file after the war, however, her parents died in 1939.

3. Archive of Warsaw University, file WL/RP 1843, unpaginated.

4. Stanisławów is the Polish name. The city, which is now in Ukraine, is today called Ivano-Frankivs'k.

5. Akta osobowe [Personal record], questionnaire filled out by Salomea Falk. IPN, collection of the MSW, archival no. BU 0993/1452.

6. Interview with Feliks Falk, Warsaw, Nov. 8, 2004 and Nov. 28, 2006.

7. The main sources for details about the Sławny family are "Władysław Sławny, Akta Osobowa Cudzoziemca [Personal record of a foreigner]" in IPN, collection of the MSW, archival no. BU 1368/5137; interviews with the Sławnys' sons, Francis and Jan Sławny, by the author, Paris, March 13, 2007; an interview with Antonina Sławna's niece, Yvette Metral, by the author, Paris, March 15, 2007; and personal papers provided by Metral and the Sławny brothers.

8. On Broderzon, see Gilles Rozier, "Moyshe Broderzon," trans. by Cecilia Grayson, in *The YIVO Encyclopedia of Jews in Eastern Europe,* ed. Gershon David Hundert, 242–244 (New Haven, Conn.: Yale University Press, 2008).

9. J. Hoberman, *Bridge of Light: Yiddish Film Between Two Worlds* (New York: Museum of Modern Art and Schocken Books, 1991), 281–285, 329, 340. Hoberman cites an interview with Berg by Michael Alpert for information about the role of her family's Chasidic background in her choreography.

10. Jaff Schatz estimates that 5,000–10,000 members of the Communist Party of Poland were of Jewish descent in interwar Poland, comprising approximately 22–26 percent of the total number of communists but less than 0.2 percent of Polish Jewry. About 75 percent of the party's publishing and propaganda apparatus was Jewish, he estimated. The percentage of Jews in the prewar Communist Party of Poland was higher in certain years, reaching a peak in 1930 at 35 percent, and the percentage of Jews in the communist youth movements was even higher than in the movement itself. Schatz notes, however, that the high percentage of Jews in the party leadership also meant that Jews were probably killed in higher proportions during the Stalinist purges, although the exact numbers are not known. See Jaff Schatz, *The Generation: The Rise and Fall of the Jewish Communists of Poland* (Berkeley: University of California Press, 1991). Jeffrey Kopstein and Jason Wittenberg estimated from their analysis of voting and census records that 7 percent of Jewish voters supported communist-affiliated parties in Poland in 1928, among the lowest level of support among Jews for any political grouping; six years earlier, that number was 2–4 percent. In 1928 14 percent of the vote for communist-affiliated parties came from Jews, they found. Jeffrey Kopstein and Jason Wittenberg, "Who Voted Communist? Reconsidering the Social Bases of Radicalism in Interwar Poland," *Slavic Review* 62, no. 1 (Spring 2003): 87–109, esp. 99 and 105.

11. In central and eastern Poland, for example, Belorussians made up 43 percent of voters for communist-affiliated parties, according to Kopstein and Wittenberg. They attribute this high percentage to "affinity for their east Slavic co-religionists in the Soviet Union." In southern Poland 46 percent of voters for communist-affiliated parties were Ukrainian. Kopstein and Wittenberg, "Who Voted Communist?" 103, 105. I am grateful to Zvi Gitelman for pointing out, however, that the weak national identity of the Belorussian population at the time challenges this explanation.

12. Interview with Stefania Fedecka, Survivors of the Shoah Visual History Foundation, Warsaw, 1996.

13. "Wspomnienie o działalności KZM Warszawy w 1926–1929 [Recollections about the Communist Union of Youth of Warsaw in 1926–1929]." AAN, KC PZPR, Zbiór akt osobowych działaczy ruchu robotniczego, archival no. Z2187, file of Ignacy Kruc, 8600, subfolder 2.

14. File of Stanisława Kruc in IPN, collection of the MSW, archival no. BU 1368/633; file of Stanisława Kruc in AAN, Zbiór akt osobowych działaczy ruchu robotniczego, archival no. Z2187.

15. The Tyszelmans' history draws on Józef Tyszelman's personnel file at Book and Knowledge, unpaginated; personal papers of Liliana Tyszelman; and interview with Liliana Tyszelman, Warsaw, Dec. 1, 2006, and July 3, 2007.

16. The essay is cited by Horwitz's great-niece in her memoirs. Joanna Olczak-Ronikier, *W ogrodzie pamięci* [In the garden of memory] (Krakow: Znak, 2003), 121.

17. "Życiorys" [Biography], August 20, 1949, in AAN, Zbiór akt osobowych działaczy ruchu robotniczego, archival no. 1474, file of Ernest Falk, 4–5; and interview with Feliks Falk, Nov. 8, 2004, and Nov. 28, 2006.

18. Aleksander Rafałowski, ... *I spoza palety: wspomnienia* [And from behind the palette: Memoirs] (Warsaw: Państwowy Instytut Wydawniczy, 1970), 23–24. The book does not refer to the family's Jewish background, nor to his brother Leopold, whose murder at Katyń would have been politically sensitive at the time of publication, when the massacre by the Soviets was a taboo topic.

19. After the war Samuel Neftalin recounted to his son Jurek that he was first deported from Łódź to a concentration camp in Germany, from which he escaped and returned to Łódź before fleeing east. Interview with Jurek Neftalin by the author, Warsaw, Nov. 14–15, 2006.

20. Stefania Fedecka's history is based mainly on her interview by the Survivors of the Shoah Visual History Foundation, Warsaw, 1996; an interview by the author with Fedecka, Warsaw, Nov. 12, 2006; and an interview by the author with her son, Paris, March 16, 2007.

21. Fedecka displayed the photographs during her interview for the Survivors of the Shoah Visual History Foundation.

22. Interview with Stefania Fedecka by the Survivors of the Shoah Visual History Foundation, Warsaw, 1996.

23. Telephone interview with Bernard Krutz by the author, Fair Lawn, N.J., July 8, 2007.

24. Archive of the Jewish Historical Institute [Żydowski Instytut Historyczny, ŻIH], collection of the Hebrew Immigrant Aid Society, folder 351/147, subfolder "Zygmunt Kaczyński"; alphabetical registry of Polish Jews who survived the Second World War, letter K, list nr. 3, Warsaw, January 1947: Ryszard Kaczyński, 1238; Zygmunt Kaczyński, 1240; Halina Kaczyńska, 1233, in ŻIH, collection of the Central Committee of Polish Jews[Centralny Komitet Żydów Polskich, CKŻP]; and an interview with Ryszard Kaczyński, Feb. 22, 2007.

25. The details of Nina Sztuczyńska's life are based on interviews by the author with Nina's sons, Jurek Neftalin, Warsaw, Nov. 14–15, and Piotr Sztuczyński, Warsaw, Nov. 10, Nov. 20, Nov. 24, 2006; an interview with her cousin, Gustawa Maślankiewicz, by the Survivors of the Shoah Visual History Foundation, Jan. 15, 1996; an interview by the author with Gustawa's daughter, Krystyna Heldwein, Warsaw, June 23, 2007; and AAN, Zbiór akt osobowych działaczy ruchu robotniczego, archival no. 8677, file of Nina Sztuczyńska.

26. Interviews with Gustawa Maślankiewicz by the Survivors of the Shoah Visual History Foundation, Jan. 15, 1996; with Gustawa's daughter, Krystyna Heldwein, Warsaw, June 23, 2007; and with Jurek Neftalin by the author, Warsaw, Nov. 14–15, 2006. See also AAN, Zbiór akt osobowych działaczy ruchu robotniczego, archival no. 8677, file of Nina Sztuczyńska. The file contains the transcript of a Nov. 20, 1957, interview in which she describes the communist youth underground in occupied Warsaw.

27. Interviews with Piotr Sztuczyński by the author, Warsaw, Nov. 10, Nov. 20, Nov. 24, 2006; and with Krystyna Heldwein by the author, Warsaw, June 23, 2007.

28. There is a growing literature about these pogroms, most importantly Jan Gross's *Neighbors: The Destruction of the Jewish Community in Jedwabne, Poland* (Princeton, N.J.: Princeton University Press, 2001). The most comprehensive collection of documents about these pogroms is included in a two-volume report from the Institute for National Remembrance: Paweł Machcewicz and Krzysztof Persak, eds., *Wokół Jedwabnego* (Warsaw: Instytut Pamięci Narodowej, 2002). See also Andrzej Żbikowski, *U genezy Jedwabnego: Żydzi na kresach północno-wschodnich II Rzeczypospolitej, wrzesień 1939–lipiec 1941* (Warsaw: Żydowski Instytut Historyczny, 2006).

29. Personnel file of Barbara H. at Book and Knowledge, unpaginated; interview with Włodek Paszyński by the author, Warsaw, Nov. 4, 2004. The Union of Polish Patriots was organized in Moscow in 1943 and was dominated by communists.

30. Interview with Stefania Fedecka, Survivors of the Shoah Visual History Foundation, 1996.

31. "Życiorys" [Biography], 3–4; and "Opinia o Towarzyszu Edwardzie S." [Opinion about Comrade Edward S.], 6, in AAN, KC PZPR, Zbiór akt osobowych działaczy ruchu robotniczego, archival no. 10546, file of Edward Jan S.; and interview by the author with their son, Paris, March 16, 2007.

32. Interviews by the author with Piotr Sztuczyński, Warsaw, Nov. 10, Nov. 20, Nov. 24, 2006; and Jurek Neftalin, Warsaw, Nov 14–15, 2006.

33. Approximately 275,000 Jews lived in Poland between the summer of 1944 and the summer of 1947, according to Łucjan Dobroszycki. However, an additional 18,000 Polish Jews remained in the Soviet Union until the repatriation between 1955 and 1959. See Bernard D. Weinryb, "Poland," in *The Jews in the Soviet Satellites*, ed. Peter Meyer et al. (Syracuse, N.Y.: Syracuse University Press, 1953); and Lucjan Dobroszycki, *Survivors of the Holocaust in Poland: A Portrait Based on Community Records 1944–1947* (Armonk, N.Y.: M. E. Sharpe, 1994). Their estimates are supported by more recent research by Albert Stankowski, who estimated that more than 280,000 Jews emigrated from Poland between 1944 and 1970 and that 20,000 remained after 1972. See Albert Stankowski, "Nowe spojrzenie na statystyki dotyczące emigracji Żydów z Polski po 1944 roku," in Grzegorz Berendt, August Grabski, and Albert Stankowski, eds., *Studia z historii Żydów w Polsce po 1945 r.* [Studies from the history of Jews in Poland after 1945] (Warsaw: Żydowski Instytut Historyczny, 2000), 103–151.

34. See Natalia Aleksiun, *Dokąd Dalej? Ruch syjonistyczny w Polsce (1944–1950)* [Where to? The Zionist movement in Poland (1944–1950)] (Warsaw: Trio, 2002).

35. Interview with Genia Adler by Marek Pelc, Göttingen, Germany, Aug. 19, 1996. In 1945, Genia, Emil, and Stefan had not yet registered with the Central Committee of Jews in Poland.

36. "Poylishe yidn in Magnitogorsk—der onheyb fun der repatriatsye fun ural" [Polish Jews in Magnitogorsk—the beginning of the repatriation from the Urals], *Dos naye lebn*, March 23, 1946. By the end of 1945, about 10,000 Jews had returned to Poland from the Soviet Union, most of them settling in Łódź and Kraków. Between February and June 1946, another 136,550 Jews arrived in Poland from the Soviet Union. The vast majority in this larger wave were sent to the new western territories, creating Jewish communities that were substantial in size in the context of postwar Poland: 75,000 were sent to Lower Silesia, 12,000 to Upper Silesia, and nearly 31,000 to Szczecin. Only

15,000 Jews in the first half of 1946 settled in Łódź, another 4,300 in Kraków, and just 3,000 in Warsaw.

37. Interview with Yvette Metral by the author, Paris, March 15, 2007. The Polish city with the largest Jewish population in 1949, when the first repatriation from the Soviet Union ended, was Wrocław, where an estimated 12,300 Jews lived. Wałbrzych had about 5,500 Jews in that year, while nearly 5,700 Jews made up the majority of the population in the small town of Dzierżoniów nearby. See Stankowski, "Nowe spojrzenie na statystyki dotyczące emigracji Żydów z Polski po 1944 roku."

38. Interview with Feliks Falk by the author, Warsaw, Nov. 8, 2004, and Nov. 28, 2006.

39. File of Stanisława Kruc in IPN, collection of the MSW, archival no. BU 1368/633; and telephone interview with Bernard Krutz by the author, Fair Lawn, N.J., July 8, 2007.

40. ŻIH, collection of the Hebrew Immigrant Aid Society, archival no. 351/147, subfolder "Zygmunt Kaczyński."

41. Jerzy S. Majewski, "Śródmieście i jego mieszkańcy w latach niemieckiej okupacji: październik 1939–1 sierpnia 1944. Dzień powszedni" [The city center and its residents in the years of the German occupation: October 1939–August 1, 1944. An average day], in *Straty Warszawy 1939–1945: Raport* [The losses of Warsaw, 1939–1945: Report], ed. Wojciech Fałkowski (Warsaw: Miasto Stołeczne Warszawy, 2005), 76.

3. THE ENTIRE NATION BUILDS ITS CAPITAL

1. Stankowski, "Nowe spojrzenie na statystyki dotyczące emigracji Żydów z Polski po 1944 roku."

2. "Ankiety TSKŻ 1961 r., wszystkie oddziały TSKŻ w Polsce" [Surveys of the TSKŻ in 1961, all branches of the Social-Cultural Association of Jews in Poland], in ŻIH, collection of the Towarzystwo Społeczno-Kulturalne Żydów w Polsce [Social-Cultural Association of Jews in Poland, TSKŻ], Organizational Department, archival no. 114. Compare that number with the organization's estimate of 6,200 Jews in Warsaw who had contact with Jewish institutions in 1967, according to Stankowski. In 1966 Bernard Mark, director of the Jewish Historical Institute, wrote in his diary: "They say that the number of Jews in Poland . . . consists of 25,000. I think that this number is higher, since we do not know about all Jews. There are those who do not have any contact and do not come to the Jewish theater, they do not take matzah and they do not even come to the ghetto [uprising] commemoration." Diary of Bernard Mark in the Goldstein-Goren Diaspora Research Center at Tel Aviv University, Bernard and Ester Mark Bequest, P-69, 1997, entry of January 14, 1966. I am grateful to Joanna Nalewajko-Kulikov and Audrey Kichelewski for calling my attention to this diary and its archival location. Akiva Kohane of the American Jewish Joint Distribution Committee office in Geneva had a different view from Bernard Mark's. He wrote in 1961 to the organization's New York office: "No one knows how many marani [marranos] there are in Poland, there might be thousands, although I do not believe that." Cited in Stankowski, who gives the archival source as AJJDC, Givat Ram Joint Archives, Poland 1961, box. 76b, OP 263–61, "Letter from the representative of the JDC in Geneva Akiva Kohane to the representative of the JDC in New York Boris Sapir from 15.05.1961 r. about. the establishment of the JDC's statistical data for 1960." See Stankowski, "Nowe spojrzenie na statystyki dotyczące emigracji Żydów z Polski po 1944 roku." The Social-Cultural Association of Jews in Poland was the main postwar Jewish organization and was focused on secular and cultural life.

The Związek Religijny Wyznania Mojżeszowego (Religious Union of the Jewish Faith) oversaw religious life.

3. Lewis Mumford, *The Culture of Cities* (New York: Harcourt, Brace, 1938), 4.

4. Krystyna Kersten argues that wartime destruction, the long Nazi occupation, international diplomacy that favored the Soviet Union, and the failure of the uprising weakened society's morale, and that Polish society began working with the new authorities even in 1944 and early 1945 to rebuild the country, compelled to compromise because of political reality. She disputes the more widespread view that Polish society mounted a civil war against the communist authorities. See Krystyna Kersten, *The Establishment of Communist Rule in Poland,* trans. John Micgiel and Michael H. Bernhard (Berkeley: University of California Press, 1991). For an example of the opposing interpretation, see Norman Davies, *God's Playground: A History of Poland,* vol. 2 (New York: Columbia University Press, 1982), 560–561.

5. Jerzy Cegielski, *Stosunki mieszkanowe w Warszawie w latach 1864–1964* [Apartment conditions in Warsaw in 1864–1964] (Warsaw: Arkady Warszawy, 1968). Kersten, *The Establishment of Communist Rule in Poland.*

6. The nucleus of the postwar government was established in Lublin in July 1944 with the formation of the Polish Committee for National Liberation (Polski Komitet Wyzwolenia Narodowego, PKWN), which was presented as a coalition based on democratic principles, leftist but not communist. In fact, according to Kersten, although its manifesto listed Chełm as the place of publication, the PKWN was formed in Moscow. It constituted a kind of second, competing Polish government in opposition to the government-in-exile in London, the latter consisting of prewar authorities. See Kersten, *The Establishment of Communist Rule in Poland, 1943–1948.* The meeting about Warsaw is referred to in Leon Chajn, *Kiedy Lublin był Warszawa* (Warsaw: Czytelnik, 1964), 108–110, cited in Tomasz Markiewicz, "Prywatna odbudowa Warszawy," in Jerzy Kochanowski, et al., *Zbudować Warszawę Piekną. O nowy krajobraz stolicy (1944–1956)* [To build beautiful Warsaw: About the new landscape of the capital (1944–1956)] (Warsaw: Trio, 2003), 217–218.

7. Chajn, *Kiedy Lublin był Warszawa,* 218.

8. Interview by Joanna Wiszniewicz with "Henia," in Joanna Wiszniewicz, *Życie Przecięte: Opowieści pokolenia marca* [Life cut in two: Stories of the March generation] (Wołowiec, Poland: Wydawnictwo Czarne, 2008), 84.

9. Jerzy Wiland to Bierut, March 10, 1945, cited in Jerzy Kochanowski, "Balast przeszłości usunęła wojna . . . Rok 1945: trzy pomysły na odbudowę Warszawy" [The war expelled the burden of the past . . . Year 1945: Three thoughts about rebuilding Warsaw], in Kochanowski, et al., *Zbudować Warszawę Piekną,* 15–21. Kochanowski acknowledges that careerism might have motivated correspondents who wrote to leaders, but he indicates that Wiland's letter and two others he cites were representative of opinions in other letters in the same collection.

10. Henri Lefebvre, *The Production of Space,* trans. Donald Nicholson-Smith (Oxford: Blackwell, 1991), 416.

11. Leopold Tyrmand, *Dziennik 1954* [Diary 1954] (Warsaw: Res Publica, 1989), 68.

12. Roman Jasiński, *Zmierzch starego świata: Wspomnienia, 1900–1945* [Twilight of the old world: Recollections, 1900–1945] (Kraków: Wydawnictwo Literackie, 2006).

13. On the eve of the Second World War, approximately 60 percent of Warsaw Jews lived in the neighborhoods of Muranów, Grzybów, and adjacent areas; approximately

70 percent of the population in these districts was Jewish. See Eleonora Bergman, "Zydzi—nie tylko na Nalewkach" [Jews—not only on Nalewki], in *Straty Warszawy 1939–1945: Raport* [The losses of Warsaw, 1939–1945: Report], ed. Wojciech Falkowski, (Warsaw: Miasto Stołeczne Warszawy, 2005), 182–201.

14. The State Archive of the Capital City of Warsaw [Archiwum Państwowy Miasta Stołecznego Warszawy], collection of registration ledgers, aleje Ujazdowskie 16, 1903–1945, archival no. 1073/855; and aleje Ujazdowskie 16, 1942–1950, archival no. 1072/854.

15. Apolinary Hartglas, *Na pograniczu dwóch światów* [On the border of two worlds] (Warsaw: Oficyna Wydawnicza, 1996), 58. The description of Lindenfeld is from Jasiński, *Zmierzch starego świata*, 58.

16. Olczak-Ronikier, *W ogrodzie pamięci*, 100.

17. The building's heirs are listed in the State Archive of the Capital City of Warsaw, collection of registration ledgers, aleje Ujazdowskie 16, 1903–1945, archival no. 1073/855. The reference to Władysław Lindenfeld is in *Gazeta Żydowska*, March 18, 1941. Berta Lindenfeld is listed in "2001 List of Swiss Bank Accounts from the ICEP Investigation," 225, accessed on the website of the Claims Resolution Tribunal of the Holocaust Victim Assets Litigation against Swiss Banks and other Swiss Entities, http://www.crt-ii.org/2001_list/sba_publication.pdf.

18. Jan Górski, *Warszawa w latach 1944–1949:Odbudowa* [Warsaw in 1944–1949: Reconstruction] (Warsaw: PWN, 1990), 226.

19. Henryk Grynberg, *Memorbuch* (Warsaw: W.A.B., 2000), 11.

20. Interview with Wojciech Chodorowski by the author, Warsaw, Feb. 14, 2007.

21. A 1948 report indicated that Book and Knowledge owned the building, but a 1963 review of the real estate of the government's umbrella publishing institution, RSW-Prasa (Robotnicza Spółdzielnia Wydawnicza—Prasa; Workers' Publishing Cooperative—Press), lists 16 Ujazdowskie Avenue as one of its properties. For the 1948 report, see AAN, KC PPR, archival number 295/XVII-24, p. 7, pp. 51–52. For the 1963 report, see "RSW 'Prasa' Main Governing Board, Economic Department—Department of Planning, Statistics and Audits, Report of the Governing Board of Warsaw Real Estate of RSW 'Prasa' from 1962–63," 256, in AAN, RSW "Prasa," archival number 16/99.

22. Interview with Wojciech Chodorowski by the author, Warsaw, Feb. 14, 2007.

23. Interviews by the author with Jurek Neftalin, Warsaw, Nov. 14–15, 2006; and with Włodek Paszyński, Warsaw, Nov. 4, 2004 and Nov. 30, 2006.

24. Jerzy Urban, "Dom i Kamienica" [Home and tenement], in Jerzy Urban, *Cały Urban* (Warsaw: Książka i Wiedza, 1989), 86.

25. The State Archive of the Capital City of Warsaw, collection of registration ledgers, archival no. 1073/855, aleje Ujazdowskie 16, 1903–1945, and archival no. 1072/854, aleje Ujazdowskie 16, 1942–1950. Also see Jasiński, *Zmierzch starego świata*, 58.

26. Interview with Wojciech Chodorowski by the author, Warsaw, Feb. 14, 2007.

27. Szymon Rudnicki recalled that after the emigration wave of 1968 to 1970, a police employee and his family moved into an apartment at 16 Ujazdowskie Avenue. I was not able to confirm this with archival documentation, but his recollection dovetails with a point raised by the historian Jerzy Eisler, who asked: "What happened to the several thousand apartments left by the emigrants? This embarrassing question is rarely posed. If we assume that on average four people lived in one apartment, we are talking about 4,000 apartments, often in prime locations. Someone had to move in after the emigrants left. It is hard to believe it was the proverbial Łódź weaver with six children or a worker

from the Warsaw Steel Mills. It seems much more probable that the apartments were given to those who distinguished themselves in the antisemitic campaign." See Jerzy Eisler, "1968: Jews, Antisemitism, Emigration," *Polin* 21 (2009): 58.

28. The State Archive of the Capital City of Warsaw, collection of registration ledgers, archival no. 1073/855, aleje Ujazdowskie 16, 1903–1945, and archival no. 1072/854, aleje Ujazdowskie 16, 1942–1950. See also "Alphabetical registry of Polish Jews who survived the Second World War," in ŻIH, collection of the CKŻP, folders: Apolonia Miller, archival no. 18497; Izak Miller, 18518; Paulina Miller, 18530; Małgorzata Lebiediew, 16022; Ilia Lebiediew, 16021; Michał Lebiediew, 16024; Jerzy Gelbfisz, 2654; Zygmunt Gelbfisz, 2663; Dyoniza Gelbfisz, 2656; and interview with Wojciech Chodorowski by the author, Feb. 14, 2007.

29. "Alphabetical registry of Polish Jews who survived the Second World War" in ŻIH, collection of the CKŻP, folders: Jerzy Gelbfisz, 2654; Zygmunt Gelbfisz, 2663; Dyoniza Gelbfisz, 2656. Three boys who grew up in the building's front section after the war—Ryszard Kaczyński as well as the brothers Jurek Neftalin and Piotr Sztuczyński —remembered another Jewish family in the back, that of Jerzy Mering, an attorney and communist party member who provided legal help to the Home Army soldier Władysław Bartoszewski during his Stalinist-era imprisonment for wartime activity in the Polish underground. Bartoszewski was imprisoned in 1946 and again in 1949 on accusations of spying. He was released in 1954. According to a book-length interview with Bartoszewski published in 2006, Mering immigrated to Israel with his family in 1957. However, there is no documentation in the city building registry or the CKŻP registry that Mering and his family lived at 16 Ujazdowskie Avenue. Michał Komar, *Władysław Bartoszewski: Skąd pan jest? Wywiad rzeka* (Warsaw: Świat Książki, 2006), 182–183, 187.

30. Błażej Brzostek, *Za progiem. Codzienność w przestrzeni publicznej Warszawy lat 1955–1970* [Beyond the threshhold: Daily life in the public sphere of Warsaw in 1955–1970] (Warsaw: Trio, 2007), 48; and David Crowley, "Warsaw Interiors: The Public Life of Private Spaces, 1949–65," in *Socialist Spaces: Sites of Everyday Life in the Eastern Bloc*, ed. David Crowley and Susan E. Reid, 181–206 (Oxford: Berg, 2002).

31. Interviews by the author with Waleria M., Warsaw, Aug. 17, Sept. 13, Sept. 20, and Oct. 4, 2004; and with Krystyna Heldwein, Warsaw, June 23, 2007.

32. Cited in Brzostek, *Za progiem*, 50.

33. Telephone interview with Bernard Krutz, Fair Lawn, N.J., July 8, 2007.

34. IPN, collection of the MSW, archival no. BU 0236/37, folder 6, 258.

35. See ch. 4, notes 39 and 40, of this volume.

36. Charlotte Fonrobert's studies of the *eruv* as a delineation of Jewish space that served a symbolic role in conceptualizing Jewish community point to the mutually reinforcing connections among Jewish observance, space, and community in traditional Jewish societies. See Charlotte E. Fonrobert, "The Political Symbolism of the Eruv," *Jewish Social Studies* 11, no. 3 (2005): 11; and Fonrobert, "From Separatism to Urbanism: The Dead Sea Scrolls and the Origins of the Rabbinic Eruv," *Dead Sea Discoveries* 11, no. 1 (2004): 43–71. For broader perspectives on the role of space in the construction of community and identity in Jewish history, see Barbara E. Mann, *A Place in History: Modernism, Tel Aviv, and the Creation of Jewish Urban Space* (Stanford, Calif.: Stanford University Press, 2006), ch. 1; and Charlotte Fonrobert and Vered Shemtov, "Introduction: Jewish Conceptions and Practices of Space," *Jewish Social Studies* 11, no. 3 (2005): 1–8.

37. Marsha Rozenblit, *The Jews of Vienna, 1867–1914: Assimilation and Identity* (Albany: State University of New York Press, 1983); Gary B. Cohen, *The Politics of Ethnic Survival: Germans in Prague, 1861–1914*, 2nd ed., rev. (West Lafayette, Ind.: Purdue University, 2006), 101–102; and Stanley Waterman and Barry A. Kosmin, "Residential Patterns and Processes: A Study of Jews in Three London Boroughs," *Transactions of the Institute of British Geographers*, new series, 13, no. 1 (1988): 79–95. Benjamin Nathans found a similar phenomenon in St. Petersburg among Jews whose jobs and other factors gave them permission to settle in the city. Benjamin Nathans, *Beyond the Pale: The Jewish Encounter with Late Imperial Russia* (Berkeley: University of California, 2002), 113–122.

4. STAMP OF A GENERATION

Bolesław Leśmian (1877–1937), popular Polish poet and writer of Jewish background.

1. The Adler family was required to compile a list of each book they brought with them when they emigrated. This list is in the personal papers of Emil and Genia Adler, Göttingen, Germany.

2. Emil Adler to Marian Adler, July 29, 1959, Personal papers of Emil and Genia Adler, Göttingen, Germany. When an individual celebrates a birthday, the expression in Polish is literally to "finish the year," so when Marian turned twelve, the expression would have been to "finish the twelfth year" and begin his thirteenth year. This seems to be the basis for Emil's reference to his son "reaching the thirteenth year" on his son's twelfth birthday. It is unclear, however, whether Emil's letter on Marian's twelfth birthday is connected with this Polish expression or with the Jewish custom by which the father sometimes begins preparing the son for his bar mitzvah after he turns twelve.

3. The phrasing "liturgical vestments" is a literal translation from Emil Adler's Polish, and the explanation of tefillin is Adler's as well. The characterization of Marian's childhood understanding of his Jewish background is based on an interview with Marian Adler by the author, Göttingen, Germany, Dec. 2–3, 2006.

4. Underlined phrases are in the original.

5. Personal papers of Emil and Genia Adler, Göttingen, Germany, for example letter from Genia to Emil, June 5, 1946. The recollection of the families sharing an apartment is from an interview with Zofia Zarębska by the author, Warsaw, July 12, 2004, and Aug. 2, 2004.

6. Emil Adler to Genia Adler, July 24, 1946, 1. Personal papers of Emil and Genia Adler, Göttingen, Germany.

7. Ibid., 2.

8. Emil Adler, "W Łódźi na Piotrkowskiej" [In Łódź on Piotrkowska Street], 4. Personal papers of Emil and Genia Adler, Göttingen, Germany. The Book offices in early postwar Łódź were on Piotrkowska Street.

9. Stankowski, "Nowe spojrzenie na statystyki dotyczące emigracji Żydów z Polski po 1944 roku."

10. In a 1971 document in Germany after the Adlers' emigration, Genia explained that after the Kielce pogrom, she changed her parents' names on all official documents, substituting "Moszek and Mariem Sztarksztejn, maiden name Szulman," with "Kazimierz and Maria Zagielski, born Rakowska." In this 1971 document Genia provides her given name as Gita. Zagielski was based on her deceased husband's surname Zagiel. Personal papers of Emil and Genia Adler, Göttingen, Germany.

11. AAN, Main Commission for Control of the Press, Publications and Performances [Główny Urząd Kontroli Prasy Publikacji i Widowisk, GUKPPiW], archival no. 146 (31/39), 105–107. *Mendel Gdański* was first published in 1890 in a literary journal in Warsaw.

12. AAN, GUKPPiW, archival number 146 (31/45), p. 127. *Mirtala* is set in Rome after the failure of the first-century Jewish rebellion against the Romans and the destruction of Jerusalem, and the novel describes increasingly strained relations between Jews and Romans in Rome. Because Orzeszkowa published her novel in 1886, some readers interpreted it as a commentary on the Warsaw pogrom five years earlier, according to Israel Bartal and Magdalena Opalski's analysis of Polish positivist novels with Jewish themes. However, Bartal and Opalski note that Orzeszkowa intended the story as an allegory for Russian persecution of Poles and the continued goal of Polish independence. Orzeszkowa cited this motivation in a letter to her editor, according to their research. See Magdalena Opalski and Israel Bartal, *Poles and Jews: A Failed Brotherhood* (Hanover, N.H.: Brandeis University Press, 1992), 126–127; and Eliza Orzeszkowa, *Mirtala: Powieść* (Warsaw: S. Lewental, 1886).

13. The report to the censor is in AAN, GUKPPiW, archival no. 146 (31/45), 202, referring to Eliza Orzeszkowa's *Meir Ezofowicz*, which was first published in 1878.

14. Interview with Jurek Neftalin by the author, Warsaw, Nov. 14–15, 2006.

15. Interview with Liliana Tyszelman by the author, Warsaw, Dec. 1, 2006.

16. Surveillance from the apartment was cited in a file containing information about a resident of 16 Ujazdowskie Avenue in the Ministry of Internal Affairs archive at the Institute for National Remembrance. No other information could be located. For privacy reasons, I have not cited the name of the family in whose apartment the surveillance took place or the specific archival file.

17. Postcard from Stefan Bergman to Emil and Genia Adler, June 28, 1981. Personal papers of Emil and Genia Adler, Göttingen, Germany.

18. Interview with Daniel Passent by the author, Warsaw, Aug. 29, 2004, and Oct. 23, 2004. Passent is now a prominent writer for the Polish newsweekly *Polityka*.

19. Personnel file of Barbara H., archive of Book and Knowledge, unpaginated.

20. Minutes from this March meeting are missing from the archive. However, reference to the meeting and what was described as a summary of the discussion are located in a document titled "Protocol no. 11. From the closed meeting of the POP PZPR KiW [Primary Party Cell of the Polish United Workers' Party of Book and Knowledge] /Smolna Street 13/ on 14 April 1956," 66–90, in the State Archive of the Capital City of Warsaw, collection of the Publishing Cooperative "Book and Knowledge" Primary Party Cell of the PZPR. A translation of Khrushchev's speech is in Ronald Grigor Suny, ed., *The Structure of Soviet History: Essays and Documents* (New York: Oxford University Press, 2003).

21. Protocol no. 11, 66–90. It is unclear whether the Book and Knowledge leaders eventually submitted the minutes to the authorities; they could not be located in the party cell records or in records of the party's Central Committee in the AAN.

22. Protocol no. 11, 76–77.

23. AAN KC PZPR, archival no. 237/VIII-1110, 1, 6, 9, 10, 18–21, 26–28.

24. Protocol no. 12, 104–106, in the State Archive of the Capital City of Warsaw, collection of the Publishing Cooperative "Book and Knowledge" Primary Party Cell of the PZPR.

25. Ibid., 106.

26. "Undzer veytik un undzer treyst" [Our pain and our consolation], *Folks-shtime*, April 4, 1956. See also Smolar, *Oyf der letster pozitsye*, 215–221.

27. Protocol 21, meeting of the presidium on April 29, 1957, addendum 1, in the Archive of the Main Governing Board of the TSKŻ.

28. For reports on this incident and more minor ones in this period, see, among others, in the collection of TSKŻ's Organizational Department in the ŻIH archives: letters from the TSKŻ's Dzierżoniów branch from September to December 1956, archival no. 89; meeting minutes of the Wrocław branch's presidium on March 6, 1957, archival no. 118; and minutes of the TSKŻ main governing board meeting on October 29, 1956, archival no. 102, Łódź branch.

29. Smolar, *Oyf der letster pozitsye*, 251–258.

30. The security police compiled dozens of folders on Ekerling and Jewish communal organizations as part of their investigation into Piasecki's murder. They are located in IPN, collection of the MSW, including archival no. MSW/SGO 0747/116; archival no. MSW/SGO 0747/118; and archival no. MSW/SGO 0747/30, folders 1–35.

31. See Eleonora Bergman, "Yiddish in Poland after 1945," in *Yiddish and the Left*, ed. Gennady Estraikh and Mikhail Krutikov (Oxford: Oxford University Press, 2001), 167–176.

32. Protocol 1, meeting of the presidium, Jan. 3, 1957, Archive of the Main Governing Board of the TSKŻ.

33. David Sfard, *Mit zikh un mit andere: Oytobiyografye un literarishe eseyen* [By oneself and with others: Autobiography and literary essays] (Jerusalem: Farlag Yerushalaymer almanakh, 1984), 222–224. Sfard quotes here from Kon's untitled poem that begins "I have a vast, endless cemetery," in Naftali Herts Kon, *Farshribn in zikorn* [Written down in memory] (Tel Aviv: Aliyah Press, 1966), 96.

34. IPN, collection of the MSW, archival no. 00231/209, folder 13, 167–169.

35. Ibid.

36. Interview with Jan and Francis Sławny by the author, Paris, March 13, 2007.

37. "Władysław Sławny, Akta Osobowe Cudzoziemca" [Personal record of a foreigner], 3, in IPN, collection of the MSW, archival no. BU 1368/5137.

38. "Stanisława Kruc, Akta Osobowe Cudzoziemca" [Personal record of a foreigner], Jan. 23, 1957, in IPN, collection of the MSW, archival no. BU 1368/633. Interview with Stefania Fedecka's son by the author, Paris, March 15, 2007.

39. Interview with Lena Rabinowicz by the author, Warsaw, July 3, 2007. The Przewalskis' role in hiding the girl is cited in Władysław Bartoszewski and Zofia Lewinówna, *Ten jest z ojczyzny mojej* [This is from my homeland] (Warsaw: Żydowski Instytut historyczny and Świat Książki, 2007), 187–189.

40. It is unclear whether Nina Sztuczyńska's postwar residence in the same building as Edward was coincidental or the result of wartime connections. Both Nina, in a conversation with her son Jurek Neftalin, and Edward, in a postwar record, indicated that communist circles through which they provided assistance to Jews in Warsaw during the war were connected with Teodor Duracz, a lawyer for whom Edward worked before the war and who was active in the prewar publishing house Book, which was a precursor of Book and Knowledge. See the collection of Teodor Duracz in AAN, archival no. 105/II-6; and "Życiorys," 3–4, in AAN, Zbiór akt osobowych działaczy ruchu robotniczego, archival no. 10546. Sztuczyńska knew another non-Jewish neighbor at 16 Ujazdowskie Avenue, the Teslar family, before the war. Interview with Jurek Neftalin by the author, Warsaw, Nov. 14–15, 2006.

41. Genia Adler to Emil Adler, December 27, 1959. Personal papers of Emil and Genia Adler, Göttingen, Germany.

42. Szymon Rudnicki, "Wspomnienia: Stefan Bergman," *Kwartalnik Historii Żydow*, no. 211 (2004): 414.

43. Ibid.

44. Interview with Marian Adler by the author, Göttingen, Germany, Dec. 2–3, 2006. A request that Emil Adler submitted in April 1968 to the rector of Warsaw University for two days off to travel to Brody for family reasons supports Marian's collection. Archive of Warsaw University, file of Emil Adler, archival no. 5186, unpaginated.

45. Emil Adler, *Herder i Oświecenie Niemieckie* [Herder and the German Enlightenment] (Warsaw: PWN, 1965), 356–357. The parenthetical phrase is Adler's.

46. Adler wrote about Spinoza several times in the early 1960s. A review essay, "Spinozyzm a Spór o 'Prometeusza'" [Spinozism and the Dispute about "Prometheus"], for example, includes this passage: "It might seem strange that the philosophy of Spinoza was the source of such deep humanistic inspiration for Herder (and for Goethe). Because such direct conclusions did not arise from Spinoza's system. Not only opponents of the thinker, but also his adherents saw this. Heine, responding to the accusation of atheism, which ' . . . could only be found in Spinoza's scholarship out of stupidity and envy,' added, 'Rather than saying that Spinoza renounces God, it would be possible to say that he renounces man.'" Emil Adler, "Spinozyzm a Spór o 'Prometeusza,'" *Studia Filozoficzne* 4 no. 25 (1961): 202. Annette Aronowicz has explored the influence of, and interest in, Spinoza by Jewish communists; see Annette Aronowicz, "Spinoza among the Jewish Communists," *Modern Judaism* 24, no. 1 (2004): 1–35.

5. OSTRICHES IN THE WILDERNESS

The phrase "ostriches in the wilderness" is from an interview by the sociologist Joanna Wiszniewicz with a Polish Jew who emigrated after 1968, describing assimilating children who attended his Jewish summer camp in Poland in the 1960s. The words are from the biblical verse Lamentations 4:3: "Even jackals offer their breast and suckle their young ones; the daughter of my people has become cruel, like the ostriches in the wilderness." The phrase in the interviewee's usage seems to refer to the absence of Jewish identity transmitted from parents to children.

1. Interview with Genia Adler by Marek Pelc, Göttingen, Germany, Aug. 19, 1996.

2. As a result of the anti-Jewish purges, which reached their height between March and June 1968, 5,000–6,000 people of Jewish origin were fired from jobs or expelled from the party. Jerzy Eisler estimates the number at 9,000. See Paul Lendvai, *Antisemitism without Jews: Communist Eastern Europe* (Garden City, N.Y.: Doubleday, 1971) 136, 173, 188; Jerzy Eisler, *Polski Rok 1968* (Warsaw: IPN, 2006). There are no decisive data on the number of émigrés after the start of the antisemitic propaganda in 1967 and in the wake of the March protests in 1968. The Dutch embassy in Poland, acting on Israel's behalf, issued about 20,000 visas, although it is difficult to confirm how many recipients used the documents. Albert Stankowski, using varied archival sources, gives the figure of 12,927 for the number of émigrés between 1968 and 1972, and 11,185 for the years 1967 to 1970, without determining a figure for the entire period between 1967 and 1972. Stankowski's numbers are conservative, and Eisler, in particular, is critical of the lower estimates. He places the number of émigrés at 15,000–20,000. See Stankowski, "Nowe spojrzenie na

statystyki dotyczące emigracji Żydów z Polski po 1944 roku"; and Eisler, "1968: Jews, Antisemitism, Emigration," 55.

3. IPN, collection of the MSW, archival no. BU 0204/111, 21–23.

4. Interview with Włodek Paszyński by the author, Warsaw, Nov. 30, 2006.

5. Ibid. In the poem, Mickiewicz yearns for Lithuania, which was part of the Polish-Lithuanian Commonwealth until the partitions of Poland at the end of the eighteenth century. The first lines read: "O Lithuania, my country, thou art like good health; I never knew till now how precious, till I lost thee. Now I see thy beauty whole, because I yearn for thee." Adam Mickiewicz, *Pan Tadeusz*, trans. Kenneth R. Mackenzie (New York: Hippocrene Books, 1992), 2.

6. Interview with Włodek Paszyński by the author, Warsaw, Nov. 4, 2004, and Nov. 30, 2006.

7. Ibid.

8. Interview with Szymon Rudnicki by the author, Warsaw, Nov. 19, 2006.

9. Archive of the TPD, Wydział Szkół, Kat. A, IV 5S, 26, "Statystyka szkół TPD, rok 1954/55 i 1955/56 (i przedszkoli)" [Statistics of the TPD schools, 1954/55 and 1955/56 (and preschools)]. Joanna Wiszniewicz conducted the first research on the attendance of Jewish youth at the schools of the Society for the Friends of Children, based on extensive interviews. In English, see "Jewish Children and Youth in Downtown Warsaw Schools of the 1960s," *Polin: Studies in Polish Jewry* 21 (2008): 204–229.

10. Interviews by the author with Szymon Rudnicki, Warsaw, May 15, 2004; and with Włodek Paszyński, Warsaw, Nov. 30, 2006.

11. Wiszniewicz makes this argument as well. See Wiszniewicz, "Jewish Children and Youth in Downtown Warsaw Schools of the 1960s," 213–215.

12. Wilhelm Dichter, *Koń pana boga, Szkoła bezbożników* [God's horse: School of the Godless] (Kraków: Znak, 2003), 295. Dichter's building was at Puławska 26a, south of the city center, and was home to party officials, including several of Jewish background.

13. About Jewish schools in early postwar Poland, see Helena Datner-Śpiewak, "Instytucje opieki nad dzieckiem i szkoły powszechne Centralnego Komitetu Żydów Polskich w latach 1945–1946" [Institutions of care for children and elementary schools of the Central Committee of Jews in Poland in 1945–1946], *Biuletyn Żydowskiego Instytutu Historycznego* 117 (1981): 37–52; and Helena Datner, "Szkoły Centralnego Komitetu Żydów w Polsce w latach 1944–1949" [Schools of the Central Committee of Jews in Poland in 1944–1949], *Biuletyn Żydowskiego Instytutu Historycznego* 169–171 (1994): 103–119.

14. Interview with Jurek Neftalin by the author, Warsaw, Nov. 14–15, 2006.

15. Ibid.

16. Interviews by Wiszniewicz with Marta Petrusewicz and Władek Poznański in Wiszniewicz, *Życie Przecięte*, 35–56, 211.

17. For the development of the image of the Jew as the "other," see Joanna Michlic, *Poland's Threatening Other: The Image of the Jew from 1880 to the Present* (Lincoln: University of Nebraska Press, 2006).

18. Archive of the Ministry of Education, collection of the Office of the Minister, archival no. 144, 1957, 85–88 and 267.

19. Letter to the governing board of the Society for the Friends of Children, February 6, 1957, in the Archive of the Ministry of Education, collection of the Office of the Minister, archival no. 144, 1957, 298–299, 136–137.

20. According to the *Folks-shtime,* the Society for the Secular School was established by parents, teachers, and "education activists" in response to the December 1956 decrees on religious instruction. "Geshafn a gezelshaft far veltlekhe shuln in Poyln" [A society of secular schools in Poland is established], *Folks-shtime,* Jan. 26, 1957. It is unclear whether the new society was connected informally to the TPD or whether the government was behind its establishment, but according to a letter from Bishop Choromański to the minister of education, "all 18 secular schools existing in Warsaw had been under the patronage of the TPD before 1956, so they are located in new, spacious buildings and modernly equipped." Antoni Dudek, *Komuniści i Kościół w Polsce, 1945–1989* (Kraków: Znak, 2003), 129. Documents in the Ministry of Education from 1957 often refer to "former TPD schools" when referring to controversies over religious instruction.

21. Archive of the Ministry of Education, collection of the Office of the Minister, archival no. 145, 1957, 145–146.

22. Report dated Oct. 11, 1958, in the archive of the Ministry of Education, collection of the Office of the Minister, archival no. 146, 1958, 178–187. The letter from Wyszyński is cited in Dudek, *Komuniści i Kościół,* 153.

23. Stankowski, for example, cites a June 1956 case in which a student wrote "away with the Jews" on the blackboard of a tenth-grade class at a Society for the Friends of Children school in Łódź. Stankowski, "Nowe spojrzenie na statystyki dotyczące emigracji Żydów z Polski po 1944 roku." In the 1960s, as Audrey Kichelewski noted, incidents at school were common among parents' complaints to the authorities about antisemitism. See Audrey Kichelewski, "A Community under Pressure: Jews in Poland, 1957–1967," *Polin: Studies in Polish Jewry* 21 (2009): 176.

24. Tosia Klugman and Aleksander Klugman, ... *A droga wiodła przez Łódź* [And the road passes through Łódź] (Łódź: Biblioteka "Tygla Kultury," 2004), 92–96. Roman Zambrowski, "Dziennik" [Diary], *Krytyka* 6 (1980): 76, cited in Dudek, *Komuniści i Kościół,* 121–122. Zambrowski's son Antoni, who attended a Society for the Friends of Children elementary school with Szymon Rudnicki, was at least twenty-one by 1956, so Zambrowski would not have been referring to his own son's experiences at the time.

25. Interview by Wiszniewicz with "Ewa" in Wiszniewicz, *Życie Przecięte,* 63. Juliusz Słowacki, like Mickiewicz, was one of the most beloved nineteenth-century Polish poets and playwrights of the Romantic period.

26. In January 1966 an informant reported to the security police about a meeting of the youth commission of the Social-Cultural Association's main governing board. According to her report, a board member told the gathering that "Jewish society in Poland, as a result of continued and systematic emigration, to a large degree will continue to shrink in the future. Aside from this, there exists the process of assimilation, which causes the Polonization of Jewish society, which will not comprise a separate group in any real sense. This process, in Łozowski's [?] opinion, will take place regardless of the efforts to counteract it." The speaker continued, according to the informant, that the board must "come to terms with the fact that Polish Jews who do not emigrate will assimilate." Although other evidence of the speech could not be found and informants' reports are not necessarily accurate, the report reflects sentiments expressed elsewhere. In Bytom in western Poland, for example, the topics discussed by the Jewish youth club each Sunday reflected divergent and diverse concerns, including "The problem of assimilation among Jewish youth in Poland," "Perspectives for Jews in Poland," and "Relationship to the state of Israel—a representative of Jews in the world." IPN, collection

of the MSW, archival no. BU 0236/85, 10; and IPN, collection of the MSW, archival no. 00231/229 folder 29, 48–49.

27. In the 1957–1958 school year, for example, the Social-Cultural Association reported that repatriation had made it possible to maintain attendance in its schools, citing 150 children of repatriate families who had registered in Legnica and 80 each in Wrocław and Łódź. In 1953, however, Jewish schools in Kraków and three smaller cities were closed because of the small number of students, angering parents, but in the 1960–1961 school year, after the emigration wave of the second half of the 1950s, the numbers had decreased only slightly, with just under 1,570 students attending ten elementary schools and 250 students in three lyceum. See "Informacja o szkołach z dodatkową nauką języka żydowskiego" [Information about schools with additional instruction in Yiddish], 16–22; and "O szkolnictwie z żydowskim językiem nauczeniem" [About schooling with Yiddish language instruction], 3–4, in IPN, collection of the MSW, archival no. MSW II 9150. The numbering in the archival folder is not consecutive.

28. Interview by Wiszniewicz with "Marek," in Wiszniewicz, *Życie Przecięte*, 163–164.

29. "Projekt preliminarza budżetowego akcji kolonii letnich na rok 1967" [Plan for the preliminary budget for the operation of summer camps in 1967], 1–2, in IPN, collection of the MSW, archival no. MSW II 9145. In the 1964–1965 school year, the Social-Cultural Association operated five elementary schools with 424 students and three middle schools with 248 students, a decline of two-thirds from the 1960–1961 school year. IPN, collection of the MSW, archival no. MSW II 9150, 16–17. The 1967 population number is from Stankowski.

30. IPN, collection of the MSW, archival no. MSW II 9145, 1–2. In 1967, 2,200 youth attended fourteen camps operated by the Social-Cultural Association throughout Poland.

31. IPN, collection of the MSW, archival no. MSW II 9150, 45–47. A separate report in 1968 about the youth clubs indicated that an estimated 195 individuals were enrolled in Yiddish courses in fifteen cities, including about 20 in Warsaw. IPN, collection of the MSW, archival no. MSW II 9143. The reference to the *Nasz Głos* offices is from an interview with Marek Web by the author, New York, Dec. 20–21, 2007.

32. Kichelewski, "A Community under Pressure," 172.

33. In a 1966 Social-Cultural Association report, a section on "Our youth" referred to "3,000 children and youth grouped around the TSKZ—in state Jewish schools, summer camps, youth clubs, student circles. Our youth generally have respectable and positive relations to the Association. But there are also among them those for whom the issues of Jewish circles are still not entirely understood. Some youth have various doubts regarding Jewish culture in our country and in the world. Some of them have succumbed to nationalist sentiments." See "Referat sprawozdawczy Zarządu Głównego Towarzystwa Społeczno-Kulturalnego Żydów w Polsce za okres od IV-go do V-go Krajowego Zjazdu (grudzień 1961-marzec 1966). Do użytku wewnętrznego" [Report summary of the Main Governing Board of the Social-Cultural Association of Jews in Poland for the period from the Fourth to the Fifth National Convention (December 1961 to March 1966). For internal use], 6–7, in IPN, collection of the MSW, archival no. BU MSWII 830, 13v–14. In a different report, the association's leaders noted that in 1965, emigration to Israel was a "constant topic among youth" in Jewish schools. Correspondence with friends who had already emigrated had a particular influence on the students, the leaders reported. See IPN, collection of the MSW, archival no. MSWII 9150, 20. Kichelewski cites similar concerns among leaders of the TSKŻ's women's section about what they referred to as

"nationalist deviation" among youth in Łódź. See Kichelewski, "A Community under Pressure," 171.

34. Interview by Wiszniewicz with Bronka Karst in Wiszniewicz, *Życie Przecięte*, 47–48.

35. Conversation with Teresa Pollin by the author, Washington, D.C., September 2008; and interview by Wiszniewicz with Leon Rozenbaum, in Wiszniewicz, *Życie Przecięte*, 121.

36. Interview by Wiszniewicz with Leon Rozenbaum, in Wiszniewicz, *Życie Przecięte*, 122.

37. In 1967 there were twenty-one clubs for younger Jewish children and five for older students. IPN, collection of the MSW, archival no. MSW II 9150, 45–47. According to a Social-Cultural Association report, 1,450 students belonged to twenty youth clubs in the 1966–1967 school year. The largest clubs were in Wrocław, with 300 students; Legnica, with 160 students; Warsaw, with 150 students; and Łódź, with 120 students. IPN, collection of the MSW, archival no. MSW II 9143.

38. Interview by Wiszniewicz with "Ewa," in Wiszniewicz, *Życie Przecięte*, 58–59. The Polish-Jewish writer Henryk Grynberg wrote about the youth, "They did not understand a word of Yiddish and they were not interested even a little in what we staged there [at the Jewish theatre]." Grynberg, "Wygnania z Polski" [Exile from Poland], in *Kultura* (Paris), no. 11, cited in Alina Cała and Helena Datner, eds., *Dzieje Żydów w Polsce, 1944–1968* [The history of Jews in Poland, 1944–1968] (Warsaw: Żydowski Instytut Historyczny, 1997), 261–262.

39. Eisler, *Polski Rok 1968*, 62.

40. Interview by Wiszniewicz with Marta Pertusewicz, in Wiszniewicz, *Życie Przecięte*, 40.

41. Ibid., 39.

42. Both Jerzy Eisler and Jacek Kuroń refer to disagreements among the circles, mainly one group centered on Adam Michnik and the other on Józef Dajczgewand. Less-privileged students from outside Warsaw who lived in university dormitories were among the latter group, which accused the Michnik circle of being isolated from the concerns of most students. See Eisler, *Polski Rok 1968*, 65–66, 83–84; and Jacek Kuroń, *Autobiografia* (Warsaw: Wydawnictwo Krytyki Politycznej, 2009).

43. Kuroń, *Autobiografia*. Eisler cites an estimate of twenty to one hundred individuals associated with the "komandości" group. Eisler, *Polski Rok 1968*, 84–85. One of Wiszniewicz's interviewees noted that although students in Michnik's club were generally wealthier and came from more privileged families than her own, the group was not a closed circle. Interview by Wiszniewicz with Małgorzata Tal in Wiszniewicz, *Życie przecięte*, 106–108.

44. Eisler, *Polski Rok 1968*, 56.

45. "Chamy" i "Żydy" referred to groupings within the communist party after 1956: the Puławy grouping, which was relatively reformist and included a significant number of Jews, and the Natolin grouping, which were more nationalist and emphasized the presence of Jews among their opponents.

46. "Excerpt from protocol no. 31/176/63," December 2, 1963, in the archive of Book and Knowledge, personnel file of Stefan Bergman, unpaginated; and "Minutes from the meeting of the presidium of Book and Knowledge's supervisory board," January 18, 1963, Book and Knowledge archive, personnel file of Józef Tyszelman, unpaginated.

47. "Minutes from the meeting of the presidium of Book and Knowledge's supervisory board," January 18, 1963, in the Book and Knowledge archive, personnel file of Józef Tyszelman, unpaginated.

48. Leszek W. Głuchowski and Antony Polonsky, "Introduction," *Polin* 21 (2009): 6. Audrey Kichelewski emphasizes the economic decline in Poland and cutbacks in staffing in the party and state administration after 1956 into the 1960s as context for the dismissals of Jews. See Kichelewski, "A Community under Pressure," 166–167.

49. "Notatka w sprawie wyników kontroli gospodarki transportowej RSW 'Prasa'" [Note on the results of the inspection of the transport management of RSW "Prasa"], May 8, 1964, in AAN, KC PZPR, archival no. VII/21, 488–495; and "Note on the matter of the responsibility of the Governing Board of RSW 'Prasa' for the misappropriation of funds and economic harm ensuing at the cooperative," in AAN KC PZPR, archival no. VII/21, 496–498.

50. Diary of Ber Mark, entry of December 23, 1965. For a Polish translation by Joanna Nalewajko-Kulikov, see Bernard Mark, "Dziennik (Grudzień 1965-Luty 1966)," *Kwartalnik Historii Żydow*, no. 226 (2008): 156–192.

51. Mark diary, entry of December 23, 1965.

52. Ibid.

53. For more on this incident, see Lendvai, *Antisemitism without Jews*, 189; and Eisler, *Polski Rok 1968*, 158–164.

54. Mark diary, entry of December 23, 1965. The assertion from former colleagues about tensions between Smolar and Mark is from Yankev Vasershtrum [Jakub Wasersztrum], "Oyfklerungen un bamerkungen (Clarifications and comments)," in *Der Tsadik in Pelts: Zamlung fun artiklen* (Tel Aviv: Orli, 1985), 37–38. I am grateful to August Grabski for calling my attention to this publication.

55. Mark diary, entry of December 23, 1965.

56. Ibid., entry of January 5, 1966.

57. Ibid., entry of January 12, 1966.

58. Ibid., entry of January 10, 1966. For Mark's biography, see Joanna Nalewajko-Kulikov, "O marcu przed marcem. Wprowadzenie do zapisków Bernarda Marka" [About March before March. Introduction to Bernard Mark's Notes], *Kwartalnik Historii Żydów*, no. 226 (2008): 153–155.

59. Szymon Datner to the Minister of Internal Affairs, Aug. 20, 1969, ŻIH, collection of the secretariat, incoming and outgoing correspondence from 1969, unpaginated.

60. Interview by Wiszniewicz with "Włodek," in Wiszniewicz, *Życie Przecięte*, 341–342.

61. IPN, collection of the MSW, archival no. BU 0296/135 folder 1, page 22.

62. Report from June 26 (28?), 1967, "Data of people of Jewish nationality employed in essential economic institutions and other institutions (data incomplete)," in IPN, collection of the MSW, archival no. BU 0365/41, folder 5, 167–170.

63. Report from June 16, 1967, 3–5, in AAN, archival no. 237/XIX-191. See also Eisler, *Polski Rok 1968*, 104. The security police alleged that young people made up most of the audience, but according to Eisler, citing his interview with Henryk Szlajfer, a student opposition leader who was at the meeting, most of the audience consisted of older people. Eisler, "1968: Jews, Antisemitism, Emigration," 43. For the security police's evaluation, see Grzegorz Sołtysiak and Józef Stępień, *Marzec '68. Między tragedią a podłością* (Warsaw: Profi, 1998), 11.

64. For a narrative of the events, see especially Eisler, *Polski Rok 1968;* Eisler, "1968: Jews, Antisemitism, Emigration"; and Dariusz Stola, "The Hate Campaign of March 1968: How Did It Become Anti-Jewish?" *Polin: Studies in Polish Jewry* 21 (2009): 16–36.

65. Cited in Stola, "The Hate Campaign of March 1968," 20. Stola notes that the government's antisemitic campaign beginning in 1967 and its attempt to stifle the political opposition did not coalesce until the March events. Only then did the "anti-Zionist" campaign become a tool of the crackdown on the students. See Stola, "The Hate Campaign of March 1968," 17.

66. IPN, collection of the MSW, archival no. BU, MSW II 831, 438–439.

67. "Sytuacja w wydawnictwie 'idisz buch'—na rece sekretarza ZG TSKŻ, tow. E. Rajber" [Situation in the publishing house "Yiddish Book"—for the secretary of the main governing board of the Social-Cultural Association of Jews in Poland, Comrade E. Rajber], January 28, 1969, in IPN, collection of the MSW, archival no. MSW II 9153, 40–45 [alternative numbering 18–23]. David Sfard, *Mit zikh un mit andere: Oytobiyografye un literarishe eseyen* [With oneself and with others: Autobiography and literary essays] (Jerusalem: Farlag Yerushalaymer almanakh, 1984), 289; cited also in Joanna Nalewajko-Kulikov, *Obywatel Jidyszlandu: Rzecz o żydowskich komunistach w Polsce* [Citizen of Yiddishland: About the Jewish communists in Poland] (Warsaw: Neriton, 2009), 273.

68. Wasersztrum, "Oyfklerungen un bamerkungen," 42.

69. "Sytuacja w wydawnictwie 'idisz buch'—na rece sekretarza ZG TSKŻ, tow. E. Rajber" [Situation in the publishing house "Yiddish Book"—for the secretary of the main governing board of the Social-Cultural Association of Jews in Poland, Comrade E. Rajber], January 28, 1969, in IPN, collection of the MSW, archival no. MSW II 9153, 40–45 [alternative numbering 18–23].

70. Artur Eisenbach to the main governing board of the Jewish Historical Institute, June 19, 1968, in ŻIH, collection of the secretariat of ŻIH, incoming and outgoing correspondence for 1968, unpaginated.

71. Teresa Torańska, *Jesteśmy: Rozstania '68* [We are: Parting '68] (Warsaw: Świat Książki, 2008), 72. Documents on Book and Knowledge's involvement with the "anti-Zionist" propaganda are in AAN, KC PZPR, archival no. 237/VIII-1110, 1, 6, 9, 10, 18–21, 26–28.

72. Artur Eisenbach to T. Daniszewski, on April 6, 1968, ŻIH, secretariat of ŻIH, incoming and outgoing correspondence for 1968, unpaginated.

73. Torańska, *Jesteśmy: Rozstania '68,* 199.

74. Interview with Zofia Zarębska by the author, Warsaw, July 12, 2004, and Aug. 2, 2004. A letter from Emil Adler to his wife, Genia, in 1946 referred to the party leadership's decision not to publish either Adler's or Bergman's names in the translations, although Emil did not explain why. Emil Adler to Genia Adler, June 4, 1946. Personal papers of Emil and Genia Adler, Göttingen, Germany.

75. Zygmunt Trawiński, "Mój jubileusz" [My jubilee], in *Książka i Wiedza: przeszłość i teraźniejszość, 1918–1968* [Book and Knowledge: Past and present, 1918–1968], ed. T. Bujnowska, Z. Słowik, and T. Weintraub (Warsaw: Książka i Wiedza, 1968), 116. Karl Kautsky, *Are the Jews a Race?* (New York: International Publishers, 1926), trans. from the 2nd German ed.

76. Stola, "The Hate Campaign of 1968," 32.

77. Interview by Wiszniewicz with "Henia" in Wiszniewicz, *Życie Przecięte,* 364–365.

78. For an analysis of the government's emigration policy for those of Jewish background in this period, see Dariusz Stola, *Kampania antysyjonistyczna w Polsce 1967–1968* [Anti-Zionist campaign in Poland, 1967–1968] (Warsaw: Instytut Studiów Politycznych Polskiej Akademii Nauk, 2000), 207–216.

79. See, among others, IPN, collection of the MSW, archival no. BU 00236/215, folders 1–4, 6, 8 part 2; BU 0236/157; BU 0236/37, folders 2–5.

80. IPN, collection of the MSW, archival no. BU 0236/37, folder 7. The translation of the phrase *Ubi bene ibi patria* in the excerpt is from the letter-writer's Polish translation.

81. IPN, collection of the MSW, archival no. BU 0236/37, folder 7, 271.

82. IPN, collection of the MSW, archival no. MSW II 4524, 1–308.

83. Interview with Włodek Paszyński by the author, Warsaw, Nov. 4, 2004, and Nov. 30, 2006.

84. IPN, collection of the MSW, archival no. BU 0204/111, 21–23.

85. Interview with Jurek Neftalin by the author, Warsaw, Nov. 14–15, 2006.

86. Interview with Piotr Sztuczyński by the author, Warsaw, Nov. 10, Nov. 20, Nov. 24, 2006.

87. Telephone interview with Bernard Krutz by the author, Fair Lawn, N.J., July 8, 2007.

88. Ibid.

6. FINDING THE OBLITERATED TRACES OF THE PATH

1. Itche Goldberg and Yuri Suhl, eds., *The End of a Thousand Years. The Recent Exodus of the Jews from Poland* (New York: Committee for Jews of Poland, 1971).

2. Michael Steinlauf, *Bondage to the Dead: Poland and the Memory of the Holocaust* (Syracuse, N.Y.: Syracuse University Press, 1997), 94; and interview with Konstanty Gebert by the author, Warsaw, Oct. 20, 1998. Accounts differ over how participants at the retreat began discussing their Jewish background. According to one version, the idea for a group on Jewish identity arose from an earlier session, during which one of the psychologists in attendance began talking, unprompted, about concentration camps. In a different account, a participant suggested a group about Jews when the retreat broke down into smaller sessions on specific topics.

3. Interviews by the author with Konstanty Gebert, Warsaw, Oct. 20, 1998; and with Ryszarda Zachariasz, October 1998.

4. Steinlauf, *Bondage to the Dead*, 94.

5. Interview with Helena Datner by the author, Warsaw, October 1998.

6. Steinlauf, *Bondage to the Dead*, 94.

7. Interviews by the author with Konstanty Gebert, Warsaw, Oct. 20, 1998, and with Helena Datner, Warsaw, October 1998. Datner's recollection of Edelman's statement was that "Jewish life in Poland is nothing. It's over." Datner's father, Szymon Datner, was a Jewish historian and served briefly as director of the Jewish Historical Institute. Helena Datner, like Ryszarda Zachariasz, had a stronger connection to her Jewish background than the other participants, occasionally attending services, for example, in the Jewish community building with her father.

8. Interview by the author with Konstanty Gebert, Warsaw, Oct. 20, 1998, and with Ryszarda Zachariasz, Warsaw, October 1998. See also Steinlauf, *Bondage to the Dead*, 94.

9. Marek Edelman, *Getto walczy /udział Bundu w obronie getta warszawskiego /* [The ghetto fights /the participation of the Bund in the defense of the Warsaw ghetto/] (Warsaw, 1983). Cited also in Steinlauf, *Bondage to the Dead*, 107–108.

10. Interview with Konstanty Gebert by the author, Warsaw, Oct. 20, 1998.

11. Stefan Bergman to Genia Adler, Warsaw, March 19, 1973. The word "my" was underlined in the original. Personal papers of Emil and Genia Adler, Göttingen, Germany.

12. Marci Shore, *Caviar and Ashes: A Warsaw Generation's Life and Death in Marxism, 1918–1968* (New Haven, Conn.: Yale University Press, 2006), 130–135.

13. Bergman added a handwritten postscript that the priest was the poet Jan Twardowski.

14. Stefan Bergman to Emil and Genia Adler, July 8, 1976. Personal papers of Emil and Genia Adler, Göttingen, Germany.

15. Stefan Bergman to Emil and Genia Adler, June 4, 1973. Personal papers of Emil and Genia Adler, Göttingen, Germany. Stefan makes an unclear reference to an incident in early postwar Łódź regarding the Polonization of a friend's name. "Ischias (like it is written in Polish) has a Polish name: 'rwa kulszowa' [sciatica]." The parenthetical phrase is Bergman's.

16. Stefan Bergman to Genia Adler, April 16, 1973; and Stefan Bergman to Genia Adler, July 26, 1980. Personal papers of Emil and Genia Adler, Göttingen, Germany.

17. Stefan Bergman to Genia Adler, December 6, 1978. Personal papers of Emil and Genia Adler, Göttingen, Germany.

18. Stefan Bergman to Emil and Genia Adler, March 9, 1979. Personal papers of Emil and Genia Adler, Göttingen, Germany.

19. Stefan Bergman, "Przedmowa [Foreword]," in Józef Łukaszewicz, *Pierwszy marca 1887 roku: Wspomnienia Józefa Łukaszewicz* [The first of March 1887: Memoirs of Józef Łukaszewicz], ed. and trans. from Russian by Stefan Bergman (Warsaw: Panstwowy Instytut Wydawniczy, 1981), 5.

20. Bergman, "Przedmowa," 10.

21. Ibid., 10–11.

22. Ibid., 12.

23. Ibid.

24. Ibid., 12–13.

25. Jan Josef Lipski, *KOR: Workers' Defense Committee in Poland, 1976–1981* (Berkeley: University of California Press, 1985).

26. Stefan Bergman to Emil and Genia Adler, undated. Personal papers of Emil and Genia Adler, Göttingen, Germany.

27. IPN, collection of the MSW, archival no. 0331/214; IPN, collection of the MSW, archival no. 0247/1373; and interviews by the author with Szymon Rudnicki, Nov. 19, 2006, and Andrzej Friedman, Nov. 20, 2006.

28. Interview with Szymon Rudnicki by the author, Warsaw, Nov. 19, 2006.

29. Ibid.

30. Archiwum Fundacji "Karta," Archiwum Opozycji, file of Włodek Paszyński, unpaginated.

31. Interview with Feliks Falk by the author, Warsaw, Nov. 8, 2004, and Nov. 28, 2006.

32. Interview with Jan and Francis Sławny by the author, Paris, March 13, 2007.

33. Interview with Stefania Fedecka's son by the author, Paris, March 16, 2007.

34. Interview with Stefania Fedecka, Survivors of the Shoah Visual History Foundation, 1996.

EPILOGUE

1. Iwona Irwin-Zarecka, *Neutralizing Memory: The Jew in Contemporary Poland* (New Brunswick, N.J.: Transaction Publishers, 1989), 33.

2. The two citations on the grave are in a different order than in Tuwim's poem. The translation here is taken from the edition of the poem edited by Chone Shmeruk and published in Polish as well as in English, Hebrew, and Yiddish translation. See Julian Tuwim, "*My, Żydzi Polscy . . . We, Polish Jews . . .* ed. Chone Shmeruk (Jerusalem: Magnes Press, 1984), 20, 24.

3. *Gazeta Wyborcza*, August 12, 1996, issue 187, section "Kultura," 11.

4. Wiktoria Śliwowska, ed., *The Last Eyewitnesses: Children of the Holocaust Speak*, trans. and annot. by Julian and Fay Bussgang, 2nd ed. (Evanston, Ill.: Northwestern University Press, 1999), 217.

BIBLIOGRAPHY

ARCHIVES

Archiwum Akt Nowych [Central Archives of Modern Records, AAN], Warsaw.
    Główny Urząd Kontroli Prasy Publikacji i Widowisk [Main Commission for Control of the Press, Publications and Performances, GUKPPiW].
    Komitet Centralny Polskiej Partii Robotniczej [Central Committee of the Polish Workers' Party, KC PPR].
    Komitet Centralny Polskiej Zjednoczonej Partii Robotniczej [Central Committee of the Polish United Workers' Party, KC PZPR].
    Ministerstwo Edukacji w Warszawie [Ministry of Education in Warsaw].
    Papers of Teodor Duracz.
    Robotnicza Spółdzielnia Wydawnicza "Prasa-Ksiązka-Ruch" [Workers' Publishing Cooperative "Prasa-Ksiązka-Ruch," RSW "Prasa"].
    Towarzystwo Przyjaciół Dzieci, Zarząd Główny w Warszawie, 1945–1953 [Society for the Friends of Children, Main Governing Board, 1945–1953].
    Zbiór akt osobowych działaczy ruchu robotniczego [Collection of individual records of activists of the workers' movement].
    Związek Patriotów Polskich w ZSRR [Union of Polish Patriots in the USSR].
Archiwum Fundacji "Karta" [Archive of the "Karta" Foundation], Warsaw.
    Archiwum Opozycji [Archive of the Opposition].
Archiwum Ksiązki i Wiedzy [Archive of Book and Knowledge], Warsaw.
Archiwum Ministerstwa Edukacji [Archive of the Ministry of Education], Warsaw.
Archiwum Państwowy Miasta Stołecznego Warszawy [State Archive of the Capital City of Warsaw].
    Podstawowa Organizacja Partyjna Polskiej Zjednoczonej Partii Robotniczej w Spółdzielnii Wydawniczej "Ksiązka i Wiedza" [Primary Party Cell of the Polish

United Workers' Party in the Publishing Cooperative "Książka i Wiedza," POP PZPR "KiW"].

Zbiór Ksiąg Meldunkowych [Collection of Registration Books].

Archiwum Towarzystwa Przyjaciół Dzieci [Archive of the Society for the Friends of Children, TPD], Warsaw.

Zarząd Główny [Main Governing Body].

Archiwum Towarzystwa Spółeczno-Kulturalnej Żydów w Polsce [Archive of the Social-Cultural Association of Jews in Poland, TSKŻ], Warsaw.

Archiwum Uniwersytetu Warszawskiego [Archive of Warsaw University].

Archiwum Żydowskiego Instytutu Historycznego [Archive of the Jewish Historical Institute, ŻIH], Warsaw.

Centralny Komitet Żydow Polskich [Central Committee of Polish Jews, CKŻP].

Hebrew Immigrant Aid Society (HIAS).

Papers of Artur Eisenbach.

Papers of Szymon Datner.

Sekretariat Żydowskiego Instytutu Historycznego [Secretariat of the Jewish Historical Institute].

Towarzystwo Spółeczno-Kulturalne Żydów w Polsce [Social-Cultural Association of Jews in Poland, TSKŻ].

Diaspora Research Center, Tel Aviv University, Tel Aviv, Papers of Bernard Mark.

Instytut Pamięci Narodowej [Institute for National Remembrance, IPN], Warsaw.

Ministerstwo Spraw Wewnętrznych [Ministry of Internal Affairs, MSW].

Medem Library, Paris.

Papers of Lili Berger.

Personal papers of the Adler family, Göttingen, Germany.

Personal papers of the Metral family, Paris [partial].

Personal papers of the Tyszelman family, Warsaw.

YIVO, New York.

Papers of Dina Abramowicz.

Papers of Naftali Herts Kon.

INTERVIEWS CONDUCTED BY THE AUTHOR

Adler, Marian. Göttingen, Germany, Dec. 2–3, 2006.

Bilewicz, Aleksander. Warsaw, May 27, 2004, and June 3, 2004.

Bramley, Halina Adler. Sharon, Mass., Jan. 7, 2007

Chodorowski, Wojciech. Warsaw, Feb. 14, 2007.

Datner, Helena. Warsaw, October 1998; May 16, 2004; and May 20, 2004.

Dubaj, Zygmunt. Warsaw, May 14, 2007.

Eilstein, Helena. Warsaw, Nov. 29, 2006.

Falk, Feliks. Warsaw, Nov. 8, 2004, and Nov. 28, 2006.

Fedecka, Stefania. Warsaw, Nov. 12, 2006.

Friedman, Andrzej. Warsaw, Dec. 1, 2004, and Nov. 20, 2006.

Gebert, Konstanty. Warsaw, Oct. 20, 1998.

Heldwein, Krystyna. Warsaw, June 23, 2007.

Kaczyński, Ryszard. Warsaw, Feb. 22, 2007.

Kaja. Warsaw, May 12, 2004.

Krajewski, Stanisław. Warsaw, July 11, 2004.
Krajewski, Władysław. Warsaw, Aug. 31, 2004.
Krutz, Bernard. Fair Lawn, N.J. (by telephone), July 8, 2007.
M., Waleria. Warsaw, Aug. 17, Sept. 13, Sept. 20, and Oct. 4, 2004.
Metral, Yvette. Paris, March 15, 2007.
Neftalin, Jurek. Warsaw, Nov. 14–15, 2006.
Olczak-Ronikier, Joanna. Kraków, Sept. 4, 2004.
Passent, Daniel. Warsaw, Aug. 29 and Oct. 23, 2004.
Paszyński, Włodek [Włodzimierz]. Warsaw, Nov. 4, 2004, and Nov. 30, 2006.
Rabinowicz, Lena. Warsaw, July 3, 2007.
Redlich, Shimon. Providence, R.I., May 15, 2005.
Rudnicki, Szymon. Warsaw, May 15, 2004, and Nov. 19, 2006.
Sławny, Jan and Francis. Paris, March 13, 2007.
Sławny, Józef. Blacksburg, Va., Oct. 3, 2007.
Sztuczyński, Piotr. Warsaw, Nov. 10, Nov. 20, and Nov. 24, 2006.
Szwarcman, Bella. Warsaw, Sept. 23, 2004.
Toeplitz, Krzysztof Teodor. Warsaw, March 9, 2007.
Tramer, Andrzej. Paris, March 14, 2007.
Tyszelman, Liliana. Warsaw, Dec. 1, 2006, and July 3, 2007.
Web, Marek. New York, Dec. 20–21, 2007.
Zachariasz, Ryszarda. Warsaw, October 1998.
Zarębska, Zofia. Warsaw, July 12 and Aug. 2, 2004.
Zozula, Andrzej. Warsaw, May 11, 2004.

INTERVIEWS FROM OTHER SOURCES

Adler, Genia. Survivors of the Shoah Visual History Foundation, Aug. 19, 1996. Transcribed and translated from Polish by Halina Adler Bramley.
Fedecka, Stefania. Survivors of the Shoah Visual History Foundation, 1996.
Heldwein, Krystyna. Survivors of the Shoah Visual History Foundation, Jan. 15, 1996.
Maślankiewicz, Gustawa. Survivors of the Shoah Visual History Foundation, Jan. 15, 1996.

PERIODICALS

Dos Naye Lebn, Łódź.
Folks-shtime, Warsaw.

MEMOIRS

Budzyńska, Celina. *Strzępy rodzinnej sagi.* Warsaw: Żydowski Instytut Historyczny, 1997.
Dichter, Wilhelm. *Koń pana boga, Szkoła bezbożników.* Kraków: Znak, 2003.
Egit, Jacob. *Tsu a nay lebn (tsvey yor yidishe yeshuv in nidershlezye).* Wrocław: Farlag Nidershlezye, 1947.
Gebert, Konstanty. "The Keeper of Memory." In *The Jews in Poland,* ed. Sławomir Kapralski, 2:45–48. Kraków: Judaica Foundation, 1999.

Halkowski, Henryk. *Żydowskie Życie*. Kraków: Austeria, 2003.

Klugman, Tosia, and Aleksander Klugman. *... a droga wiodła przez Łódź*. Łódź: Biblioteka "Tygla Kultury," 2004.

Mark, Bernard. "Dziennik," trans. from Yiddish by Joanna Nalewajko-Kulikov. *Kwartalnik Historii Żydow*, no. 226 (2008): 156–192.

Markiewicz, Henryk. *Moj Życiorys Polonistyczny z historią w tle*. Conversation with the author conducted by Barbara N. Lopienska. Kraków: Wydawnictwo Literackie, 2003.

Olczak-Ronikier, Joanna. *W ogrodzie pamięci*. Kraków: Znak, 2003.

Rafałowski, Aleksander. *... I spoza palety: wspomnienia*. Warsaw: Państwowy Instytut Wydawniczy, 1970.

Sfard, David. *Mit zikh un mit andere: oytobiyografye un literarishe eseyen*. Jerusalem: Farlag Yerushalaymer almanakh, 1984.

Smolar, Hersh. *Oyf der letster pozitsye, mit der letster hofenung*. Tel Aviv: Farlag I. L. Peretz, 1982.

Toeplitz, Krzysztof Teodor. *Rodzina Toeplitzów: Książka mojego ojca*. Warsaw: Iskry, 2004.

Treper (Domb), Leopold. *Di royte kapelye*. Jerusalem: Yerushalaymer Alamanakh, 1978.

PUBLISHED BOOKS AND ARTICLES

Adler, Emil. *Herder i Oświecenie Niemieckie*. Warsaw: PWN, 1965.

———. "O przyjacielu ... " In *Jakub Prawin (Wspomnienia)*. Warsaw: Książka i Wiedza, 1959.

———. "Spinozyzm a Spór o 'Prometeusza.'" *Studia Filozoficzne*, no. 4 (1961): 197–208.

Aleksiun, Natalia. *Dokąd dalej? Ruch syjonistyczny w Polsce (1944–1950)*. Warsaw: Trio, 2002.

Andrzejewski, Adam. *Polityka mieszkaniowa*. Warsaw: Państwowe Wydawnictwo Ekonomiczne, 1987.

Araszkiewicz, Feliks. *Z dziejów walki o laicyzacje szkoły i wychowania w Polsce w latach 1914–1939*. Warsaw: Centralny Ośrodek Doskonalenia Kadr Laickich, 1969.

Aronowicz, Annette. "Spinoza among the Jewish Communists." *Modern Judaism* 24, no. 1 (2004): 1–35.

Banas, Josef. *The Scapegoats: The Exodus of the Remnants of Polish Jewry*. London: Weidenfeld and Nicolson, 1979.

Bauman, Zygmunt. "Exit Visas and Entry Tickets: Paradoxes of Jewish Assimilation." *Telos* 77 (1988): 45–77.

Berendt, Grzegorz. *Życie żydowskie w Polsce w latach 1950–1956*. Gdańsk: Wydawnictwo Uniwerystetu Gdańskiego, 2006.

———. *Żydzi na gdańskim rozdrożu: 1945–1950*. Gdańsk: Wydawnictwo Uniwersytetu Gdańskiego, 2000.

Berendt, Grzegorz, August Grabski, and Albert Stankowski. *Studia z historii Żydów w Polsce po 1945 r.* Warsaw: Żydowski Instytut Historyczny, 2000.

Bergman, Aleksandra. *Rzecz o Bronisławie Taraszkiewiczu*. Warsaw: Książka i Wiedza, 1977.

Bergman, Eleonora. "Yiddish in Poland after 1945." In *Yiddish and the Left*, ed. Gennady Estraikh and Mikhail Krutikov, 167–176. Oxford: Oxford University Press, 2001.

———. "Żydzi—nie tylko na Nalewkach." In *Straty Warszawy 1939–1945: Raport*, ed. Wojciech Fałkowski, 182–201. Warsaw: Miasto Stołeczne Warszawy, 2005.

Bergman, Stefan. " Przedmowa." In *Józef Łukaszewicz, Pierwszy marca 1887 roku: Wspomnienia Józefa Łukaszewicza*, ed. and trans. from Russian by Stefan Bergman. Warsaw: Państwowy Instytut Wydawniczy, 1981.

Bilewicz, Michał, and Bogna Pawlisz, eds. *Żydzi i komunizm*. Warsaw: Jidele, 2000.

Blejwas, Stanislaus A. "Polish Positivism and the Jews." *Jewish Social Studies* 46, no. 1 (1984): 21–36.

———. *Realism in Polish Politics: Warsaw Positivism and National Survival in Nineteenth Century Poland*. New Haven, Conn.: Yale University Press, 1984.

Brzostek, Błażej. *Za progiem. Codzienność w przestrzeni publicznej Warszawy lat 1955–1970*. Warsaw: Trio, 2007.

Buchli, Victor. *An Archaeology of Socialism*. Oxford: Berg, 1999. Esp. chapter 4, "The Narkomfin Communal House and the Material Culture of Socialism."

Bujnowska, T., Z. Słowik, and T. Weintraub, eds. *Książka i Wiedza: przeszłość i teraźniejszość, 1918–1968*. Warsaw: Książka i Wiedza, 1968.

Butrymowicz, Brygida, and Leszek Gomółka. *Pedagogika Towarzystwa Przyjaciół Dzieci*. Warsaw: PWN, 1975.

Cała, Alina. "An Attempt to Recover Its Voice: The Towarzystwo Społeczno-Kulturalne Żydów w Polsce, the Jewish Community, and the Polish State, 1956–1960." *Polin* 19 (2007): 557–568.

Cała, Alina, and Helena Datner. *Dzieje Żydów w Polsce 1944–1968*. Warsaw: Żydowski Instytut Historyczny, 1997.

Cegielski, Jerzy. *Stosunki mieszkaniowe w Warszawie w latach 1864–1964*. Warsaw: Arkady Warszawy, 1968.

Checinski, Michael. *Poland: Communism, Nationalism, Antisemitism*. Trans. Tadeusz Szafar. New York: Karz-Cohl, 1982.

Cichopek, Anna. *Pogrom Żydów w Krakowie 11 sierpnia 1945 r.* Warsaw: Żydowski Instytut Historyczny, 2000.

Cohen, Gary B. *The Politics of Ethnic Survival: Germans in Prague, 1861–1914*. 2nd ed. West Lafayette, Ind.: Purdue University Press, 2006.

Crowley, David. "Warsaw Interiors: The Public Life of Private Spaces, 1949–65." In *Socialist Spaces: Sites of Everyday Life in the Eastern Bloc*, ed. David Crowley and Susan E. Reid, 181–206. Oxford: Berg, 2002.

Czaplicka, John, ed. *Lviv: A City in the Crosscurrents of Culture*. Cambridge, Mass.: Ukrainian Research Institute and Harvard University Press, 2005.

Datner, Helena. "A First Glance at the Results of the Survey 'Poles, Jews and Other Ethnic Groups.'" *East European Jewish Affairs* 23, no. 1 (1993): 33–48.

———. "Szkoły Centralnego Komitetu Żydów w Polsce w latach 1944–1949." *Biuletyn Żydowskiego Instytutu Historycznego* 169–171 (1994): 103–119.

Datner-Śpiewak, Helena. "Instytucje opieki nad dzieckim i szkoły powszechne Centralnego Komitetu Żydów Polskich w latach 1945–1946." *Biuletyn Żydowskiego Instytutu Historycznego* 117 (1981): 37–52.

Der tsadik in pelts. Zamlung fun artiklen. Tel Aviv: "Orly," 1985.

Davies, Norman. *God's Playground: A History of Poland.* Vol. 2. New York: Columbia University Press, 1982.

Dobroszycki, Łucjan. "Restoring Jewish Life in Postwar Poland." *Soviet Jewish Affairs* 3, no. 2 (1973): 58–72.

———. *Survivors of the Holocaust in Poland: A Portrait Based on Community Records 1944–1947.* Armonk, N.Y.: M. E. Sharpe, 1994.

Dudek, Antoni. *Komuniści i Kościół w Polsce, 1945–1989.* Kraków: Znak, 2003.

Edelman, Marek. *Getto walczy /udział Bundu w obronie getta warszawskiego/.* Warsaw, 1983.

Eisler, Jerzy. *Marzec 1968: Geneza, Przebieg, Konsekwencje.* Warsaw: Państwowe Wydawnictwo Naukowe, 1991.

———. "Młodzież akademicka w Łodzi w 1968 roku." In *Opozycja i Opór Społeczny w Łodzi 1956–1981,* ed. Krzysztof Lesiakowski, 64–72. Warsaw: IPN, 2003.

———. *Polski Rok 1968.* Warsaw: IPN, 2006.

———. "1968: Jews, Antisemitism, Emigration." *Polin* 21 (2009): 37–61.

Fałkowski, Wojciech, ed. *Straty Warszawy 1939–1945: Raport.* Warsaw: Miasto Stołeczne Warszawy, 2005.

Fijałkowska, Barbara. *Borejsza i Różański: przyczynek do dziejów Stalinizmu w Polsce.* Olsztyn, Poland: Wyższa Szkoła Pedagogiczna, 1995.

Fik, Marta. *Marcowa Kultura.* Warsaw: Wydawnictwo Wodnika, 1995.

Fonrobert, Charlotte E. "From Separatism to Urbanism: The Dead Sea Scrolls and the Origins of the Rabbinic Eruv." *Dead Sea Discoveries* 11, no. 1 (2004): 43–71.

———. "The Political Symbolism of the Eruv." *Jewish Social Studies* 11, no. 3 (2005): 9–35.

Fonrobert, Charlotte E., and Vered Shemtov. "Introduction: Jewish Conceptions and Practices of Space." *Jewish Social Studies* 11, no. 3 (2005): 1–8.

Frankel, Jonathan, ed. "Dark Times, Dire Decisions: Jews and Communism." *Studies in Contemporary Jewry* 20 (2004).

Friedlander, Judith. *Vilnius on the Seine: Jewish Intellectuals in France since 1968.* New Haven, Conn.: Yale University Press, 1990.

Gajewski, Jan, ed. *Książka i Wiedza. Sześćdziesiąt lat działalności.* Warsaw: Książka i Wiedza, 1978.

Gebert, Konstanty. "The Keeper of Memory." In *The Jews in Poland,* vol. 2. Kraków: Judaica Foundation Center for Jewish Culture, 2001.

Gerasimova, Katerina. "Public Privacy in the Soviet Communal Apartment." *Socialist Spaces: Sites of Everyday Life in the Eastern Bloc,* ed. David Crowley and Susan E. Reid, 207–230. Oxford: Berg, 2002.

———. "The Soviet Communal Apartment." In *Beyond the Limits: The Concept of Space in Russian History and Culture,* ed. Jeremy Smith, 107–130. Helsinki: SHS, 1999.

Gitelman, Zvi, Barry Kosmin, and András Kovács, eds. *New Jewish Identities: Contemporary Europe and Beyond.* Budapest: Central European University Press, 2003.

Głuchowski, Leszek, and Antony Polonsky, eds. "1968: Forty Years After." Special issue, *Polin: Studies in Polish Jewry* 21 (2009).

Goldberg, Itche, and Yuri Suhl, eds. *The End of a Thousand Years. The Recent Exodus of the Jews from Poland.* New York: Committee for Jews of Poland, 1971.

Gordon, Milton M. *Assimilation in American Life: The Role of Race, Religion, and National Origins.* New York: Oxford University Press, 1964.

Górski, Jan. *Warszawa w latach 1944–1949: Odbudowa.* Warsaw: PWN, 1990.

Grabski, August. *Działalność komunistów wśród Żydów w Polsce (1944–1949).* Warsaw: Trio, 2004.

———. "Sytuacja Żydów w Polsce, 1950–1957." *Biuletyn Żydowskiego Instytutu Historycznego* 196 (2000): 504–519.

Grabski, August, and Grzegorz Berendt. *Między emigracją a trwaniem: Syjoniści i komuniści żydowscy w Polsce po Holocauście.* Warsaw: Żydowski Instytut Historyczny, 2003.

Gross, Jan. *Fear: Antisemitism in Poland after Auschwitz: An Essay in Historical Interpretation.* New York: Random House, 2006.

———. *Neighbors: The Destruction of the Jewish Community in Jedwabne, Poland.* Princeton, N.J.: Princeton University Press, 2001.

Gross, Natan. *Film żydowski w Polsce.* Kraków: Rabid, 2002.

Grupińska, Anka. *Po kole. Rozmowy z żydowskimi żołnierzami.* Warsaw: Alfa, 1991.

Grynberg, Henryk. *Memorbuch.* Warsaw: W.A.B., 2000.

———. *Prawda Nieartystyczna.* West Berlin: Archipelag, 1984.

Grynberg, Michał. *Żydowska spółdzielczość pracy w Polsce w latach 1945–1949.* Warsaw: PWN, 1986.

Hartglas, Apolinary. *Na pograniczu dwóch światów.* Warsaw: Oficyna Wydawnicza, 1996.

Hoberman, J. *Bridge of Light: Yiddish Film Between Two Worlds.* New York: Museum of Modern Art and Schocken Books, 1991.

Hołub, Barbara. "Stefan Bergman: Jerozolima Północy." In *Przy wileńskim stole,* ed. Barbara Hołub, 191–205. Warsaw: Książka i Wiedza, 1992.

Hurwic-Nowakowska, Irena. *A Social Analysis of Postwar Polish Jewry.* Jerusalem: Zalman Shazar Center for Jewish History, 1986.

Irwin-Zarecka, Iwona. *Neutralizing Memory: The Jew in Contemporary Poland.* New Brunswick, N.J.: Transaction Publishers, 1989.

Jasiński, Roman. *Zmierzch starego świata: Wspomnienia, 1900–1945.* Kraków: Wydawnictwo Literackie, 2006.

Jaworski, Wojciech. "Jewish Religious Communities in Upper Silesia 1945–1970." In *Jews in Silesia,* ed. Marcin Wodziński and Janusz Spyras, 247–263. Kraków: Księgarnia Akademicka, 2001.

———. *Żydzi na Górnym Śląsku, 1945–1970.* Sosnowiec, Poland: Wojciech Jaworski, 2001.

Kainer, A. [Stanisław Krajewski]. "Żydzi a komunizm." *Krytyka* 15 (1983): 214–247.

"Katolicyzm-Judaizm. Żydzi w Polsce i w Świecie." Special issue, *Znak* 35, nos. 2–3 (1983).

Kenney, Padraic. "Whose Nation, Whose State? Working-Class Nationalism and Antisemitism in Poland, 1945–1947." *Polin: Studies in Polish Jewry* 13 (2000): 224–235.

Kersten, Krystyna. *The Establishment of Communist Rule in Poland, 1943–1948.* Trans. John Micgiel and Michael H. Bernhard. Berkeley: University of California Press, 1991.

———. *Polacy, Żydzi, Komunizm: Anatomia półprawd 1939–1968.* Warsaw: Niezależna Oficyna Wydawnicza, 1992.

———. *Repatriacja ludności polskiej po II wojnie światowej (studium historyczne).* Warsaw: Polska Akademia Nauk, 1974.

Kichelewski, Audrey. "A Community under Pressure: Jews in Poland, 1957–1967." *Polin: Studies in Polish Jewry* 21 (2009): 159–186.

Kochanowski, Jerzy. "Balast przeszłości usunęła wojna . . . Rok 1945: trzy pomysły na odbudowę Warszawy." In Jerzy Kochanowski et al., *Zbudować Warszawę Piękną. O nowy krajobraz stolicy (1944–1956)*, 15–21. Warsaw: Trio, 2003.

Kon, Naftali Herts. *Farshribn in zikorn*. Tel Aviv: Aliyah Press, 1966.

Kopstein, Jeffrey, and Jason Wittenberg. "Who Voted Communist? Reconsidering the Social Bases of Radicalism in Interwar Poland." *Slavic Review* 62, no. 1 (Spring 2003): 87–109.

Kotkin, Stephen. *Magnetic Mountain: Stalinism as a Civilization*. Berkeley: University of California Press, 1995. Esp. part 2, "Living Socialism: The Little Tactics of the Habitat."

Krajewski, Władysław. "Fakty i mity: O roli Żydów w okresie stalinowskim." *Więź* 5 (1997): 109–122.

Kula, Marcin. *Religiopodobny Komunizm*. Kraków: Nomos, 2003.

Kumaniecka, Janina. *Saga rodu Słonimskich*. Warsaw: Iskry, 2003.

Kuroń, Jacek. *Autobiografia*. Warsaw: Wydawnictwo Krytyki Politycznej, 2009.

Landau-Czajka, Anna. *Syn będzie Lech . . . Asymilacja Żydów w Polsce międzywojennej*. Warsaw: Neriton, 2006.

Lefebvre, Henri. *The Production of Space*. Trans. Donald Nicholson-Smith. Oxford: Blackwell, 1991.

Lehrer, Erica. "'Jewish Like an Adjective': Confronting Jewish Identities in Contemporary Poland." In *Boundaries of Jewish Identity*, ed. Susan A. Glenn and Naomi B. Sokoloff, 161–187. Seattle: University of Washington Press, 2010

———. "'Shoah-business,' 'Holocaust Culture,' and the Repair of the World in 'Post-Jewish' Poland: A Quest for Ethnography, Empathy, and the Ethnic Self after Genocide." Diss., University of Michigan, 2005.

Lendvai, Paul. *Antisemitism without Jews: Communist Eastern Europe*. Garden City, N.Y.: Doubleday, 1971.

Levy, Richard. *Ana Pauker. The Rise and Fall of a Jewish Communist*. Berkeley: University of California Press, 2001.

Lichten, Joseph. "Notes on the Assimilation and Acculturation of Jews in Poland, 1863–1943." In *The Jews in Poland*, ed. Chimen Abramsky, Maciej Jachimczyk, and Antony Polonsky, 106–129. Oxford: Basil Blackwell, 1986.

Lipski, Jan Josef. *KOR: Workers' Defense Committee in Poland, 1976–1981*. Berkeley: University of California Press, 1985.

Łukaszewicz, Józef. *Pierwszy marca 1887 roku: Wspomnienia Jozefa Łukaszewicz*. Ed. Stefan Bergman. Warsaw: Państwowy Instytut Wydawniczy, 1981.

Machcewicz, Paweł. "Antisemitism in Poland in 1956." *Polin: Studies in Polish Jewry* 9 (1996): 170–183.

Machcewicz, Paweł, and Krzysztof Persak, eds. *Wokół Jedwabnego*. Warsaw: Instytut Pamięci Narodowej, 2002.

Madajczyk, Piotr. "Mniejszości narodowe a Październik 1956 roku." *Dzieje Najnowsze* 1 (1995): 89–105.

Madej, Krzysztof. *Spółdzielczość mieszkaniowa. Władze PRL wobec niezależnej inicjatywy społecznej (1961–1965)*. Warsaw: Trio and IPN, 2003.

Mann, Barbara E. *A Place in History: Modernism, Tel Aviv, and the Creation of Jewish Urban Space*. Stanford, Calif.: Stanford University Press, 2006.

Markiewicz, Tomasz. "Prywatna odbudowa Warszawy." In Jerzy Kochanowski et al., *Zbudować Warszawę Piękną. O nowy krajobraz stolicy (1944–1956)*, 217–218. Warsaw: Trio, 2003.

Melchior, Małgorzata. *Zagłada a Tożsamość*. Warsaw: Wydawnictwo Instytutu Filozofii i Socjologii PAN, 2004.

Melzer, Emanuel. *No Way Out: The Politics of Polish Jewry, 1935–1939*. Cincinnati: Hebrew Union College Press, 1997.

Mendelsohn, Ezra. *The Jews of East Central Europe between the World Wars*. Bloomington: Indiana University Press, 1983.

Mezglewski, A. *Szkolnictwo wyznaniowe w Polsce w latach 1944–1980: studium historyczno-prawne*. Lublin: KUL, 2004.

Michlic, Joanna. *Poland's Threatening Other: The Image of the Jew from 1880 to the Present*. Lincoln: University of Nebraska Press, 2006.

Mumford, Lewis. *The Culture of Cities*. New York: Harcourt, Brace, 1938.

Nalewajko-Kulikov, Joanna. "O marcu przed marcem. Wprowadzenie do zapisków Bernarda Marka." *Kwartalnik Historii Żydów*, no. 226 (2008): 153–155.

———. *Obywatel Jidyszlandu: Rzecz o żydowskich komunistach w Polsce*. Warsaw: Neriton, 2009.

Nathans, Benjamin. *Beyond the Pale: The Jewish Encounter with Late Imperial Russia*. Berkeley: University of California, 2002.

Natkowska, Monika. *Numerus clausus, getto ławkowe, numerus nullus, paragraf aryjski. Antysemityzm na Uniwersytecie Warszawskim 1931–1939*. Warsaw: Żydowski Instytut Historyczny, 1999.

Opalski, Magdalena, and Israel Bartal. *Poles and Jews: A Failed Brotherhood*. Hanover, N.H.: Brandeis University Press, 1992.

Osęka, Piotr. *Marzec '68*. Kraków: Znak, 2008.

———. *Rytuały stalinizmu: oficjalne święta i uroczystości rocznicowe w Polsce 1944–1956*. Warsaw: Trio, 2007.

———. *Syjoniści, inspiratorzy, wichrzyciele. Obraz Wroga w Propagandzie Marca 1968*. Warsaw: Żydowski Instytut Historyczny, 1999.

Parush, Iris. *Reading Jewish Women: Marginality and Modernization in Nineteenth Century Eastern European Jewish Society*. Trans. Saadya Sternberg. Hanover: University Press of New England for Brandeis University Press, 2004.

Persak, Krzysztof. *Sprawa Henryka Hollanda*. Warsaw: IPN, 2006.

Polonsky, Antony, ed. *My Brother's Keeper: Recent Polish Debates on the Holocaust*. London: Routledge, 1990.

———, ed. *Polin: Studies in Polish Jewry*. Vol. 9: *Jews, Poles, Socialists: The Failure of an Ideal*. Oxford: Littman Library of Jewish Civilization, 1996.

Rosenson, Claire. "Jewish Identity Construction in Contemporary Poland: Dialogue between Generations." *East European Jewish Affairs* 26, no. 2 (1996): 66–78.

Rozenblit, Marsha. *The Jews of Vienna, 1867–1914: Assimilation and Identity*. Albany: State University of New York Press, 1983.

Ruchniewicz, Małgorzata. *Repatriacja ludności polskiej z ZSRR w latach 1955–1959*. Warsaw: Volumen, 2000.

Rudnicki, Szymon. "From 'Numerus Clausus' to 'Numerus Nullus,'" in *From Shtetl to Socialism: Studies from Polin,* ed. Antony Polonsky, 359–381. London: Littman Library of Jewish Civilization, 1993.

———. "Wspomnienia: Stefan Bergman (1904–2002)." *Kwartalnik Historii Żydów,* no. 211 (2004): 411–415.

Sandauer, Artur. *O sytuacji pisarza polskiego pochodzenia żydowskiego w XX wieku. (Rzecz, ktora nie ja powinienem był napisać . . .).* Warsaw: Czytelnik, 1982.

Schatz, Jaff. *The Generation: The Rise and Fall of the Jewish Communists of Poland.* Berkeley: University of California Press, 1991.

Sfard, David. *Mit zikh un mit andere: Otobiyografye un literarishe esayen.* Jerusalem: Farlag Yerushalaymer almanakh, 1984.

Shatzky, Jacob. "Alexander Kraushar and His Road to Total Assimilation." *YIVO Annual of Jewish Social Science* 7 (1952): 146–174.

Shore, Marci. *Caviar and Ashes: A Warsaw Generation's Life and Death in Marxism, 1918– 1968.* New Haven, Conn.: Yale University Press, 2006.

———. "Children of the Revolution: Communism, Zionism, and the Berman Brothers." *Jewish Social Studies* 10, no. 3 (2004): 23–86.

———. "Język, pamięć i rewolucyjna awangarda: kształtowanie historii powstania w getcie warszawskim w latach 1944–1950." *Biuletyn Żydowskiego Instytutu Historycznego* 188 (1998): 44–61.

Slezkine, Yuri. *The Jewish Century.* Princeton, N.J.: Princeton University Press, 2004.

———. "The USSR as a Communal Apartment, or How a Socialist State Promoted Ethnic Particularism." *Slavic Review* 53, no. 2 (Summer 1994): 414–452.

Smolar, Aleksander. "Tabu i niewinność." *Aneks* 41/42 (1986): 89–133.

Sorkin, David. *The Transformation of German Jewry, 1780–1840.* Detroit: Wayne State University Press, 1999.

Stankowski, Albert. "Nowe spojrzenie na statystyki dotyczące emigracji Żydów z Polski po 1944 roku." In *Studia z historii Żydów w Polsce po 1945 r,* ed. Grzegorz Berendt, August Grabski, and Albert Stankowski, 103–151. Warsaw: Żydowski Instytut Historyczny, 2000.

Steinlauf, Michael C. *Bondage to the Dead: Poland and the Memory of the Holocaust.* Syracuse, N.Y.: Syracuse University Press, 1997.

Stola, Dariusz. "The Hate Campaign of March 1968: How Did It Become Anti-Jewish?" *Polin: Studies in Polish Jewry* 21 (2009): 16–36.

———. *Kampania antysyjonistyczna w Polsce 1967–1968.* Warsaw: Instytut Studiów Politycznych Polskiej Akademii Nauk, 2000.

Stołtysiak, Grzegorz, and Józef Stępień. *Marzec '68. Między tragedią a podłością.* Warsaw: Profi, 1998.

Suleja, Włodzimierz. *Dolnośląski Marzec '68.* Warsaw: IPN, 2006.

Szaynok, Bożena. "The Bund and the Jewish Fraction of the Polish Workers' Party in Poland after 1945." *Polin: Studies in Polish Jewry* 13 (2000): 206–223.

———. *Ludność żydowska na Dolnym Śląsku.* Wrocław: Wydawnictwo Uniwersytetu Wrocławskiego, 2000.

———. *Z historią i Moskwą w tle. Polska a Izrael 1944–1968.* Warsaw: IPN, 2007.

Szlajfer, Henryk. *Polacy/Żydzi. Zderzenie stereotypów. Esej dla przyjaciół i innych.* Warsaw: Scholar, 2003.

Szwankowski, Eugeniusz. *Ulice i Place Warszawy.* Warsaw: PWN, 1963.

Torańska, Teresa. *Jesteśmy. Rozstania '68.* Warsaw: Świat Książki, 2008.

———. *"Them." Stalin's Polish Puppets.* New York: Harper & Row, 1987. Shortened English translation of *Oni.* London: Aneks, 1985.

Tyrmand, Leopold. *Dziennik 1954.* Warsaw: Res Publica, 1989.

Urban, Jerzy. *Cały Urban.* Warsaw: Książka i Wiedza, 1989.

Vasershtrum, Yankev [Jakub Wasersztrum]. "Oyfklerungen un bamerkungen." In *Der Tsadik in Pelts: Zamlung fun artiklen.* Tel Aviv: Orli, 1985.

Ward, Graham, ed. *The Certeau Reader.* Oxford: Blackwell, 2000.

Waszkiewicz, Ewa. "The Religious Life of Lower-Silesian Jews in 1945–1968." In *Jews in Silesia,* ed. Marcin Wodziński and Janusz Spyra, 239–246. Kraków: Księgarnia Akademicka, 2001.

Waterman, Stanley, and Kosmin, Barry A. "Residential Patterns and Processes: A Study of Jews in Three London Boroughs," *Transactions of the Institute of British Geographers,* new series, 13, no. 1 (1988): 79–95.

Webber, Jonathan, ed. *Jewish Identities in the New Europe.* London: Littman Library of Jewish Civilization, 1994.

Weinryb, Bernard D. "Poland." In *The Jews in the Soviet Satellites,* ed. Peter Meyer et al. Syracuse, N.Y.: Syracuse University Press, 1953.

Wiszniewicz, Joanna. "Jewish Children and Youth in Downtown Warsaw Schools of the 1960s." *Polin: Studies in Polish Jewry* 21 (2009): 204–229.

———. *Życie przecięte: Opowieści pokolenia marca.* Wołowiec: Wydawnictwo Czarne, 2008.

Zagajewski, Adam. *Two Cities: On Exile, History, and the Imagination.* Trans. Lillian Vallee. New York: Farrar, Straus & Giroux, 1995.

Zaremba, Marcin. *Komunizm, Legitymacja, Nacjonalizm.* Warsaw: Trio, 2001.

———, ed. *Marzec 1968: Trzydzieści lat później. Dzień po dniu w raportach SB oraz Wydziału Organizacyjnego KC PZPR.* Warsaw: PWN, 1998.

Żbikowski, Andrzej. *U genezy Jedwabnego: Żydzi na kresach północno-wschodnich II Rzeczypospolitej, wrzesień 1939–lipiec 1941.* Warsaw: Żydowski Instytut Historyczny, 2006.

Żydowski Instytut Historyczny. 50 Lat Działalności. Materiały z konferencji jubileuszowej. Warsaw: Żydowski Instytut Historyczny, 1996.

INDEX

Adler, Emil, xv, 19–23, 29, 46, 47, 84–90,
  95, 96, 97, 109–114, 136, 151, 153, 160–162,
  170, 187, 197nn10–14, 201n35, 206nn1–3,
  206nn5–8, 207n17, 209n41, 209nn44–
  46, 215n74, 217n11
Adler, Eugenia, xv, 14–20, 23, 29, 42, 50,
  84, 88–90, 95, 96, 97, 109–110, 113–114,
  141, 153, 160–162, 170, 187, 196n1, 197n6,
  201n35, 206n1, 206nn5–8, 206n10,
  207n17, 209n41, 209n1, 215n74, 217n11
Adler, Marian, xv, 84–86, 89, 96, 110,
  112, 114, 153, 168, 187–188, 197nn8–9,
  206nn2–3, 209n44
Adler family, 159, 196n9, 206n1
Adler-Bramley, Halina, xv, 86, 89, 110, 114,
  142, 153, 168, 196n1, 197n8
American Jewish Joint Distribution Committee, 101, 181, 202n2
Antisemitism: in early postwar Poland,
  90–91; in interwar Poland, 5–6, 9, 16,
  18, 22, 25, 32–33, 36–37, 39–40; in 1956–
  1957, 102–104, 211nn23–24; at prewar
  universities in Poland, 32, 37, 197n5. *See
  also* "anti-Zionist" campaign; pogroms
"anti-Zionist" campaign, 5, 6, 9–10, 17–18,
  71, 110, 114, 126, 129, 134, 141–156, 165,

190, 209n2, 214n48, 215n65; emigration during and after, 17, 113–114, 116,
  138–139, 147–155, 166, 190, 204n27,
  209n2, 216n78. *See also* student protests in 1968
Armia Krajowa. *See* Home Army
Asch, Sholem, 83
assimilation, definition of, 10, 196n6
Auschwitz, 19, 89, 110
Australia, 10, 186

Babel Club, 128–129, 140, 141, 143–144, 152
Bałaban, Majer, 19
Baranowicze, xvii, 48
Bartoszewski, Władysław, 205n29
Bauman, Zygmunt, 151
Beit Warszawa, 179
Benjamin, Walter, 3
Berg, Judyta, 41, 46, 35, 199n9
Bergman, Aleksandra, xvi, xix, 1–3, 14, 24,
  26–29, 38, 41, 48, 88, 93, 98, 109, 113, 160,
  161, 162, 167, 171, 186, 191, 198n20
Bergman, Eleonora, xvi, 3, 88, 166–167,
  186, 188, 189
Bergman, Paulina, xvi, xviii, xix, 24, 28,
  29, 93, 108–109, 171, 191

KAREN AUERBACH is Kronhill Lecturer in East European Jewish History at Monash University in Melbourne, Australia. A former journalist, she reported for the *Philadelphia Inquirer,* the *Star-Ledger* of Newark, and the *Forward.*